新英汉
New English & Chinese

9分达人®

新航道雅思研发中心
[英]詹姆斯(James Foster) ◎ 编著

雅思口语宝典

2020—2023年雅思口语新题 + 4套全真模拟题

☑ 考官视角 解读评分标准 剖析得分要点
☑ 教学视角 精析外教范文 学习地道表达
☑ 考生视角 打造一题双解 积累口语素材

U0114976

2023.1
Describe a time when you missed
an important appointment.

2023.5
Describe the last book you read.

2023.1
Describe an event in history in
your country.

2023.1
Describe an interesting old person you would
like to meet.

2022.1
Describe a place in a village that
you visited.

2022.9
Describe a café you like to visit.

2022.5
Describe a family member who you
want to work with in the future.

2022.9
Describe a quiet place you like to go.

2021.9
Describe a time when you were
stuck in a traffic jam.

2022.5
Describe an interesting song.

全新真题

世界知识出版社

图书在版编目（CIP）数据

9 分达人雅思口语宝典 / 新航道雅思研发中心，（英）詹姆斯
（James Foster）编著. -- 北京：世界知识出版社，2023.7
ISBN 978-7-5012-6663-0

Ⅰ.① 9… Ⅱ.①新… ②詹… Ⅲ.① IELTS —口语—自学参考
资料 Ⅳ.① H319.9

中国国家版本馆 CIP 数据核字（2023）第 108865 号

责任编辑	谢　晴
特约编辑	龚玲琳
特邀编辑	葛亚芬　　杜修丽　　王丽娜
责任出版	赵　玥
责任校对	张　琨

书　　名	**9 分达人雅思口语宝典**
	9 Fen Daren Yasi Kouyu Baodian
编　　著	新航道雅思研发中心　[英]詹姆斯（James Foster）
出版发行	世界知识出版社
地址邮编	北京市东城区干面胡同 51 号（100010）
网　　址	www.ishizhi.cn
电　　话	010-65265923（发行）　　010-85119023（邮购）
经　　销	新华书店
印　　刷	清淞永业（天津）印刷有限公司
开本印张	787 毫米 × 1092 毫米　1/16　22¾ 印张
字　　数	518 千字
版次印次	2023 年 7 月第 1 版　2023 年 7 月第 1 次印刷
标准书号	ISBN 978-7-5012-6663-0
定　　价	69.00 元

新航道 图书编委会

主　任　胡　敏

委　员　（按姓氏笔画排序）

邓碧云　　冉　维

兰　熙　　李　纯

李　建　　杨　宏

陈采霞　　罗　霄

赵学敏　　胡　敏

Congratulations on taking a step forward to achieving an improved IELTS Speaking score!
恭喜你，在提高雅思口语成绩之路上又迈进了一步！

To begin with, some figures. According to the 'Test taker performance 2022' statistics, the Academic Mean Performance of Chinese Candidates was less than 6, 5.6, to be precise. (You can find this information here – https://www.ielts.org/for-researchers/test-statistics/test-taker-performance.) However, an IELTS score of 6.5, 7.0 or maybe even higher is required to study at a highly-ranked university in the UK. This is the primary reason for this book – to help students improve their IELTS exam score to obtain a university offer successfully, not just in the UK but in other countries too, as the IELTS Test is recognised worldwide.

首先分享几个数据。根据"2022年考生成绩表现"统计，中国考生的学术平均成绩不到6，更准确地说是5.6。（你可以从这里找到相关信息 https://www.ielts.org/for-researchers/test-statistics/test-taker-performance。）然而，要申请英国排名靠前的大学，雅思必须考到6.5分、7分甚至更高。本书旨在帮助学生提高雅思考试成绩并成功获得英国或其他国家的大学录取通知书，因为雅思考试在世界范围内都能得到认可。

I have designed this book, as part of the 9 Fen Daren series, to help IELTS candidates know and fully understand what the examiners are listening for when assessing candidates during an exam, namely the IELTS Speaking criteria. I will describe, in detail, the reasons for some of the administration and the three parts of the exam: Part 1 – Introduction, Part 2 – The individual long turn, and Part 3 – Two-way discussion. I will also go through several example answers using real questions and marks, comment and give tips, advice and useful phrases that can be used.

我创作的这本书属于"9分达人"系列，能帮助雅思考生充分理解考官在评估考生时所听的内容，即雅思口语评分标准。我将详细描述一些评分的理由和口语考试的三个部分：Part 1简介、Part 2个人陈述、Part 3双向讨论。我还会以真题为例，给出多个答案，评论并给出提示、建议和有用的短语。

There are many links, QR codes, tips and information where you can find several viewable or downloadable resources. I firmly believe that using the knowledge of the criteria can help you on the path to passing the IELTS exam at your required level. It should be understood that this is NOT a 'quick fix' book, but one that can point you in the right direction to improve.

本书包含许多链接、二维码、提示和信息，为你提供可查看或可下载的资源。我坚信，使用评分标准可以帮助你在雅思考试中达到应有的水平。你要明白，这不是一本"快速通关"指南，而是一本给你指明改进方向的书。

▌ Some details about the exam procedure 考试流程细节

The Speaking exam consists of three parts, aptly named Part 1, Part 2 and Part 3 and takes between 11 and 14 minutes to complete. Each IELTS exam is done individually, that is, one-to-one, and is NEVER performed in pairs or groups. You do not need to bring anything with you to this exam, other than your brain, to complete it.

口语考试由3部分组成，即Part 1、Part 2和Part 3，考试时间是11到14分钟。每位考生的口语考试都是单独进行的，也就是一对一，从来**没有**成对或者分组考试的情况。除了你的大脑，你不需要带任何其他东西来完成这项考试。

After opening the door, the examiner will ask a few questions before he allows you into the room. Typically, they will ask whether you have your ID with you, will check that you don't have your phone with you (this should be left with the administration staff) and will check that the number on your wristband matches the examination room number. Once these checks have been successfully completed, the examiner will invite you in and show you where you can be seated.

开门后，考官会问几个问题，然后才让你进入房间。通常，他们会询问你是否带了身份证，检查你是否带了手机（手机需由工作人员保管），最后检查你腕带上的号码是否与考场号码匹配。一切无误后，考官会邀请你进房间，坐在指定的位置上。

Once you've sat down, the exam officially starts, and the examiner will speak into the recording device and give details about you as a candidate, them as an examiner, and some information about the Examination centre. They will then ask you for your name and to see your ID so that they can check it against the details that they have for you. This is just a simple, further, security check, so don't worry. Once this is done, you will be asked, 'What should I call you?'. Here, you can give them your English name or your Chinese name. It doesn't matter which one you give as, in my experience, examiners will only use it sparingly, if at all.

坐下之后，考试就正式开始了，考官会对着录音设备说话，介绍考生和考官的详细情况以及一些关于考试中心的信息。然后，他们会询问你的姓名，查看你的身份证以再次核对信息。这只是一个简单的二次安全检查，所以不用担心。核对完成后，考官会问"What should I call you?"（我该怎么称呼你？）。你可以回答英文名字或中文名字。根据我的经验，你用哪一个名字并不重要，因为考官基本用不上。

重要信息： 所有的口语考试都是录音的，而且录音在考官开门之前就已经开始了。这是标准程序，不用担心。录音有多种原因，其中一个主要原因是重新评分。如果一位考生认为需要重新评估口语考试，录音通常会发给一位级别更高的新考官，以便回顾整场口语考试。

Tiny Tip: *Many countries, including China, are now offering more and more Speaking Exams online. The process is fundamentally the same, except that you will do it online in front of a computer screen rather than in person. The questions, marking system etc., are all the same.*

小提示： 包括中国在内的许多国家现在提供越来越多的在线口语考试。考试流程基本相同，只是你要在电脑屏幕前完成，而不是面对真人考官，问题、评分系统等都一样。

■ The Examination Structure 考试组成

Part 1　*Introducing Yourself/The Interview – four to five minutes* 自我介绍 / 问答 4—5 分钟

This is sometimes referred to as 'The Interview' because the examiner typically asks questions about likes and dislikes, habits, culture etc. You should also answer each question fully and use extended answers wherever possible. I prefer to think of this part as a chance to introduce yourself and use vocabulary that is very common and well-known (My name is ... etc.) to try and relax for the rest of the exam.

Part 1有时被称为"面试"，因为考官通常会问一些关于好恶、习惯、文化等方面的问题。你应该完整回答每个问题，并尽可能扩展答案。我倾向于把这一部分当成一个自我介绍的机会，使用非常常见和熟悉的词汇（My name is ... 等），在接下来的考试中尽量放松。

Tiny Tip: *The introduction and ID checking will take around 30 seconds. Then, there will be approximately four and a half minutes to complete 12 questions – four questions from three different topics. Without boring you with the mathematics, it means that each answer should be around 20 seconds. That would generally be about three sentences.*

小提示： 自我介绍和证件检查大约需要30秒。接着考生会在大约四分半钟的时间里回答12个问题，三个不同的主题下各有四个问题。不劳你计算，每个回答应该说20秒左右，通常是三句话。

Another Tiny Tip: *Within the criteria, these are referred to as 'Familiar' topics.*

另一个小提示： 在评分标准中，这些问题属于"熟悉的"主题。

The individual long turn – three to four minutes 个人陈述 3—4 分钟

In this part, you are given a topic card (as shown below) and 1 minute to make notes on what you want to say. You must then speak for 1 to 2 minutes about the topic shown or until the examiner stops you.

在 Part 2，考官会给你一张话题卡（如下所示），你有 1 分钟的时间来记下你想说的内容。然后你必须就所给的话题说 1—2 分钟，或者一直说到考官打断你为止。

Describe your favourite singer or actor.

You should say:

　　who he/she is

　　what his/her personality is

　　what kind of style his/her music/acting belongs to

and explain why he/she is your favourite singer/actor.

Important Information: *Make sure that you start making notes immediately after you are given the topic card. The examiner won't remind you to begin as he has already given you the instructions for this part of the test and asked whether you understood them.*

重要信息：拿到话题卡后务必立即开始做笔记。考官不会提醒你开始，因为他已经告知过你这部分考试的说明，并问你是否理解。

Tiny Tip: *Although you can speak for less than two minutes, you probably wouldn't get any higher than a 6 for Fluency. It's best to continually talk for the full two minutes and have the examiner stop you after the time is up.*

小提示：虽然你可以说不到两分钟，但你的流利性的得分可能不会超过 6 分。最好是连续讲满两分钟，时间到了之后让考官打断你。

The two-way discussion – four to five minutes 双向讨论 4—5 分钟

Although still a question-and-answer session, this last section of the exam can be looked at as more of a discussion between two people. The examiner will ask questions related to the topic card in part 2 and ask you for your opinion, thoughts and hypotheses. Similarly to Part 1, you should also give complete sentences and extended answers.

虽然仍然是一问一答，但 Part 3 更像是两个人之间的讨论。考官会问与 Part 2 话题卡相关的问题，并询问你的观点、想法和假设。同 Part 1 一样，你也应该给出完整的句子和扩展的答案。

Tiny Tip: *You will be asked six to eight questions, meaning your answers need roughly 35 seconds each to fill the time. This would be around 4 or 5 sentences in length.*

小提示： 你会被问六到八个问题，这意味着你的回答需要 35 秒左右，大约说四五句话。

Another Tiny Tip: *Within the criteria, Parts 2 and 3 are referred to as 'Unfamiliar' topics. Read the following chapters for information on the differences between these and 'Familiar' topics.*

另一个小提示： 在评分标准中，Part 2 和 Part 3 被称为"不熟悉的"话题。请阅读后面的章节，了解这些话题与"熟悉的"话题之间的区别。

It should also be CLEARLY understood that the examiners mark the WHOLE exam as one unit, not in separate parts. They DON'T give a mark for Part 1, and a different mark for Parts 2 and 3. It's simply all put together and assessed at the end. In many ways, this is useful for the candidate because, if they haven't included much in the form of Paraphrasing in Part 1, they have the opportunity to add more during Parts 2 and 3, which means that the examiner is able to increase the score for that particular element.

你还应该**清楚地**认识到，考官是将整个考试作为一个**整体**来评分，而不是分成单独的部分。他们**不是**分别给 Part 1、Part 2 和 Part 3 打分，而是合在一起，最后进行评估。从很多方面来说，这对考生是有利的，因为他们如果在 Part 1 中较少使用改述，还有机会在后面两个部分中补充，也就是说考官能够增加该评分维度的分数。

■ The Band Scores 分数表

There is no pass or fail in the IELTS Exam, simply different levels or 'Band Scores' as they are officially known. The table below shows the nine different levels of IELTS. I have also added TOEFL iBT, CEFR and this book's Star (★) system so you can easily compare them. Some scores don't match each other exactly, so use this as a rough guide.

雅思考试没有及格或不及格的说法，只有不同的水平或官方"分数"。下表显示了雅思考试的九个不同级别。我还添加了托福网考、欧标 CEFR 和本书的星级（★）系统以方便比较。有些分数与等级之间并不完全匹配，因此仅供粗略参考。

IELTS Score	TOEFL iBT	CEFR	James' Stars
9 – Expert User	118	C2	
8 – Very Good User	110	C1	★★★★★
7 – Good User	94		★★★★
6 – Competent User	60	B2	★★★
5 – Modest User	35	B1	★★
4 – Limited User		A2	★
3 – Extremely Limited User	0 - 31		
2 – Intermittent User		A1	
1 – Non User			

Often, candidates will receive half marks (5.5 or 6.5, for example). This is because the overall score is the calculated mean average from the individual scores of each exam element. See below for an example:

通常，考生的分数会出现半分的情况（例如 5.5 或 6.5 ）。这是因为总分是根据每个单项分数计算出的平均分。请参见下例：

Listening	Reading	Writing	Speaking	Overall
7	6.5	6	6	6.5

Tiny Tip: *Individual element Scores are rounded down, whereas, to balance things, Overall scores are rounded up.*

小提示：单项分数向下取整，为了平衡，总分向上取整。

■ ChatGPT and other Chatbots ChatGPT 及其他聊天机器人

A recent technological development is that of AI, particularly ChatGPT. At the time of writing, early 2023, it has been all over the news and Internet for weeks and a lot of people are unsure how they can, or will be, incorporated into learning and education.

最近的技术发展当属人工智能，特别是 ChatGPT。撰写本书时正值 2023 年初，它连续数周出现在新闻和互联网上，许多人还不确定能否或者如何将其应用于学习和教育中。

Many teachers and universities have already raised the questions of plagiarism and copyright and, to my knowledge, there aren't any definite answers at the moment. Having looked at and used it a little myself, I would have to say that if you just copy/memorise the answers given for the IELTS speaking exam, it will be very obvious.

许多老师和大学已经提出了剽窃和版权的问题，据我所知，目前还没有任何明确的解决方案。我自己了解并尝试了一下，不得不说，如果你全部复制或记忆它提供的雅思口语考试答案，考官能明显看出是机器生成的。

I say this for two reasons. The first is that the answers are given in a more written format rather than spoken and the second is that the structures of the answers are always the same, quite often with the same vocabulary being used.

我这样说有两个原因。第一，答案更像是书面语，而不是口语；第二，所有答案的结构几乎一致，使用的词汇也是。

I realise that Baidu, Alibaba and other such companies will all be bringing their own versions out in the near future, and I wish them luck, but DON'T use them to give you answers that you can memorise. It's possible that you could get away with it once, or even more than that, but if you think about this logically, it will be that there are thousands of people doing exactly the same and producing VERY similar answers, so if an examiner hears the same response from multiple students, they are likely to raise questions and report candidates to the administration team.

我知道百度、阿里巴巴和其他类似的公司都将在不久的将来推出自己的版本，我祝他们好运，但请不要用人工智能给你提供能记住的答案。你可能会侥幸成功一次，甚至更多次，但如果你从逻辑上思考这个问题，会发现有成千上万的人在做完全相同的事情，并给出**非常**相似的答案，如果考官听到多个学生的回答相同，他们很可能会提出质疑，将考生情况报告给管理团队。

I would advise using them to give you ideas and maybe even facts and then use your knowledge and language to describe those ideas. This will not only help you improve your English, but also help you understand how to improve your grammar and idea development.

我的建议是仅让它们提供想法或者一些实例，然后用你的知识和语言来描述这些想法。这不仅能帮助你提高英语水平，还能帮助你理解如何提升语法和构思拓展。

■ Some 'Thank yous' 致谢

Before I get into the book proper, I'd like to thank some people who helped make this book a reality.
进入正文之前，我想感谢以下这些人，他们的帮助使这本书成为现实。

Cindy Ge, from New Channel, her constant advice and support were invaluable in keeping me motivated during this content's design and actual writing. Shelley Du, from New Channel, who helped with the content design and supplied me with more than enough questions to complete this first edition. Zhang Long, from New Channel, whose expertise in online development allowed us good access to the online content. Edward Lou, for his ideas for specific Chinese Student answers and the help with deliberate errors common to Chinese Students. Jia Jingjing and Wang Yu were both a great help with the audio recordings. Finally, Stuart Jones, whose advice and support with some of the higher-level answers, was invaluable. I'm sure that without all their help and the rest of the New Channel team, this would at least be a very different book and, at worst, not a book at all.

新航道的葛亚芬老师持续给予我宝贵的建议与支持，是我构思和创作的动力来源；杜修丽老师帮我构思内容，为我提供丰富的真题以完成本书第一版；张龙老师用在线开发的专业知识让我们能够便捷访问在线内容；娄雨润为我提供中国学生的具体答案和常见错误；贾京京和王宇在音频录制时给予了很大的帮助；最后，斯图亚特·琼斯（Stuart Jones）为我提供宝贵的建议和部分高分答案。我敢肯定，如果没有他们和新航道其他成员的帮助，这本书会截然不同，甚至难以成形。

詹姆斯
2023年5月

新航道"9分达人"系列图书已面世十余载，陪伴雅思考生走过了许多备考的日日夜夜。雅思口语分册迄今共出版了两册，五年磨一剑，在2023年，本系列迎来了全新的版本。这本《9分达人雅思口语宝典》在原来的基础上，与时俱进更新了题库，选取了2020—2023年的高频考题，第一次从考官的角度对评分标准进行了具体的阐述，并通过线上平台的方式，解决了口语换题季的更新问题。希望在全新的视角和学习方式的助力下，考生能够精准备考，提高考试成绩和口语能力。

本书由新航道雅思研发中心与詹姆斯（James Foster）共同创作出版，目的是"明确考官想要的，提供考生要学的"。詹姆斯在英语教学的各个方面都有着丰富的经验。作为一名前雅思考官，他先后在北京多所大学工作，已有15年的在华教学经验，对中国学生的需求有着独特的见解。有感于中国学生在学习英语和通过雅思考试方面所面临的困难，他非常期待通过本书，为考生提供帮助。以下是本书在编排上的几个特色。

1. 考官视角解读评分标准　剖析得分要点

市场上雅思口语方面的参考用书，有的事无巨细，从字、词、句、语法等各个环节手把手教导；有的提供方法论，从思维方式的角度进行分析和引导，各有千秋。然而，本书另辟蹊径，从剑桥雅思官方的评分标准出发，逐条分析并举例说明，将标准中"极少""偶尔""有时""明显"等表达具象化，从而向考生更好地阐明在雅思考试过程中，考官到底看重什么。不仅如此，作者还展示了从4分到7分四大标准的不同例子，让考生能更好地了解自己的水平以及进步空间。

本书不仅从文本上对 Lexical Resource（词汇多样性）和 Grammar Range and Accuracy（语法多样性及准确性）进行条分缕析，同时在 Fluency（流利度）和 Pronunciation（发音）这两个图书上不易展示的方面，也给出了多个范例，并由詹姆斯亲自语音示范，从而让考生能更好地理解评分规则，更有针对性地进行备考。

2. 教学视角精析外教范文　学习地道表达

作为前雅思口语考官，詹姆斯多年的任教经验让他在编写参考范文时，能充分了解考生日常会踩的"坑"，并巧妙地融合到答案范例和评析建议中去，让学生看到就能产生"是我了"的熟悉感，从而绕道而行。为了向考生提供更加精准的备考建议，本书在 Section Ⅱ 提供了口语 Part 1 范文及完整答案解析（包含四个评分标准的详细分析以及星级，小部分1星答案，大部分为3星及以上答案），尤其是对流利度和发音部分提供了预估评分，希望能让考生明白，文本与口音是相辅相成的，并不存在满分的文本一定有9分的评分，也并不是发音决定分数的上限，而是表达的完整性。因此，在 Part 1部分的答案中，会出现一些学生惯常容易出现的错误表达，并在评分解析中进行分析和修改。Part 2/3都是高分范例（4星及以上），提供不同角度的回答方式，方便学生积累和学习语料，所以只提供文本维度的评分标准分析，不再提供发音和流利度方面的演示。这样的设计是考虑到发音和流利度这两个方面的演示相对主观，千人千面，不会因为 Part 1或者 Part 2题目不同而出现很大的分数差异，因此集中放在 Part 1部分进行阐述。Part 2/3部分对内容、框架和词汇语法等方面考查更多，所以提供高分范例，更方便考生进行积累和学习。在范文的正文部分，本书编者将得分要点和地道表达做了专色和角标的处理，在不影响学生理解范文的同时，突出作者想要引起注意的内容，在反复中加强考生对标准的印象和理解。

3. 考生视角打造一题双解　积累口语素材

长久以来，考生一直在准备口语方面，都对参考答案有很强的依赖性，认为口语备考，必然是要看地道的答案、满分的示范，甚至于陷入"背答案"的误区。"9分达人"系列图书的口语部分固然为考生准备了专家打造的范文，然而如何使用、如何借鉴、如何在考场上自如地表达，不是简单背诵能解决的。本书作者希望考生能够带着考官评分所遵循的各项标准，去形成自己的答案。为了达到这个目标，本书为每道题提供"一题双解"。两个答案，有的分数差异较大（如2星和4星），用以突出哪一项或几项得分标准影响最大；有的分数段十分接近（如3星与4星），主要是让学生通过对比细节的表达区别，理解得分差异，揣摩在内容相似的情况下，到底是什么影响了得分高低。Part 2/3部分根据话题和问题类型，从不同的立场、角度编写了两份答案，这样不仅可以拓展答题维度，积累更多样的语料，而且包含更多地道的表达，内容更丰富。

为了更符合阅读习惯，更方便对比学习，本书的"一题双解"可以在同一个左右跨页上展示出来，既免去了翻页，又方便做交叉对比，能把两份答案的精髓完整地把握住，对形成自己的答题思路大有帮助。

4. 与时俱进搭建线上平台　提供多元信息

与以往的传统图书相比，本书力求在立体化出版方面做更多尝试，从而更好地满足口语学习的需求。对于大多数解读，文中将给出示例，同时也可以扫描书中的二维码，访问"9分达人在线学习系统"来获取在线信息。此外，微信扫一扫图书封底"新英汉"APP二维码可收听随书的音频。

考试的准备功在朝夕，口语的进步除了仔细了解考试方式和参考范文，更重要的是明白，表达的根本是沟通与交流。希望本书能够架起考官与考生之间的桥梁，传达考官所需要的，给予考生所要学的，能助力考生通过孜孜不倦的积累与日复一日的训练，成为在考场上能侃侃而谈的那个闪亮的人。感谢本书作者詹姆斯将多年的心得一字一句地传授给考生，也感谢为本书提供翻译的蔡杰老师，感谢新航道雅思研发中心每一位为本书辛勤付出的老师们。欢迎各位读者朋友们提出宝贵意见与建议，共同翻越语言的障碍，更流畅地与世界对话！

CONTENTS
目　　　录

Section II   Part 1 Preparation and Topics 如何准备 Part 1

Section III   Parts 2&3 Preparation and Topics 如何准备 Parts 2&3

附录 Module Tests and Sample Answers 真题模拟及参考答案

Section I

The IELTS Speaking Criteria

雅思口语评分标准

I believe that understanding the IELTS Speaking Criteria is fundamental to getting a good score in the IELTS. Unless you know, and understand, what the examiners are listening for when they are marking you, it is challenging to obtain higher scores as you're not sure what is needed. To get scores of six and above, examiners listen for specific things, and you can increase your score relatively quickly. In contrast, scores of five and below typically indicate the lack of, or inaccuracy of, the required elements.

我认为了解雅思口语评分标准是在雅思考试中获得好成绩的基础。除非您知道并理解考官在给您评分时在听什么，否则获得更高的分数是具有挑战性的，因为您不确定需要说些什么。要获得6分及以上的分数，考官会听取具体细节，知道这一点，您可以相对较快地提高分数。相比之下，5分及以下的分数通常说明缺乏必要信息或表达不准确。

Tiny Tip: *The overall Speaking score is the average of the score of each element rounded down. For example, 6 6 5 5 is an overall score of 5.5, but so is 6 6 6 5.*

小提示：口语分数是每个分项分数的平均值。例如，单项6、6、5、5的总分是5.5，但6、6、6、5也是如此。

The following section of this book will go through the criteria in detail through all four areas: Fluency and Coherence, Lexical Resource, Grammatical Range and Accuracy, and Pronunciation, and levels four to seven in each.

本书第一部分将详细介绍以下四个方面的标准：流利性和连贯性、词汇多样性、语法多样性和准确性以及发音，以及每个标准4分到7分是如何打分的。

Important Information: *Unless ALL the positive criteria are met within a given score, that score CANNOT be awarded. Many of the decisions are subjective, meaning there are no actual absolute times or quantities in scoring, which in turn means that each examiner's score may vary.*

重要信息：除非满足给定的分数段内**所有的**标准，否则考官将不会给出这个分数。许多决定都是主观的，这意味着评分实际上并没有绝对的时长和内容要求，这反过来意味着每个考官给出的分数可能会有所不同。

Tiny Tip: *When looking at the criteria, also try to understand what's NOT there. This may help you understand it more. For example, in Fluency Level 7, it doesn't mention 'content related' hesitation, which means that if your pauses are content related, an examiner will look at 8 rather than 7 for this part.*

小提示：在查看标准时，要试着理解其中**没有**要求什么，这可能有助于你更好地理解它。例如，在流利程度7分水平中，它没有提到"与内容相关"的停顿会扣分，这意味着如果你的停顿与内容相关，考官在这一部分的打分会偏向于8分而不是7分。

IELTS Examiners are trained and need to pass a test to allow them to examine candidates, and they will NOT vary in their scoring by much. However, it must be understood that examiners are human beings and will think differently occasionally.

雅思考官是经过培训，需要通过测试才能对考生进行考试，因此他们的评分标准不会有太大差异。然而，必须理解的是，考官是人，偶尔会有不同的想法。

For most explanations, examples will be given, and you can access the 9 Fen Daren Online Learning System(OLS) at any time to access the audio samples. Simply scan the QR Code below.

对于大多数解读，文中将给出示例，您也可以随时扫描下面的二维码，访问"9分达人在线学习系统"（OLS）来获取在线信息。

在线学习系统入口

Chapter 1 Fluency and Coherence
流利性与连贯性

Fluency generally covers your ability to speak naturally and without hesitation, too many pauses or going back and correcting yourself if you think you have said something wrong. Now listen to examples of both bad and good Fluency:

流利性通常包括说话时表现自然、没有犹豫、没有过多停顿或自我纠正。现在来听一下流利度好与不好的例子。

· **Example 1 – Bad** ·   🎧 001

> *Examiner: Do you have a job, or are you a student?*
>
> *Candidate: Well, at the ... er ... moment ... er ... um .... I'm a ... er ... I'm a Student and ... er ... um ... student ... and I study ... I study Ma ... Mathema ... Mathematics at ... erm ... University.*

With this example, the candidate stumbles after one or two words and constantly repeats what they say. This is not considered a good level of fluency.

在这个例子中，考生每说一两个词就磕磕绊绊、不断重复所说的话，是流利性不好的表现。

· **Example 2 – Good** ·   🎧 002

> *Examiner: Do you work, or are you a student?*
>
> *Candidate: Well, er ... at the moment, I'm a student, and I study Mathematics at University.*

Here, even though the candidate does 'er' a little, which is normal sometimes, it would be considered a good level of fluency.

在这个例子中，即使考生"呃"了一下也是正常的，仍是流利性好的体现。

Coherence is all about whether you can make yourself 'coherent', which means 'understood', but also, in this context, means 'logical'. The examiner will listen to the structure of your speech and whether you follow a logical order. Now listen to examples of both bad and good coherence:

连贯性是你能不能让自己的表达"连贯"，即"能被理解"，在这个语境下也"合乎逻辑"。考官会听你言语的结构以及你是否遵循逻辑顺序。现在来听一下连贯性好与不好的例子。

· **Example 1 – Bad** · 　　　　　　　　　　　　　　　　　　🎧 003

> ***Examiner:*** *Do you play any musical instruments?*
>
> ***Candidate:*** *Guitar. I now play guitar ... before nothing. In my band ... I am singer and play lead. I think music is good to learn and everyone should have a band. Oh, I forgot I ... used to play piano before learning guitar.*

With this example, the order of the musical instruments is not in any kind of order, whether chronological or emphatic.

在这个例子中，考生谈论乐器时没有遵循任何顺序，既没有按时间顺序也没有按主次顺序。

· **Example 2 – Good** · 　　　　　　　　　　　　　　　　　　🎧 004

> ***Examiner:*** *Do you play any musical instruments?*
>
> ***Candidate:*** *No - not anymore. When I was a small child of about 10 or 11, I used to learn the violin but stopped when I was 16 because I was too busy with the exams. One instrument I have always wanted to know how to play, though, is the drums! But I think I might annoy my neighbours too much with the noise! Ha Ha Ha!*

In this example, it is clear that it follows a chronological (time) order, namely from a small child to now.

在这个例子中，考生明显遵循时间顺序，即从小时候到现在的顺序回答。

	Fluency and Coherence	流利性与连贯性
Level 4	•cannot respond without noticeable pauses and may speak slowly, with frequent repetition and self-correction •links basic sentences but with repetitious use of simple connectives and some breakdowns in coherence	•作答有明显停顿，且语速有时缓慢，出现频繁重复及自我纠正 •能连接简单句子，但重复使用简单的连接词，有时缺乏连贯性

▶ **cannot respond without noticeable pauses 作答有明显停顿**

This comes down to what the examiner believes is a 'noticeable pause'. In my teaching experience, I would judge a pause as two seconds or maybe even three. Any more than this, I'd be looking at dropping the score to a 3.

这取决于考官对"明显停顿"的理解。根据我的教学经验，我会把停顿两秒甚至三秒判断为"明显停顿"。停顿再久一点，我会考虑打 3 分。

`· Example ·` 🎧 005

... My ... name is ... Wang Yu. You ... can call ... me ... Michaela.

▶ **... and may speak slowly 或者语速缓慢**

This, again, is a down to the judgement of the examiner. If they feel that the candidate is speaking slower than 'normal' and certainly slower than a native, they will undoubtedly consider a 4. This is quite often considered more in Part 2 of the exam if the examiner feels the candidate is speaking slowly to fill the 2-minute guideline.

这同样取决于考官的判断。如果他们认为考生说得比"正常情况"慢，而且当然比母语者说得慢，他们无疑会考虑给 4 分。在 Part 2 部分，如果考官觉得考生降低语速是为了说够 2 分钟，那么他们会着重考虑这一点。

`· Example ·` 🎧 006

Well, the ... famous ... building ... I'd ... like ... to ... talk ... about ... is ....

▶ **... with frequent repetition 频繁重复**

Another subjective one for the examiner. For many, once is OK, twice is enough, and three times is repetitive. Certainly if it was in the same sentence, but also within an entire answer.

这也涉及考官的主观判断。对许多考官来说，重复一次没问题，两次就够了，三次就啰嗦了。当然，不论这种重复出现在同一个句子里，还是在整个回答过程中。

`· Example ·` 🎧 007

My name ... my ... name ... my name is ... James.

 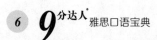

▶ ... and self-correction 自我纠正

Again, this element comes down to how the examiner feels, as there is no definite number of occasions for this. For me, and my experience, it would also come down to the speed of the correction. So if the quantity was three or more and the error types were simple, 4 would be seriously considered.

同样，这也取决于考官的感受，因为纠正次数与分数之间没有明确的对应关系。以我的经验来说，这也取决于自我纠正的速度。如果大于等于三次，并且错误类型很简单，那么我将考虑给4分。

> · **Example** ·　　　　　　　　　　　　　　　　　🎧 008
>
> *When I goes out ... go out for walking, I will ... for a walk, I will always takes ... take my phone.*

▶ links basic sentences but with repetitious use of simple connectives 能连接简单句子，但重复使用简单的连接词

Tiny Tip: *Connectives are words like 'and', 'or', 'but', etc. They will connect one half of a sentence with the other or maybe one sentence to another. Scan the QR code for a list of commonly used Connectives.*

小提示：连接词包括 and、or、but 等。这些词把一个句子的一部分和另一部分连接起来，或者把一个句子和另一个句子连接起来。扫描二维码，查看常用连接词列表。

连接词与语篇标记

This part refers to Grammar and Vocabulary. Firstly, the candidate only uses basic/simple sentences; secondly, they only use the most basic connectives like: and, or, but.

这部分指的是语法和词汇。第一，考生只用基本句型/简单句；第二，他们只使用最基本的连接词，如 and、or、but。

> · **Example** ·　　　　　　　　　　　　　　　　　🎧 009
>
> *OK, so the city I will describe is London, and that's in England. OK, so London is very big, and I've only been there once, and it was last summer. OK so, I went with my Mum and Dad and my little brother and my Dad's friend and his wife. OK, so we arrived, and it was so noisy but ....*

▶ ... and some breakdowns in coherence 缺乏连贯性

> · **Example** ·　　　　　　　　　　　　　　　　　🎧 010
>
> *Firstly, I went to London, then I went to Bath. Before that, I visited Cambridge, and at the beginning, I went to Winchester.*

	Fluency and Coherence	流利性与连贯性
Level 5	•usually maintains flow of speech but uses repetition, self-correction and/or slow speech to keep going •may over-use certain connectives and discourse markers •produces simple speech fluently, but more complex communication causes fluency problems	•通常能保持语流，但需通过重复、自我纠正和（或）降低语速来维持表达 •过度使用某些连接词及语篇标记 •能用简单的语言进行流利的表达，但在进行更为复杂的交流时则表达不畅

▶ **usually maintains flow of speech but uses repetition, self-correction and/or slow speech to keep going** 通常能保持语流，但需通过重复、自我纠正和（或）降低语速来维持表达

Tiny Tip: *This is basically the same as Level 4, just without the pausing part and not 'frequent' repetition, but still repeating sometimes.*

小提示：基本和 4 分水平一样，只是没有停顿和"频繁"的重复，但有时仍会重复。

For this part, the candidate doesn't pause too much, so they generally keep going with their speaking, but they repeat and/or correct themselves and/or speak slower than what would be expected as 'normal'.

在这一水平，考生不会停顿太多次，他们通常能一直说，但他们会重复、纠正自己、说得比"正常情况"慢。

· Example · ◌ 011

> *My name ... name is ... James and I'm from England. Now, I lived in ... live in China.*

▶ **may over-use certain connectives and discourse markers** 过度使用某些连接词及语篇标记

Tiny Tip: *Discourse Markers are words like 'Well', 'So', and 'Furthermore', generally used at the beginning of sentences, but not always. Scan the QR code for a list of commonly used Discourse Markers.*

小提示：语篇标记是 Well、So、Furthermore 之类的词，一般用在句首。扫描二维码查看常用语篇标记列表。

连接词与语篇标记

Here it is, again, utterly subjective to the examiner. There is no fixed number to 'overuse', but, in my experience, I had a student use 'Well' 36 times during a practice exam. That's certainly too much!

再次，这也完全取决于考官的主观判断。超过多少次属于"过度使用"没有规定，但是，据我回

忆，我有一个学生在一次模拟考试中使用了 36 次 Well，这当然太多了！

　　　　　　　　　　　　　　　　　　🎧 012

> *OK, so the city I will describe is London, and that's in England. OK, so London is very big, and I've only been there once besides last summer. OK so, I went with my Mum and Dad and my little brother and my Dad's friend and his wife. OK, so we arrived, and it was so noisy but ....*

▶ **produces simple speech fluently, but more complex communication causes fluency problems** 能用简单的语言进行流利的表达，但在进行更为复杂的交流时则表达不畅

This is loosely linked to grammar and vocabulary. Simple speech would be considered as short sentences with short/easy words.

这与语法和词汇有些许联系。简单的语言会被认为是使用简单单词的短句。

　　　　　　　　　　　　　　　　　　🎧 013

> **Examiner:** *Hello. How are you?*
> **Candidate:** *Hello. I'm fine, and you?*

More complex language could include discourse markers, more complex grammar and longer words (not necessarily all three).

更复杂的语言可能包括语篇标记、更复杂的语法和更长的单词（不一定要三种全有）。

　　　　　　　　　　　　　　　　　　🎧 014

> **Examiner:** *Hello. How are you?*
> **Candidate:** *Well, before you opened the door, I was just nervous. Now I'm completely petrified.*

If a candidate can't say a sentence like the one above without pausing, correcting or repeating, it would be considered a 5.

如果考生说一个像上面那样的句子做不到不停顿、不纠正或不重复，那将得 5 分。

	Fluency and Coherence	流利性与连贯性
Level 6	• is willing to speak at length, though may lose coherence at times due to occasional repetition, self-correction or hesitation • uses a range of connectives and discourse markers but not always appropriately	• 表现出充分交流的意愿，但有时由于偶尔的重复、自我纠正或犹豫而缺乏连贯性 • 能使用一系列连接词及语篇标记，但无法保持一贯恰当

▶ **is willing to speak at length 表现出充分交流的意愿**

Although this refers to ALL parts of the exam and partly to extended answers for at least some examiners, it mainly refers to the Part 2 time limit. If candidates are willing /capable of speaking for at least 1m50s and don't have any of the negative elements in 5, like speaking slowly, examiners would award a 6. If it's shorter than this, they will look more at a 5.

虽然这是口语考试**所有**部分的评分标准，对一些考官来说针对的是扩展答案，主要是 Part 2 的时间限制。如果考生愿意/有能力说至少 1 分 50 秒，并且没有 5 分标准中的任何负面因素，比如语速慢，考官会给 6 分。如果时长更短，考官会更倾向于给 5 分。

▶ **... though may lose coherence at times due to occasional repetition, self-correction or hesitation 但有时由于偶尔的重复、自我纠正或犹豫而缺乏连贯性**

Here it is down to what the examiner feels is 'occasional' and, like everything else so far, may differ slightly from one to another. As a general rule, if the candidate only repeats, self-corrects or hesitates once or twice during a topic/question, examiners are likelier to give a 6. More than that, they would gauge how many times they have over the entire exam and think about a 6 or a 5.

这取决于考官对"偶尔的"理解，就像到目前为止的其他标准一样，可能会因人而异。一般来说，如果考生在一个话题/问题中只重复、自我纠正或犹豫一两次，考官有可能给 6 分。而且，他们会计算整个考试出现这种情况的次数，再考虑给 6 分或 5 分。

▶ **uses a range of connectives and discourse markers 能使用一系列连接词及语篇标记**

There are links to what Discourse Markers and Connectives are in Level 5, above, and yet again, it varies on what an examiner might think 'range' means. For many examiners, a minimum range implies at least 3, and a 'good' range would be more like 6 or 7. Like many things in this exam, the wider the range that you can give during the exam, the higher your score.

上文 5 分标准里放有语篇标记和连接词的链接，但这同样取决于考官对"一系列"的理解。对许多考官来说，最少使用 3 个，最好使用 6 至 7 个。就像口语考试中的许多标准一样，你在考试中使用的多样性越丰富，你的分数就越高。

▶ **... but not always appropriately** 但无法保持一贯恰当

Here, it says that you can make a few mistakes using Discourse Markers or Connectives and still receive a 6. The example shown is from a mock test I conducted with one of my students a few years ago when it seemed that ALL students wanted to use the Discourse Marker 'Obviously'.

这里是说你使用语篇标记或连接词时即使犯一点错误，仍然可以得到 6 分。下面的例子来自几年前我和一个学生进行的模拟测试，当时似乎**所有的**学生都想使用 Obviously（显而易见）这个语篇标记。

· Example ·　　　　　　　　　　　　　　　　　　　　　　　6ᗡ 015

> *Examiner : What's your favourite colour?*
> *Female Candidate: Obviously, it's blue!*

Here, it wouldn't be appropriate to say 'Obviously'. Why is it obvious to an examiner what someone's favourite colour is? And blue, for a girl? It certainly wasn't obvious to me.

在这个例子中，使用 Obviously 是不合适的。为什么对考官来说，某人最喜欢的颜色是显而易见的？一个女孩最喜欢蓝色？这对我来说当然不是显而易见的。

If the candidate wore a pink ribbon in her hair, a pink dress, pink nail polish, and lipstick, it would be more appropriate as it would be reasonably clear that she likes pink.

如果考生头上扎了一条粉色的丝带，穿了一件粉色的衣服，涂了粉色的指甲油和口红，这时才更合适用 Obviously，因为她明显喜欢粉色。

Tiny Tip: *Another favourite is 'In a word, ...'. This LITERALLY means in ONE word. So you can say, 'In a word, yes.', but you can't say, 'In a word, I think that it's the best idea I've ever heard.'*

小提示：考生最喜欢用的另一个语篇标记是 In a word，这个短语的字面意思就是用一个词来总结。所以你可以说 "In a word, yes."，但你不能说 "In a word, I think that it's the best idea I've ever heard." 。

	Fluency and Coherence	流利性与连贯性
Level 7	•speaks at length without noticeable effort or loss of coherence •may demonstrate language-related hesitation at times, or some repetition and/or self-correction •uses a range of connectives and discourse markers with some flexibility	•表达详尽，并无明显困难，或不失连贯 •有时出现与语言相关的犹豫或出现重复和（或）自我纠正 •具有一定灵活性地使用一系列连接词和语篇标记

▶ **Speaks at length without noticeable effort or loss of coherence 表达详尽，并无明显困难，或不失连贯**

The most crucial element here is 'without noticeable effort'. It is a judgment of the examiner as to precisely what this means, but, at least for me, it means that I think it's easy for the candidate to speak English. The coherence is also easy to follow, and the examiner doesn't need to think at all to understand the flow of language from one part to the next.

这里最关键的标准是"无明显困难"。这取决于考官对其确切含义的判断，但是，至少对我来说，我的标准是考生说英语很容易。考生的连贯性也很好，考官根本不需要思考就能理解语言的流动。

▶ **May demonstrate language-related hesitation at times 有时出现与语言相关的犹豫**

'Language Related' refers to vocabulary rather than grammar here. So, for example, you might say, '…oh, what's the word? Enthusiasm, that's it!'. Like nearly everything else, it's up to the examiner what 'at times' means. One thing I can say is that they wouldn't be giving a 7 if nearly every sentence had a pause looking for a word, and I'd expect the word to be less common.

这里的"语言相关"指的是词汇而不是语法。例如，你可能会说："……哦，那个词是什么？热情，没错！"和几乎所有其他标准一样，取决于考官对"有时"的理解。我想说的是，如果几乎每个句子都有一个想不起词的停顿，考官就不会给7分，而且我希望这个词不那么常见。

▶ **… or some repetition and/or self-correction 或出现重复和（或）自我纠正**

For this part, 'some' would be a 'few' times over the entire exam. It would be expected most of the exam to be without self-correction or repetition.

在这部分，some指在整个考试中只出现几次，最好正常考试没有自我纠正或重复。

▶ **… uses a range of connectives and discourse markers with some flexibility 具有一定灵活性地使用一系列连接词和语篇标记**

Here, inappropriacy is not accepted, and the range should show some ability to use different examples for similar grammatical reasons.

在这里，不恰当是不被接受的，而范围是指考生应当显示出依据类似的语法结构而使用不同例子的能力。

· Example 1 ·　　🎧 016

> **Examiner:** Do you like playing sports?
>
> **Candidate:** Absolutely. Sports are a great way ....

· Example 2 ·　　🎧 017

> **Examiner:** Do you like meeting your friends?
>
> **Candidate:** Definitely. My friends are ....

Chapter 2 Lexical Resource
词汇多样性

Lexical Resource is a more formal way of saying Vocabulary. This section of the criteria is all about the words you use and whether you can use paraphrasing/synonyms to explain your ideas precisely and in detail.

词汇多样性是词汇量更正式的表达。这部分的评分标准与你使用的词汇、你是否能使用改述/同义词来精确详细地解释你的想法有关。

Quite often, people confuse elements of this with Grammar. Lexical Resource doesn't mean changing a word from a noun to a verb, like 'deployment' to 'deploy', or even tenses, like moving from the Past to the Future tense. It is simply the range of vocabulary that you have and can use when speaking about both 'Familiar' and 'Unfamiliar' topics.

人们经常会把这一点和语法多样性弄混淆。词汇多样性并不意味着将一个词从名词变成动词，例如把 deployment 换成 deploy，或者变化时态，从过去时变成将来时。词汇多样性仅仅指谈论"熟悉的"和"不熟悉的"话题时，你拥有和可以使用的词汇量。

As we go through the different criteria levels, you'll notice that 'Paraphrase' is a word that's used a lot. In my view, it's of paramount importance that when you are studying vocabulary, you also learn as many different synonyms as you can and how to use them. The online Cambridge Dictionary defines a paraphrase as 'to repeat something written or spoken using different words, often in a humorous form or in a simpler and shorter form that makes the original meaning clearer'.

当我们讨论不同级别的标准时，你会注意到"改述"是一个使用频率很高的词。在我看来，当你学习词汇时，尽可能多地学习不同的同义词以及如何使用它们是极其重要的。在线剑桥词典对"改述"的定义是"用不同的单词重复书面或口语内容，通常用幽默的或更简短的形式使原始意思更清楚"。

Important Information: *Although synonyms and paraphrases are technically different, they are often measured similarly by examiners. So, what this means is that if you can use other words to explain something, it would be included as a paraphrase. If you use different words from those used in the question, it would be a good thing.*

重要信息： 虽然同义词和改述严格来说是不同的，但考官经常采用相似的衡量标准。这就是说，如果你用其他的词来解释某事，也算改述。如果你用了不同于题干中的词，这是一件好事。

· Example ·

> **Examiner:** *What's your favourite colour?*
>
> **Candidate:** *Well, I just love blue. Out of all the colours, it's the one I like the most, by far.*

In the above example, the candidate paraphrases the question and their previous statement. So, it's clear to the examiner that you can use different words to explain 'favourite'.

在上面这个例子中，考生改写了问题和之前的表述。对考官来说，这明显表明你使用了不用的词汇来解释 favorite。

Tiny Tip: *Try using the synonyms/paraphrasing closely in your sentence. It makes it easier for the examiner to recognise.*

小提示：尽量在你的句子中频繁使用同义词 / 改述，以便考官更容易识别。

	Lexical Resource	词汇多样性
Level 4	•is able to talk about familiar topics but can only convey basic meaning on unfamiliar topics and makes frequent errors in word choice •rarely attempts paraphrase	•能谈论所熟悉的话题，但对不熟悉的话题仅能表达基本意思，且经常用词不当 •很少尝试改述

▶ **is able to talk about familiar topics 能谈论所熟悉的话题**

This refers to Part 1 of the exam as shown earlier in 'The Examination Structure'. 'Familiar topics' mean topics that are relatively commonly spoken between people during a conversation in a social context. The first 'familiar' topic of Part 1 is always either something about you – whether you work or are a student – or something about your home or hometown. Other familiar topics may include the weather, movies, music, shoes, people you know etc. You should know the words that are used within all these topics.

这指的是前面介绍的"考试组成"中的 Part 1。"熟悉的话题"指人们在社交场合中交谈相对常见的话题。Part 1中第一个"熟悉的"话题要么关于你——你工作了还是在读书？——要么关于你的家或家乡。其他熟悉的话题可能包括天气、电影、音乐、鞋子、你认识的人等。你需要知道所有这些话题中用到的单词。

Tiny Tip: *There are a variety of these familiar topics, and they change regularly.*
小提示：这些熟悉的话题有很多，而且会定期变化。

▶ **... but can only convey basic meaning on unfamiliar topics 但对不熟悉的话题仅能表达基本意思**

This refers to Part 2 and Part 3 of the exam again, as mentioned previously in 'The Examination Structure', and 'unfamiliar' topics mean those that you may not speak about daily or even weekly. Example topics may include your favourite actor, an unusual building, news you've received etc.

正如之前在"考试组成"中提到的，这指的是考试的 Part 2和 Part 3。"不熟悉"的话题是指那些你可能不会每天甚至每周都谈论的话题，可能包括你最喜欢的演员、不寻常的建筑、你看到的新闻等。

'Basic meaning' means that simple words are used, and only simple words are used to describe the topic.

"基本意思"就是用简单的词，且仅能用简单的词来描述话题。

> *I play basketball. I play with my friends, and I like basketball.*

Words like 'play' and 'like' would be considered too simple as they are some of the first words anyone would learn when studying English.

像 play 和 like 这样的词会被认为太简单，因为学英语最开始学的就是这些词。

▶ ... and makes frequent errors in word choice 经常用词不当

This part means that the words being used are incorrect in some way. It may be the verb, noun, adjective, or any other word in the sentence, but it wouldn't be related to tense.

这是指使用的单词在某些方面是不正确的。这可能是动词、名词、形容词或句子中的任何其他词用词不当，但这种用词不当与时态无关。

> *I do basketball. I do basketball with my followers.*

Here, the candidate has used 'do' rather than 'play' and 'followers' rather than 'friends' both of which would be the wrong vocabulary for this sentence.

在这个例子中，考生用 do 而不是 play，用 followers 而不是 friends。这两个词在句中都很不恰当。

▶ rarely attempts paraphrase 很少尝试改述

Similarly to some of the previous elements, there isn't a number put on 'rarely', but I believe most people would put it at one or two. Any more than this, and examiners would probably look at a five or more.

同前面其他标准一样，"很少"是几次没有规定，但我相信大多数人的理解是一两次。超过两次，考官可能会给 5 分或更多。

■ IELTS Level 5 (★ ★)

	Lexical Resource	词汇多样性
Level 5	•manages to talk about familiar and unfamiliar topics but uses vocabulary with limited flexibility •attempts to use paraphrase but with mixed success	•能谈论熟悉或不熟悉的话题，但使用词汇的灵活性有限 •尝试改述，但有时成功有时失败

▶ **manages to talk about familiar and unfamiliar topics but uses vocabulary** 能谈论熟悉或不熟悉的话题

The main difference between this level and level 4 is the ability to speak about unfamiliar topics in Parts 2 and 3. Again, you need to be able to have at least some knowledge of words within and surrounding any particular Part 2 topic.

5分水平与4分水平的主要区别是在 Part 2和 Part 3能够谈论不熟悉话题的能力。同样，你需要至少掌握一些 Part 2特定主题的词汇。

▶ **... with limited flexibility** 但使用词汇的灵活性有限

This means that although you can use some vocabulary to describe a topic, it's not sufficient that you can be precise in your descriptions.

这是指虽然你可以用一些词汇来描述一个主题，但你的描述不够精确。

· Non-Flexible Example ·

> *A sport I enjoy is basketball. I play basketball with my friends. Sport is good for me.*

· Flexible Example ·

> *The sport I enjoy is basketball. I play it with my friends. It's good for my health and keeps me fit.*

▶ **attempts to use paraphrase but with mixed success** 尝试改述，但有时成功有时失败

The critical thing to realise here is that the examiner has recognised that you are using some synonyms/paraphrasing; you just might be using some correctly and some incorrectly.

这个标准的关键是考官已经意识到你使用了一些同义词/转述，只是用对和用错的情况都有。

· Example ·

> *My favourite colour is blue, it's the best colour by far.*

In the example above, 'best' isn't really a synonym of 'favourite'. So although the candidate is attempting to paraphrase, it's not entirely correct.

在上面这个例子中，best并不算是favourite的同义词，所以即使考生尝试转述，但并不完全正确。

 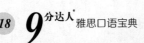

■ IELTS Level 6 (★ ★ ★)

	Lexical Resource	词汇多样性
Level 6	• has a wide enough vocabulary to discuss topics at length and make meaning clear in spite of inappropriacies • generally paraphrases successfully	• 有足以详尽讨论各种话题的词汇量，虽然有时使用不当但意思表达清晰 • 基本上能成功地进行改述

▶ **has a wide enough vocabulary to discuss topics at length** 有足以详尽讨论各种话题的词汇量

This relates to Part 2 of the exam and also is connected to Level 6 of Fluency and Coherence. The connection is the phrase 'at length'. This means that a candidate should have enough vocabulary to NOT repeat themselves during the 2 minutes allowed for Part 2. It also means that the extended answers in Part 3 have enough of a range of vocabulary for exactly the same reason.

这与考试的 Part 2 有关，也与 6 分标准的流利性和连贯性有关。这种关联在于"详尽"一词。这意味着考生应该具备足够的词汇量，在 Part 2 的 2 分钟内不重复自己的话。这还意味着，出于完全相同的原因，Part 3 的扩展答案要展现足够的词汇量。

▶ **... and make meaning clear in spite of inappropriacies** 虽然有时使用不当但意思表达清晰

The meaning here is that a candidate may use the wrong word sometimes when speaking, but this doesn't affect the examiner's understanding of what they're trying to explain.

这里的意思是，考生说话时有时可能会用错词，但这不会影响考官对他们试图解释的内容的理解。

> **· Example ·**

> *A sport I enjoy is basketball. It's good for my health, not only because it is an excellent aerobic exercise but also because I can wind down my mind, which means I can totally relax myself.*

In the above example, 'wind down my mind' and 'relax myself' aren't lexically correct in this sentence. Although I believe any examiner would understand without too much difficulty what was meant.

在上面的例子中，wind down my mind 和 relax myself 使用不当，但我相信任何考官能毫不费力地理解考生的意思。

For your reference, the correct sentence would be:

仅供参考，正确的表达应该是：

> *A sport I enjoy is basketball. It's good for my health, not only because it is an excellent aerobic exercise but also because I can mentally wind down, which means I can totally relax both body and mind.*

▶ generally paraphrases successfully 基本上能成功地进行改述

Hopefully, you have begun to see a trend here and the importance of paraphrasing. If you don't paraphrase or do so minimally, the examiner will score a 4. If candidates at least make an effort to paraphrase, they will likely be awarded a 5. Here at level 6, as long as the attempts at paraphrasing are *MOSTLY* correct, this is the score you will achieve.

希望你已经开始注意到这里的趋势以及转述的重要性。如果你不转述或极少这样做，考官会给你打4分。如果考生有朝这方向努力，他们可能会拿5分。在6分标准下，只要**大部分**转述是正确的，就能得6分。

■ IELTS Level 7 (★ ★ ★ ★)

	Lexical Resource	词汇多样性
Level 7	•uses vocabulary resource flexibly to discuss a variety of topics •uses some less common and idiomatic vocabulary and shows some awareness of style and collocation, with some inappropriate choices •uses paraphrase effectively	•灵活地使用词汇讨论各种话题 •使用一些非常见的词汇及习语，对语体及词汇搭配有所认识，但有时词语选择不甚恰当 •有效地进行改述

▶ **uses vocabulary resource flexibly to discuss a variety of topics 灵活地使用词汇讨论各种话题**

An improvement on a 6; what is important here is the removal of 'inaccuracies' from the criteria level. This means that mistakes are not going to be accepted for a 7.

要想拿6分以上，重要的是从标准层面消除"不准确性"。这意味着7分是不能有错误用词。

▶ **uses some less common 使用一些非常见的词汇**

I would define 'less common' as, quite literally, words that are not frequently (or commonly) used.

按字面意思，我对"非常见"的定义是不常用的词。

· Example ·

> *I often chat with my friends on the weekends.*

In the above example, the word 'chat' I would consider 'less common'. Quite often, candidates would use 'speak' or 'say' or even 'talk', which are used a lot, or commonly, when learning English, whereas 'chat' is something only more advanced students may know.

在上面的例子中，我认为chat这个词不太常见。很多时候，考生会用speak、say或者talk，这三个词在学习英语时经常使用，而chat可能只有水平更高的学生才知道。

▶ **... and idiomatic vocabulary 及习语**

Idiomatic vocabulary is explained as '(of a group of words) having a particular meaning that is different from the meanings of each word considered separately' or simply 'means natural in expression, correct without being too formal', according to the online 'Cambridge Dictionary'.

根据线上"剑桥词典"，习语是"（一组单词的）特定含义不同于每个单词单独的含义"，或者简单来说，指"自然、正确而不太正式的表达"。

· Example ·

> *Last weekend, it rained cats and dogs.*

Obviously, in the above example, it didn't ACTUALLY rain cats and dogs. This just means that it rained a lot. Using idiomatic language makes you sound more like a native, and a good range and understanding of when to use it will be helpful.

显然，在上面的例子中，天上**实际上**并没有下猫下狗。这句意思是雨下得很大。使用习语会让你听起来更像一个母语者，掌握一定数量的习语以及知道何时使用会很有帮助。

▶ ... and shows some awareness of style and collocation, with some inappropriate choices 对语体及词汇搭配有所认识，但有时词语选择不甚恰当

The online 'Cambridge Dictionary' defines a collocation as 'a word or phrase that is often used with another word or phrase, in a way that sounds correct to people who have spoken the language all their lives, but might not be expected from the meaning: In the phrase 'hard frost', 'hard' is a collocation of 'frost' and 'strong' would not sound natural.'

线上"剑桥词典"对搭配的定义是"经常与另一个单词或短语一起使用的单词或短语，对于说了一辈子这种语言的人来说，听起来是正确的，尽管从字面意思上来看可能不正确：在短语 hard frost 中，hard 与 frost 搭配，而 strong frost 会听起来不自然。"

There are hundreds, if not thousands, of collocations in the English language. Although nobody would expect you to know them all, learning and using some of the more common ones would undoubtedly be a good idea if you want a 7 in this section.

英语中有成百上千的搭配。虽然没人指望你知道所有的搭配，但如果你想在这一部分得到 7 分，学习和使用一些更常用的搭配无疑是个好主意。

I have compiled a list of commonly used collocations you can access from the QR code.

本书整理了一个常用搭配表，你可以扫描右侧的二维码获取。

常见搭配

▶ uses paraphrase effectively 有效地进行改述

The trend of paraphrasing continues with the indication that paraphrasing should be correct at this level. There is no concrete definition of 'effectively' in this context, but, at least for me, it would mean that multiple instances of paraphrasing are used correctly, and at a time when it is suitable.

对改述的要求继续提高，改述要正确才能达到 7 分水平。在这个语境下，"有效地"并没有具体的定义，但是，至少对我来说，它意味着在适当的时候，正确地多次使用改述。

Chapter 3 Grammatical Range and Accuracy
语法多样性及准确性

Grammar is the part of any language that most people don't like, but like any test of language, it's always included. Two things are being looked at within IELTS: Range and Accuracy.

任何语言中，大多数人都不喜欢的部分就是语法，但在任何语言测试中，语法总是必不可少的。雅思考试关注语法的两方面：多样性和准确性。

▶ Range 多样性

This specifies the different types of grammatical structures that you can use. It would include things like tenses, subject-verb agreements, plurals, conditionals, simple and complex sentence structures, to mention a few. It's beyond the scope of this book to teach you English Grammar, but you should learn as much as possible to reach the IELTS exam's higher scores.

这指的是你可以使用不同类型的语法结构，包括时态、主谓一致、复数、条件句、简单句和复杂句等。教你英语语法已经超出了本书的范围，但是想要拿到雅思考试更高的分数，你应该多学习语法知识。

▶ Accuracy 准确性

As the name implies, this is how accurate your grammar is when speaking. So, when using the different structures indicated in Range, they must be correct. The more correct sentences you can provide during the exam, the higher your score will be.

顾名思义，这是指你说话时语法准不准确。因此，使用多样性标准中指示的不同结构时，它们必须是正确的。考试时你能使用的正确句子越多，你的分数就越高。

	Grammatical Range and Accuracy	语法多样性及准确性
Level 4	•produces basic sentence forms and some correct simple sentences but subordinate structures are rare •errors are frequent and may lead to misunderstanding	•能使用基本句型并正确使用一些简单句型，但极少使用从句 •常出现错误，且会造成误解

▶ **produces basic sentence forms and some correct simple sentences** 能使用基本句型并正确使用一些简单句型

A basic sentence can be a single independent clause or a compound sentence. Typically, basic sentences are short and very simple in structure.

基本句型可以是单个独立分句，也可以是并列句。一般来说，基本句很短，结构非常简单。

· Example ·

I like books.

▶ **... but subordinate structures are rare** 但极少使用从句

This means that independent/subordinate clauses are only used a couple/few times during the whole exam. An example of a sentence with a subordinate clause:

这是指独立分句或从句在整个考试中只使用了几次。以下是使用从句的例子：

· Example ·

When I read books, I like reading Sci-Fi.

▶ **errors are frequent** 常出现错误

'Frequent', at least to me, means that there are more errors than correct sentences. This is sometimes difficult to judge as an examiner will not actually count the number of sentences. However, if they feel that the majority of sentences are incorrect in some way, you'll probably get a 4.

至少对我来说，"频繁"是指错误的句子比正确的多。这有时很难判断，因为考官实际上并不会计算句子的数量。然而，如果他们觉得大多数句子有错误，你可能会得4分。

▶ **... and may lead to misunderstanding** 且会造成误解

Generally, a simple mistake, like the example below, won't confuse the examiner.

像下例中的小错误一般不会让考官误解。

· Example ·

I likes football.

But something like the sentence below, is much more difficult to understand.

但下面这个例子则比较难理解。

·**Example**·

Tomorrow, I played football.

In this example, the beginning talks about the future but then changes to the past tense. It's difficult for the examiner to know which is correct and could be misunderstood.

在这个例子中，开头说的是将来，但马上换成过去时态。这让考官难以判断哪部分是对的，从而造成误解。

	Grammatical Range and Accuracy	语法多样性及准确性
Level 5	•produces basic sentence forms with reasonable accuracy •uses a limited range of more complex structures, but these usually contain errors and may cause some comprehension problems	•能使用基本的句型，且具有合理的准确性 •使用有限的复杂句式结构，但通常会出错且会造成某些理解困难

▶ **produces basic sentence forms with reasonable accuracy** 能使用基本的句型，且具有合理的准确性

A step up from Level 4, most of the basic sentence structures are correct. So, expanding on the previous level's example:

从4分水平再上一个台阶，大部分基本句型结构要正确。因此，把上面的例子再扩展下：

· Example ·

I like swimming, and I like basketball.

Although this sentence is a compound sentence, it's still considered a simple form. Scan the QR Code for more details about Grammar Information.

尽管这个句子是一个并列句，但它仍然是一种简单句型。扫描二维码了解更多语法信息。

四种句型

▶ **uses a limited range of more complex structures** 使用有限的复杂句式结构

If you're unsure of what a complex structure contains, please scan the QR code above, where you'll find some details and examples that will help. A 'limited range' means that although some complex structures are used, they're not varied.

如果你不确定复杂句式结构有哪些，请扫描上方的二维码，你会找到一些有帮助的细节和例子。"有限的多样性"是指尽管使用了一些复杂结构，但它们没有变化。

· Example 1 ·

When I read, I like Sci-Fi.

· Example 2 ·

When I relax, I like reading.

You can see from the example above that although the vocabulary is somewhat different, the grammatical structure is the same. This doesn't indicate that a range of complex structures is being used.

从上面的例子可以看出，虽然词汇有些不同，但语法结构是一样的。这并不表明考生使用了一系列复杂句式。

> **... but these usually contain errors and may cause some comprehension problems 但通常会出错且会造成某些理解困难**

'Usually' as given here, again, means that there are more incorrect sentences given than correct ones, but this only refers to the complex structures, NOT the basic ones. There may be some sentences the examiner doesn't understand from a grammatical point of view.

这里的"通常"也是指错误的句子比正确的多，但这是指复杂句，而不是基本句型。从语法角度来看，可能有些句子考官不理解。

■ IELTS Level 6 (★ ★ ★)

	Grammatical Range and Accuracy	语法多样性及准确性
Level 6	•uses a mix of simple and complex structures, but with limited flexibility •may make frequent mistakes with complex structures, though these rarely cause comprehension problems	•结合使用简单与复杂的句型，但灵活性有限 •使用复杂结构时经常出现错误，尽管这些错误极少造成理解困难

▶ **uses a mix of simple and complex structures, but with limited flexibility** 结合使用简单与复杂的句型，但灵活性有限

The first half of this element is self-explanatory. 'Limited flexibility' means that although more than one structural type of grammar has been used, it wouldn't really be considered a good 'range'.

这个标准的前半部分不言自明。"有限的灵活性"指尽管使用了一种以上的语法结构类型，但实际并不具有多样性。

▶ **may make frequent mistakes with complex structures, though these rarely cause comprehension problems** 使用复杂结构时经常出现错误，尽管这些错误极少造成理解困难

The most important part of this particular element is the ' rarely cause comprehension problems'. As previously stated, 'frequent', to me, means more than half, so this part is saying: 'Even though more than 50% of complex grammar structures have errors, as long as the examiner can mostly understand you, it's OK for a 6.'

这个特殊标准最重要的部分是"极少造成理解困难"。如前所述，对我来说，"频繁"意味着错误的句子超过了一半，所以这部分是在说："即使超过 50% 的复杂语法结构有错误，但只要考官能大致理解你，你还是可以拿 6 分的。"

· Example ·

> *After I play basketball, I usually goes swimming.*

In the example above, although the sentence is grammatically wrong – it should be 'go', not 'goes' – it is not difficult to understand the meaning.

在上面的例子中，应该用 go，而不是 goes，虽然句子有语法错误，但并不影响理解句意。

■ IELTS Level 7 (★ ★ ★ ★)

	Grammatical Range and Accuracy	语法多样性及准确性
Level 7	•uses a range of complex structures with some flexibility •frequently produces error-free sentences, though some grammatical mistakes persist	•较灵活地使用一系列复杂的语法结构 •虽然反复出现一些语法错误，但语句通常正确无误

▶ **uses a range of complex structures with some flexibility** 较灵活地使用一系列复杂的语法结构

Further upward movement reaching Level 7 shows that simple sentence structures have been dropped from the requirements, and it concentrates on complex structures like those discussed in our Grammar Information link.

7分水平已经删除对简单句子结构的要求，并且像我们在语法信息链接中讨论的一样，重点关注复杂的语法结构。

> · **Example 1** ·

When I want to relax after a basketball match, I often go for a swim.

> · **Example 2** ·

If I need to relax after playing basketball, I will go for a swim.

In the above examples, you can see that multiple structures can be used to say the same thing. One is an 'ordinary' complex structure, whereas the second is a conditional statement. Using different formats like this will demonstrate a good range to the examiner, and using them interchangeably will show flexibility.

在上面的例子中，你能看到可以用不同语法结构来表达同一个意思。一个是"普通的"复杂句结构，而另一个是条件从句。像这样使用不同的语法结构能向考官表明你具有很好的语法多样性，交替使用则体现出灵活性。

▶ **frequently produces error-free sentences, though some grammatical mistakes persist** 虽然反复出现一些语法错误，但语句通常正确无误

Switching now to the positive side of 'frequently', the above means that more than half of all sentences are correct. However, there are still some mistakes spoken during the test. As previously, there is no particular number for 'some', but I would expect a lot less than half.

现在切换到"反复"的积极一面，上面的意思是一半以上的句子是正确的，但是仍存在一些错误。和以前一样，"一些"是多少没有规定，但我认为是不超过一半。

Chapter 4 Pronunciation

发 音

The examiner is listening for several things when marking for pronunciation, and how much of a British accent the candidate has is NOT one of them. I want to expel this myth here and now – the examiners don't care what kind of accent you have; they simply care about the clarity of your speech and whether they can understand you.

考官在给发音打分时有几个标准，而考生有多少英国口音**不在**其中。我想在此澄清一个迷思——考官不在意你的口音，他们只在意你说话是否清晰易懂。

IELTS Exam pronunciation is measured by the following 'features'.

雅思考试发音是通过以下"特征"来衡量的。

▶ Enunciation 清晰

This is what many people think of as pronunciation. It is how clearly you pronounce words.

这是多数人对发音的理解，它是指发音的清晰度。

> · Example ·　　　　　　　　　　　　　　　　　　🎧 018
>
> *I would like to speak clearly.*

▶ Connected Speech 连读

Stringing words together in a way that sounds more like a native speaker.

把单词连在一起读，听起来更像是在说母语。

> · Example ·　　　　　　　　　　　　　　　　　　🎧 019
>
> *She can speak English better than I can.*

▶ Rhythm 节奏

The rhythm, or beat, of spoken language.

口语的节奏或节拍。

> · Example ·　　　　　　　　　　　　　　　　　　🎧 020
>
> *This is an example of the rhythm of spoken English.*

 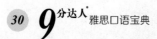

▶ Word and Sentence Stress 词句重音

Correct stressing of syllables in words, phrases or sentences.

单词、短语和句子正确的重音音节。

· Example ·　　　　　　　　　　　　　　　　　　　　🎧 021

> *Here, I'm stressing different parts of this sentence.*

▶ Chunking 断句

Grouping words, and pausing, where appropriate.

在适当的时候将单词组合在一起和停顿。

· Example ·　　　　　　　　　　　　　　　　　　　　🎧 022

> *This is an example of Chunking in the English language.*

▶ Intonation 语调

Rising and falling of pitch/tone during everyday speech.

日常说话中音调的升降。

· Example ·　　　　　　　　　　　　　　　　　　　　🎧 023

> *Sometimes, you will raise your pitch when you speak, and other times, you'll lower it.*

When looking at the criteria, one thing that's very noticeable about the Pronunciation section is that it's full of holes. Levels 3, 5 and 7 only refer to higher or lower levels. They are relatively self-explanatory, and you'll notice that they usually break down into Range – how many you use, Consistency – how much you use them, and Understandability – whether the examiner understands what you say.

发音部分的标准有一点非常值得注意，那就是它并不完整。3分、5分和7分水平仅指更低或更高的级别。它们相对来说是不言自明的，你会注意到它们通常分为多样性（你用了多少）、一致性（你用的频率）和可理解性（考官是否理解你所说的）。

	Pronunciation	发音
Level 4	•uses a limited range of pronunciation features •attempts to control features but lapses are frequent •mispronunciations are frequent and cause some difficulty for the listener	•使用有限的发音特征 •尝试表现多种发音特征，但频繁出现偏差 •经常出现发音错误，对听者理解造成一些困难

▶ **uses a limited range of pronunciation features** 使用有限的发音特征

This means exactly what it says. Only one or two of the features listed previously are used during the exam.

这就是字面意思。在考试过程中，只使用了前面列出的一两个特征。

· Example ·   ዃ 024

> *I like playing sports. It helps me keep healthy and fit.*

▶ **attempts to control features but lapses are frequent** 尝试表现多种发音特征，但频繁出现偏差

'Lapses' here means 'mistakes'. So, although a candidate may want to show that they can use intonation, for example, it's not done correctly, and the mistakes happen more than correctly pronounced words/phrases/sentences.

"偏差"在这里指"错误"。例如，虽然考生可能想表明他们可以使用不同语调，但没有表现好，导致发音错误的单词/短语/句子比正确的多。

· Example ·   ዃ 025

> *I like playing sports. It helps me keep healthy and fit.*

▶ **mispronunciations are frequent** 经常出现发音错误

The meaning of 'frequent' here is similar to that previously described in other elements and generally means 'more than half the time'.

此处"经常"的含义类似于之前在其他标准中描述的含义，通常指"超过半数"。

· Example ·   ዃ 026

> *I like playing sports. It helps me keep healthy and fit.*

▶ **... and cause some difficulty for the listener** 对听者理解造成一些困难

My measurement system here is that if I have to think about what was said and then think again and am still unsure, that would, by my reckoning, be 'difficult'. There is no number of what 'some' refers to, and like many other elements in this criteria, it is subjective and may differ depending on the examiner.

我的衡量标准是，如果我必须思考对方所说的话，反复琢磨还不确定，我会认为这对理解造成了"困难"。像许多其他标准一样，"一些"没有所指的具体数字，它是主观的，可能因考官而异。

> *Tiny Tip:* *It is worth understanding that some examiners may be new to China and therefore have more difficulty understanding the habits of Chinese speakers. For example, the 'th' and 'v' sounds are often mispronounced as those sounds aren't in the Chinese language. Someone that's been in China for several years will be used to that, whereas someone that's just arrived may not be.*

小提示：需要注意的是，一些考官可能刚来中国，因此在理解汉语使用者的表达习惯方面有更多的困难。例如，th 和 v 的发音经常发错，因为这些音不是汉语发音。已经在中国生活了几年的人会习惯这一点，而刚到中国的人可能不习惯。

■ IELTS Level 5 (★★)

	Pronunciation	发音
Level 5	•shows all the positive features of Band 4 and some, but not all, of the positive features of Band 6	•表现出4分水平中所有积极特征，但也能部分体现6分水平的积极特征

▶ **shows all the positive features of Band 4 and some, but not all, of the positive features of Band 6** 表现出 4 分水平中所有积极特征，但也能部分体现 6 分水平的积极特征

For the levels covered in this book and the online learning material, this is the first of the levels that mention the bands both above and below. You'll notice that it concentrates on 'positive' features and will require ALL of them in the lower level and some in the upper one. If the examiner feels that not all the positive features in the upper level have been met, that score will automatically, in this case, be a 5.

对于本书和在线学习材料中提到的级别，这是标准第一次涉及上下两个级别。你会注意到它关注"积极"特征，并要求具有较低级别**所有的**积极特征以及较高级别的一些特征。如果考官认为考生没有达到 6 分的所有积极特征，那么在这种情况下，分数自然是 5 分。

It is subjective as to what 'some' means here. For some examiners, it may mean that at least one of the positive features is met; for others, it may mean two of the three.

这里的"一些"指多少是主观的。对一些考官来说，可能意味着至少满足其中一个积极特征；对其他考官来说，可能意味着要满足三个特征中的两个。

Tiny Tip: *There are always three elements in the Criteria, as we have mentioned before – Range, Consistency and Understandability.*

小提示：正如我们之前提到的，标准中总是有三要素——多样性、一致性和可理解性。

For more information on the positive features mentioned in 6, please see the following page covering Level 6.

关于 6 分水平积极特征的更多信息，请参见下一页内容。

IELTS Level 6 (★ ★ ★)

	Pronunciation	发音
Level 6	•uses a range of pronunciation features with mixed control •shows some effective use of features but this is not sustained •can generally be understood throughout, though mispronunciation of individual words or sounds reduces clarity at times	•使用多种发音特征，但掌握程度不一 •展现出某些有效使用发音特点的能力，但不能持续表现这一能力 •表达过程中听者基本能理解，但部分单词或音发音不准确导致有时清晰度下降

▶ **uses a range of pronunciation features with mixed control** 使用多种发音特征，但掌握程度不一

A range here, in my mind, means using at least 3 of 6. In reality, anyone will use all of the pronunciation features. It depends on how well they do it, hence the 'mixed control'.

在我看来，这里的多样性是指至少使用6个发音特征中的3个。实际上，任何人都会使用所有的发音特征。这取决于他们的掌握程度，因此"掌握程度不一"。

▶ **shows some effective use of features but this is not sustained** 展现出某些有效使用发音特征的能力，但不能持续表现这一能力

This element means that although the pronunciation features are sometimes used well, it is not done throughout the exam.

这个标准的意思是，虽然考生的发音特征有时用得很好，但并没有在整个考试中一以贯之。

▶ **can generally be understood throughout, though mispronunciation of individual words or sounds reduces clarity at times** 表达过程中听者基本能理解，但部分单词或音发音不准确导致有时清晰度下降

'Generally' here, like nearly everything else, is subjective to the examiner. There isn't a number given to the number of times that the examiner may not understand, but I would say that around three-quarters should be understandable as a general rule.

这里的"基本"和几乎所有其他标准一样，对考官来说是主观的。考官可能不理解的次数没有规定，但我认为，一般来说应该要能理解大约四分之三的句子。

Important Information: *Some words are more difficult than others to understand depending on their length, the amount of mispronunciation and the context in which the word or phrase is used.*

重要信息： 有些单词因为其长度、容易发音错误的数量以及使用的上下文会比其他单词更难理解。

I particularly enjoy ball sports, like Baseball and Cricket. It's pretty difficult to find clubs in Beijing that play them, though, as they're not very popular.

Although the example given above is somewhat extreme, it should clearly show that it can be challenging to understand unless the pronunciation is correct.

虽然上面的例子有些极端，但它清楚地表明，如果发音不正确会难以理解。

Tiny Tip: *When learning and practising your pronunciation, I suggest you use both the phonetic alphabet and hear it said by a native speaker so that you have a solid foundation for your knowledge.*

小提示： 在学习和练习发音时，我建议你既使用音标，也要听一个以英语为母语的人朗读，以打下坚实的基础。

■ IELTS Level 7 (★ ★ ★ ★)

	Pronunciation	发音
Level 7	•shows all the positive features of Band 6 and some, but not all, of the positive features of Band 8	•表现出6分水平中所有积极特征，但也表现出8分水平中部分积极特征

▶ **shows all the positive features of Band 6 and some, but not all, of the positive features of Band 8** 表现出 6 分水平中所有积极特征，但也表现出 8 分水平中部分积极特征

This is the second of the levels covered that mentions higher and lower levels. In this case, 6 and 8. As we have already covered 6, I will talk briefly about the elements of Level 8.

这是第二次在标准中提到上下级别。在当下，即6分水平和8分水平。由于我们已经介绍了6分水平，我再简单谈谈8分水平的标准。

	Pronunciation	发音
Level 8	•uses a wide range of pronunciation features •sustains flexible use of features, with only occasional lapses •is easy to understand throughout; L1 accent has minimal effect on intelligibility	•使用多样的发音特征 •表达过程中灵活地使用多种发音特征，但偶尔出现偏差 •表达过程中始终易于听者理解，母语（L1）的口音对听者理解的影响极小

The first two elements within Level 8 are an increase in Range and Effectiveness beyond Level 6 and are relatively simple to understand. Where I wish to focus, certainly for those who are aiming for a 7, in this area is the last sentence:

8分水平中的前两个标准是在6分水平的基础上提高多样性和有效性，这相对容易理解。对于那些目标是7分的人来说，我想强调的是最后一句话：

▶ **is easy to understand throughout; L1 accent has minimal effect on intelligibility** 表达过程中始终易于听者理解，母语（L1）的口音对听者理解的影响极小

I believe this is one of the easier ones to obtain when aiming for a score of 7. 'L1' means your first language. So, for most people reading this book, it would be Chinese. The easiest way is to practice the 'th' and 'v' sounds. Although I say the 'easiest', these sounds aren't used in the Chinese language, so typically, Chinese students find this quite tricky to pronounce correctly, but if you need a 7 or higher, it must be mastered.

我相信对目标是7分的考生来说，这是较容易满足的标准。L1是指你的第一语言。所以，对于本书的大多数读者来说，L1是汉语。最简单的方法就是练习th和v音。虽然我说的是"最简单的"，但汉语并不使用这些音，所以通常情况下，中国学生很难正确发音，但如果你需要7分或更高的分数，就必须努力。

This is the end of Section 1 of this book. I hope that now you have a good understanding of the Speaking Criteria used by the examiners. Like I said during the introduction, I firmly believe that simply by understanding what the examiners are listening for, you can fully understand what parts of the English language you can concentrate on to increase your score and hopefully obtain the level you need.

这是本书 Section 1 的结尾。我希望现在你已经充分理解考官的口语标准。正如我在前言中所说的，我坚信，只要了解考官在听什么，你就应该知道要关注英语的哪些部分以提高你的分数，并有希望获得你需要的分数。

There are many resources and links in this book that you can use to improve your English, and I would highly recommend that you use them as much as possible. Simply reading this book once will NOT be sufficient. English must be studied and used daily to improve. There's an English saying, 'If you don't use it, you lose it'. It means that if you don't constantly use and practice something, in this case, English, you will forget how to use/speak it.

这本书有很多资源和链接可用来提高你的英语水平，我强烈建议你尽量利用。仅仅读一遍这本书是不够的，必须每天学习和使用英语才能提高。有句英语谚语说，"如果你不用它，你就会失去它"。因此，如果你不经常使用和练习英语，你就会忘记如何使用和说英语。

Learning a language is a process that takes time and should be adequately planned. I wouldn't advise waiting until the last minute to cram for an IELTS exam. It's incredibly difficult to raise your score by 1 or 2 points in a matter of weeks. Even if you succeeded in doing that, you would find it challenging during your studies upon your arrival in England and potentially a UK university.

学习语言是一个需要时间、充分准备的过程。我不建议等到最后一刻才临时准备雅思考试。在几周内将你的分数提高一两分非常困难。即使你成功了，当你抵达英国并进入一所英国大学时，你也会发现你的学习过程充满了挑战。

The information I have given you in this part has helped many of my past students increase their scores and feel more confident when taking the IELTS Speaking exam because they understand more about how it works from the examiner's point of view rather than the candidate's.

这一部分分享的信息已经帮助我的许多学生提高了分数，让他们在参加雅思口语考试时更加自信，因为他们能更多地从考官的角度而不是考生的角度理解评分标准。

Overall, just remember that examiners are human beings and have a job to do. If you give them the language and elements necessary for a Level 7, that's what they'll give you; if not, they won't. It's nothing personal; it's just that's what they believe they should give you according to the criteria.
总的来说，你要记住考官也是人，评分是他们的工作。如果你的语言和标准达到了 7 分所要求的，他们就会给你 7 分；如果达不到，他们就不会给。这不是针对你，只是他们认为应该根据标准给你对应的分数。

Section II

Part 1 Preparation and Topics

如何准备 Part 1

In this section, I will provide examples of topics that **may** appear in the IELTS Speaking exam. I have given two example answers for each question. The answers are similar to each other, with Answer 2 being of better quality than Answer 1. You should notice that in some of the answers, the grammatical and lexical differences are very small, yet the second score is higher. This may be because of the number of structures/less common words given, the fact that there are fewer errors, or simply that the fluency and pronunciation levels are higher. As you go through these samples, pay careful attention to the differences and refer back to the Speaking Criteria to clarify your understanding.

在本部分，我会提供一些雅思口语考试中**可能**会出现的话题。每个问题我都提供了两个答案范例。两个答案有些相似，答案二优于答案一。请注意，有时候两个答案的语法和词汇差别很小，但是答案二得分更高。原因可能是答案二的结构更多样、非常见词汇的数量更多、错误更少，或流畅性和发音水平更佳。浏览这些范例时，请注意这些差别并回头参考口语评分标准来帮助理解。

After each sample answer, I will point out/list particular language and grammar so that you can notice the idioms, collocations, and overall grammatical range. Where appropriate, I will also offer tips and information to reuse words, phrases or sentences for multiple topics. Please understand that I will NOT list EVERY instance of less common words or 'paraphrasing' etc., simply some, so that you can understand what will help improve your score.

在每个答案范例后，我会指出或列举语言点和语法点，这样你就能留意到一些习语、搭配和整体的语法表现。我还会适时地提供一些小提示，教你如何将一些单词、短语或句型重复运用到多个话题中。要清楚的是，我只会列举部分非常见的单词或同义替换，目的是希望你能明白什么样的表达能够帮你提高分数。

As mentioned in the previous section, Part 1 topics are considered 'familiar', that is, topics that could easily be part of regular conversations in everyday English. Although the questions change periodically, four topics are always considered first, which is where I'll start. You will only be asked one of the four frequently asked topics, and for Study/Work, the questions will depend on your employment situation.

正如在上个部分所提到的，**Part 1**是"常见的"话题，也就是日常英语中的常见对话。虽然题目会定期更换，但是有四个话题总会首先考到，所以我会从它们开始。你只会被问到这四个高频话题中的一个，对于其中的工作或学习类话题，你会被问到的问题取决于你的就业情况。

> *Little Reminder:* *Each answer should be around 20–25 seconds long – about 2 or 3 sentences. This would be recognised as an 'extended answer'.*

小提醒： 每个答案的长度大约是20—25秒，即两三句话。这样就可以视作"拓展答案"。

Chapter 1 Part 1 Preparation
Part 1 备考

■ Some Exam Advice for Part 1

▶ No. 1: Prepare different answers for the same question 一题备多解

You may have noticed that some of the questions are very similar in some subject areas. For example:

你可能已经注意到，某些话题的问题非常相似。例如：

> *Do you like x? or*
> *Do you think x is important?*

This means that you can potentially use a prepared answer for these questions, and it doesn't matter what the subject is. The answer 'Yes, I like x very much.' would work for 'Do you like Maths?' as well as 'Do you like History?'. This would be fine for short 'unextended' answers, but you must remember that this will not get you the higher-level scores. So, I would NOT recommend this approach.

这意味着你可以提前准备好一个答案来回答所有这类问题，而主题是什么并不重要。"是的，我非常喜欢某某。"这个答案可以用来回答"你喜欢数学吗？"以及"你喜欢历史吗？"这两个问题。这样可以得到很短的"未拓展的"答案，但是你要记住，这样做你是得不到高分的。所以，我不推荐用这种方法。

I would recommend that you prepare some discourse markers and some paraphrases that you can use to show the examiner that you can answer a similar question using different language. For example:

我建议你准备一些语篇标记和同义替换，用它们向考官展示你可以使用不同的语言来回答相似的问题。例如：

> **Examiner:** *Do you like x?*
> **Candidate:** *Actually, I love x. I find it really interesting and thoroughly enjoy my classes. I've learnt it since I was a kid and my parents always encouraged me in this subject.*

In the above sentences, we have an extended answer including a discourse marker, paraphrasing, and less common language. All of these are positive elements that the examiner is listening for and will give you higher scores.

上面的句子就是一个拓展的答案，有语篇标记、同义替换和非常见的语言。考官想听到的是这些，这样才会给你更高的分数。

> *Candidate: Totally, I adore it. I find it fascinating and always look forward to my classes. I've studied it since I started school, so when I was about five, and my folks have always supported me in this subject.*

The above example answers the question in the same way. It still has a discourse marker, paraphrasing and less common language and uses similar language. The critical word is 'similar' NOT 'same'. This is precisely what the examiners are listening for.

上面的答案范例使用了一样的方法。答案中有语篇标记、同义替换、非常见的语言，使用了相似的表达。关键是"相似"，而非"一模一样"。这才是考官想听到的。

If you simply memorise one answer for multiple questions, your scores won't be as good as if you memorise different answers for the same question. If you take a moment to think about this through, it's quite possible that throughout an exam, you may be asked whether you like different things four, five times or maybe even more. Suppose you only have one or two prepared answers for these. In that case, your answers will become repetitive, which the examiner will recognise as a lack of vocabulary range and potentially a lack of grammatical range too. In turn, this means that you won't be able to achieve more than about 6 during your exam.

如果你只记住一个答案来回答很多问题，你的分数会低于一个问题记住不同答案这种方法所得到的分数。如果花点时间想想，你就会明白在整场考试中，你可能会被问到你是否喜欢不同的事物这个问题四五次，甚至更多。假如对于这些问题你只准备了一两个答案，你的回答就会显得重复，考官会认为你词汇量欠缺、语法结构有限。这就意味着在考试中你的分数不会超过6分。

▶ No. 2: Avoid memorised responses 不要背诵答案

To illustrate this point further:

进一步举例说明：

> *Examiner: Do you like Maths?*
> *Candidate: Yes, I like Maths very much. I've studied it since I was a kid.*

> *Examiner: Do you like History?*
> *Candidate: Yes, I like History very much. I've studied it since I was a kid.*

> *Examiner : Do you like sports?*
>
> *Candidate: Yes, I like sports very much. I've studied it since I was a kid.*

(Hang on, grammar mistake here – 'it' should be 'them' and you don't 'study' sports.)

（等一下，有语法错误：it 应改为 them，"study" sports 逻辑不通。）

> *Examiner : Do you like your subject? (a typical question in the Study topic)*
>
> *Candidate: Yes, I like my subject very much. I've studied it since I was a kid.*

(Hang on, you've studied Business Studies/Economics/Physics since childhood? – assuming that you are at university or have finished high school.)

（等一下，难道你从小就开始学商务研究、经济学或物理吗？——假设你在上大学或刚刚高中毕业。）

Although these sentences are grammatically correct and answer the question(mostly), if they are repeated throughout the exam, the examiner may feel that they are simply memorised responses that you have read in a book or seen on one of the many IELTS study websites. Therefore, they may listen more intently to your answers for excessive repetition of vocabulary or grammar structures. As a final point on deterring you from simply memorising answers, here is something to bear in mind:

Lexical Resource Band 2 – 'only produces isolated words or memorised utterances'.

虽然这些句子语法正确，也能回答问题（大体上），但是如果在整场考试中重复出现，考官会觉得这些是背诵的答案，是你从某本书里读到的，或者是在某个雅思学习网站中看到的。因此，他们会越发从你的答案里听出重复性的词汇与语法结构。最后，为了劝你不要只记答案，记住下面这句话：

词汇多样性 2 分——"仅能说出零散的单词或预先背诵的几句话。"

■ Advice for Common Topics

▶ Learning Subjects 学习科目类

With this topic, knowing what the learning subject is can be essential. If you're not sure, say so and pick a subject that you do know something about. For example, pick History if you don't understand what Geography is.

对于这个话题，了解学习科目很重要。如果你不确定，可以选一个你了解的科目。比如说，如果你不了解地理学，可以选历史。

> **Examiner**: *Do you like Geography?*
>
> **Candidate**: *I'm not sure what Geography is, so I'm hoping it's like History, and the answer is yes, I dore it and have learnt it since Middle school.*

From here, for any question related to Geography, just change it as if it's related to History.

由此可见，对于任何与地理学有关的问题，可以调整为就像与历史科目有关。

Although the occasional answer may not entirely make sense, it's more likely that you can maintain your fluency and pronunciation scores if you quickly choose a topic to talk about rather than continuously stutter, hesitate, and pause because you are trying to figure out what, in the example above, Geography, is for every question.

虽然这种答案可能不完全合理，但如果快速地选定话题进行谈论，你就能保住流畅性和发音的得分，而不会因为试图想弄清楚地理学（如上例）是什么而不断地结巴、犹豫、停顿。

▶ Places 地点类

With this Topic Area I would suggest that you try and give at least two things:

关于此类话题，建议至少提供以下两条信息：

The name of the place 地点的名称

This could be a Chinese name or an English one. It doesn't really matter. Having said that, if the place is known in English, it would be better to use the English one if you know it. For example, if you don't know how to say 'London', 'Starbucks' or 'The Great Wall', try and pick a different place. But if it's only known by the Chinese name, 'XiaBu XiaBu', for example, use that.

地点的名称可能是中文，也可能是英文，这都没关系。但是，如果这个地方有英文名，最好用英文名，如果你知道的话。例如，如果你不知道用英语怎么说"伦敦""星巴克""长城"，那就试着换个地点。但是，如果一个地点只有中文名，例如"呷哺呷哺"，那就用中文名。

Details of where the place is 该场所的具体位置

Quite often, describing where something is reasonably straightforward, but can often use complex grammar structures and collocations. So, don't just say 'I live in BeiJing'. Use something like, 'I live in Beijing, which is in northern China and not far away from TianJin'. You could even add some distances or travel times:

通常，描述场所的位置很简单，但是可以使用复杂的语法结构和搭配。所以，不要只说"我住在北京"。还可以说，"我住在北京，北京在中国北方，离天津不远"，甚至还可以加上距离或出行时间：

> *It's about 100 km away.*（大约 100 公里远。）
> *It's approximately half an hour by fast train from BeiJing Railway station.*（坐高铁大约半小时到北京火车站。）

You can use these kinds of sentences to extend your answers, which can improve the Fluency scores.
你可以使用上面这些句子来展开回答，能提高流畅性的得分。

▶ Habits 习惯类

With this topic area, I would suggest that you think about the language that describes how often something happens/you do something.
关于习惯类话题，我建议你考虑描述事情发生或你做某事的频率的表达。

Something else to think about is 'Tenses'. Quite often, with questions that form habits, they can often talk about things in the past and the future, so make sure you know how to change your sentences to reflect this change in time.
另外，还可以考虑"时态"。通常，习惯类的问题通常会谈及过去和将来的事情，因此，要确保如何调整句子来体现这种时间的变化。

▶ Rest and Diet 休息与饮食类

Quite often, if the topics are related to Rest, they are often related to other topics, so examples could be work, study, travelling and then reasons for that, studying a long time, or working very hard, for example. Another element to think of is time. This might be a time of the week, Monday, Tuesday etc. or time of day – morning, afternoon, evening. It could also be a specific time, like 3 pm.
与休息有关的话题往往也与以下这些话题相关，例如工作、学习、旅行等，这些话题的理由也是相通的，例如学习时间太久或工作很努力。另一个可以考虑的因素是时间。可以是一周、周一、周二等或一天的某个时段：上午、下午、晚上。也可能是一个具体的时间，如下午三点。

With topics relating to diet, you should think about using specific names of food. Similarly to the tip in Places, if there is an English name for the food you're describing, use it. If not, you could use the

Chinese Name, or maybe a mix of the two. For example, Kung Pao Chicken is quite often used for 'Gong Bao Ji Ding'(saute diced chicken with peanuts). Think also of how the food you're talking about is prepared, cooked and potentially when it is eaten.

对于饮食相关的话题，可以考虑使用食物的具体名称。与地点类提示相似，如果你所描述的食物有英文名，就用英文名。如果没有，可以用中文名或中英混合。例如，Kung Pao Chicken 通常用来指"宫保鸡丁"。还可以考虑你所谈及的食物的烹饪方式和食用场合。

▶ Art and Hobbies 艺术与兴趣爱好类

With the Art topic, you should think about types of art, places for art, and any people that are connected to art. Artists would be the most common, but this could include teachers and other people. It wouldn't matter if you don't know the name of a famous artist, or a particular style of art, Renaissance or Impressionism, for example, but you should know some basic terms, Portrait, Landscape, Sculpture, etc.

对于艺术类话题，你应该考虑艺术类型、艺术场所，以及与艺术有关的任何人。其中最常见的是艺术家，但还包括教师等人。你是否知道某位知名艺术家的名字，或者某种艺术类型的叫法（例如，文艺复兴或印象主义）都不重要，但是，你应该了解一些基本的术语，像肖像画、风景画、雕塑等。

With Hobbies, it needs to be understood that hobbies do not include sports. Swimming, Football, and Skiing are not hobbies. Stamp collecting, drawing/painting, and playing music are hobbies. The definition of a hobby, according to the online 'Cambridge Dictionary', is *'an activity that someone does for pleasure when they are not working'*.

对于兴趣爱好类话题，需要明白的是，兴趣爱好不包括运动。游泳、足球、滑雪都不属于兴趣爱好，而集邮、绘画、演奏音乐才是兴趣爱好。线上"剑桥词典"对兴趣爱好的定义是"人们在非工作时间为了开心而采取的一种活动"。

▶ Pastimes and Sports 休闲与运动类

A variety of pastimes can be spoken about, so it's a challenge to cover them all, but they quite often cover food and travel. Preparing vocabulary for these kinds of questions would be a good idea (as well as other topics you can think of). Think of specific times, places, and activities you enjoy in your spare time and why.

有很多的休闲方式可以谈论，所以想说完所有的休闲方式很难，但是它们通常都涉及食物和旅行。准备与这些问题（以及其他你能想到的话题）相关的词汇是个好主意。可以考虑特定的时机、地点和闲暇时你喜欢的活动以及为什么喜欢。

With sports, like with other topics, it's important to think about details. If it's a general question about sports – 'Do you like Sports?' – then you can choose a sport that you enjoy and know the vocabulary. Think about the equipment that you use as well as any health benefits it may have. If it's a specific sport, skiing for example, that you don't know anything about, simply use more general language and explain that you're unfamiliar with that sport. Try and think about words you might know with regards to that sport – 'snow', and 'mountains' could be words used when talking about skiing, for example.

运动类话题跟其他话题一样，考虑细节很重要。如果是一个宽泛的运动类问题，例如"你喜欢运动吗？"，那可以选一种你喜欢、并且了解相关词汇的运动。想想你用的设备以及该运动能给健康带来的好处。如果是某种具体的你不了解的运动，比如滑雪，就用更概括的语言并解释说你对那种运动不熟。试试与那种运动相关的单词——例如，谈论滑雪时，"雪"和"高山"可能用得上。

❯ Holidays, Weekends and Traffic 假期、周末及交通类

With this group of topics, the first two elements are more about the 'where' and 'what' do you do, and the third is about the 'how you get there'.

对于这些话题，最重要的两个要素是你在"哪里"做"什么"，第三个要素是"你是如何去的"。

When talking about holidays or weekends, think of place names, festival/holiday names, and any activities you may do, for example, eat jiaozi, lie on the beach, visit family etc.

谈论假期或周末时，可以考虑场所的名称、节假日的名称，以及你可能会参加的活动，例如吃饺子、躺在沙发上、看望家人等。

When talking about travel, think more of types of travel: train, car, plane, as well as public vs. private transportation. Also, thinking about the advantages and disadvantages of each type of travel would be a good idea too.

谈论旅行时，多想想出行方式——火车、汽车、飞机，以及公共交通或私人交通。此外，考虑每种出行方式的优缺点也不错。

❯ Shopping and Fashion 购物与时尚类

With these topics, it's going to be mostly about styles and cost, with possible questions of how or where to buy.

对于这些话题，主要是关于风格和价格，可能会问怎么买或在哪儿买。

Stlyes can include the colour and type of clothing, for example, jeans, dresses, skirts, shirts and can be expensive, cheap, or discounted. You should also think about where you buy things, places in the city, what apps you use and why etc.

风格可能包括服装的颜色和类型，例如牛仔、裙装、短裙、衬衫，价格可能昂贵、便宜或有折扣。你还可以考虑购物的场所、城区的地点、你使用的应用以及为什么等。

Fashion could include the names on the fashion houses, like Chanel, Gucci etc. as well as times of year to buy certain clothes(Summer/Spring Lines). It could also include Traditional Costumes and the like, where you can still mention colour, style etc.

时尚类话题包括时尚品牌的名字，如香奈儿、古驰等，还有购买特定服装的时间（春装或夏装）。还可能包括传统服饰等，在这种情况下，你仍然可以提及颜色、风格等。

▶ People 人物类

Quite often, the topics where people are mentioned are about a famous celebrity, actor, singer or such like. Quite often what you say about an actor, you can also say about a singer so. You need to think about why you like a certain person, why they're famous, and what their character is like.

会提到人物的话题往往与名人、演员、歌手等有关。通常情况下，与演员有关的内容也适用于歌手。你需要考虑为什么你喜欢某个人，他们为什么出名，以及他们有什么样的性格。

Another side to topics including people is how you interact and communicate with others. This may mean questions about friendships and how to develop relationships and how to talk to others; different age groups, different sexes, different relationships, a student and a teacher, for example. So, make sure that you look at vocabulary about characteristics of people as well as the technology of communication – WeChat, Email etc., and the feelings they may produce.

另外，与人物有关的话题还可以讨论你是如何与他人交流的。与此相关的问题有友谊，以及如何发展友谊、如何与他人对话；不同的年龄群体、性别、人物关系等，如师生关系。因此，要确保了解有关人物性格和网络交流技术的词汇（微信、电邮等），以及与之相关的情感类表达。

▶ Objects 物品类

It is quite challenging to prepare for questions about objects as there are simply too many variants to choose from. Some typical questions though could be 'Have you used …?', 'When do you use …?, and 'Do you like …?'.

物品类的问题准备起来很有挑战性，因为可供选择的物品太多了。一些常见的问题有"你用过……吗？"、"你什么时候使用……？"，以及"你喜欢……吗？"。

If you're not sure what object you are being asked about, explain that to the examiner. As long as you can use some general language, correct grammar and remain fluent, you wouldn't lose many marks.

如果你不太了解所问的物品，跟考官解释一下。只要你能使用一些宽泛的语言和正确的语法、保证流畅性，你就不会失分太多。

▶ Media and Advertisements 媒体与广告类

Within this group of topics, you should consider when and where you watch TV, advertisements or movies, and also what equipment can be used.

对于这类话题，你应该考虑看电视、广告、电影的时间和地点，以及可以使用什么设备。

Details you can include are the name of any app you use, the kind of computer or mobile phone you use, how media makes you feel, and how it has changed over the last few years.

细节包括你所使用的任何应用的名字、电脑或手机的类型、你对媒体的感受，以及近年来媒体和媒介的变化。

▶ Nature 自然类

Most Nature topics will want you to talk about the environment in general, as well as more specific areas like trees, plants, flowers etc., so you should learn names for all these. You would need to learn many, but three or four would be a good start.

大部分自然类话题会希望你谈谈大体的自然环境，以及像树、植物、花等更具体的领域。所以，你需要了解它们的名字。你可能需要了解很多这种名字，但可以先了解三至四种。

▶ Abstract Topics 抽象类

Part 1 Topics can be about anything; don't forget that they need to be considered 'Familiar' topics, so you should have at least heard of the subject.

Part 1可能会考查任何话题，别忘了它们需要被视作"熟悉"的话题，所以你应该至少听说过这些主题。

With all these types of question you can always answer using very general words, just be careful that you don't just memorize a standard response. I would advise that every time you have a conversation, whether this is in English or Chinese, you remember the topic and some of the details you spoke about and try to either remember or learn some of the language used.

对于所有问题，你都可以使用宽泛的词汇来作答，只是要小心不要去记标准答案。我建议，每次交流时，无论是用英语还是汉语，你应该记住话题和谈论到的细节，并尝试要么记住、要么学习所使用的语言。

■ Suggested Useful Phrases/Paraphrases for Common Topics

In the tables below, I have given you some suggestions for language that can be used for some of the more commonly used questions. They are not an exhaustive list and will not always work interchangeably, so please use your knowledge of English to use them properly and adjust your grammar if necessary.

在下列表格中，我会提供一些有关常考话题的语言建议。这些只是简表，有些表达也不能完全互换，所以，请根据你的英语知识恰当地使用这些表达并在必要时调整语法。

▶ Learning Subjects group 学习科目类

Original Question	Synonym/Paraphrase	Antonym
Do you like ...?	I love, I adore, I enjoy	I dislike, I hate, I can't stand
Is ... important?	It's essential, It's crucial, It's vital	It's useless, It's pointless
Is ... difficult?	It's not easy, It's hard, It's impossible	It's easy, It's simple, It's a piece of cake, It's a doddle

▶ Places 地点类

Original Question	+ Vocab	− Vocab
Do you like ...?	I love, I adore, I enjoy	I dislike, I hate, I can't stand
Where is ...? Which part ...?	It's found at ... It's located in ... It's close to ...	It's not by ... It's nowhere near ...
How is ... different from ...? How has ... changed?	It's completely/totally/very different ... Now, it's completely/totally different ...	It's not ... It's very similar to/same as ... It hasn't ... It's still the same. Not much.

▶ Habits 习惯类

Original Question	+ Vocab	− Vocab
Have you ever ...?	all the time/every day/as often as possible	never/as little as possible/seldom/not often/regularly
Will ... change? Will you ... in the future?	Yes, I think so. I might do. That's for sure. Absolutely/Definitely.	not really/definitely not/absolutely not/not a chance

▶ Rest and Diet 休息与饮食类

Original Question	+ Vocab	− Vocab
What do you do when …?	I usually/often/sometimes …	
Why do you …?	Mostly/Sometimes because …	I never … I don't …
Do you usually … in/at the morning/evening/weekend?	I usually/often/sometimes … early/late.	
Where can you buy/eat …?	I normally go …, (name of place). It's near …	-
What can you buy/eat?	(name of food), I don't know the English name, but … is the Chinese name for it.	-

▶ Art and Hobbies 艺术与兴趣爱好类

Original Question	+ Vocab	− Vocab
What kind of …?	The type of … I …	-
Do you like …?	Yes, very much, I love …	No, I don't like … / I hate …
Are you good at …?	Yes, I am. I'm very good at …	No, I'm not, I'm useless at …
When do you …?	Everyday/Every Tuesday/Every morning.	I don't have time for …
How long have you …?	… years/weeks/days.	I've never …

▶ Pastimes and Sports 休闲与运动类

Original Question	+ Vocab	− Vocab
Is … good for your health?	Oh, definitely, It's great for my lungs/heart/muscles …	I think it can hinder more than help …
What sports do you like?	I enjoy playing/doing/going …	I hate … I don't like …
Do you watch … on TV?	Yes, all the time/occasionally. I particularly like watching (name of athlete) because they make it look so easy/simple/effortless.	Never …, I don't like watching (name of sport) …

Holidays, Weekends and Traffic 假期、周末及交通类

Original Question	+ Vocab	− Vocab
How do you celebrate …?	We take a trip to … We go and visit … We cook several dishes like …	-
Any special foods/activities?	We prepare (name of food)/ We stuff ourselves with (name of food) …	-
What is your favourite holiday/ time of the week?	Spring Festival/Christmas/Mid-Autumn Festival/weekends/ summer holiday	I don't have one, they're all great! I don't like (name of holiday).
What type of transportation do you usually use?	train/subway/metro/underground/ car/bicycle/plane	-

Shopping and Fashion 购物与时尚类

Original Question	+ Vocab	− Vocab
What is your favourite colour …?	My favourite colour is … The colour I like the most is …	I don't have a favourite colour, I like them all.
What kind of clothes do you like?	I love Jeans/T-shirts/polo shirts …	-
Have you ever bought … online?	I buy online all the time. Often and regularly.	No, never. I prefer Brick and Mortar shops.
Do you like wearing …?	Yes, I do./Absolutley, I wear … all the time.	Not at all. No, I never wear …

People 人物类

Original Question	+ Vocab	− Vocab
Do you like spending time by yourself/with other people?	Yes, absolutely. I find being with others/alone …	No, I hate being alone/in a crowd. Sometimes, but I also like occasionally being alone/in a group.
Do you keep in contact with …?	Yes, we WeChat each other all the time. Yes, normally via WeChat.	No, we lost touch. No, we stopped communicating.
Have you ever met a …?	Maybe surprisingly, yes. I met …	No, like most people, I watch them from afar.

▶ Objects 物品类

Original Question	+ Vocab	− Vocab
Do you use ...?	Yes, all the time. Yes, occasionally.	No, never. Not often, no.
When would you use ...?	Everyday. All the time. Only when I need it.	I wouldn't. If I had one, I suppose I'd use ...
Do you have a ...?	I've had one for ages. Yes, I own a ...	No, I don't own a ... No, and I don't want one/some.

▶ Media and Advertisements 媒体与广告类

Original Question	+ Vocab	− Vocab
Are you interested in ...?	Yes, I'm fascinated by ... Indeed, I'm captivated by ...	Not at all. Not really, I've never done it.
What are the impacts of ...?	Well, I think ... would happen.	-
When was the first time ...?	Last week/year ... When I was ... years old.	I've never ... I wouldn't ...
How have TV/adverts/movies/radio changed ...?	Previously ... was ... A few years ago, ...	I don't hink they have ... They're not that different ...

▶ Nature 自然类

Original Question	+ Vocab	− Vocab
How can we protect ...?	We can look after ... We can start by ...	I don't believe we can ...
Have you ever ...?	Yes, a little/long while ago I ...	No/Never, but ...
Do you like ...?	Absolutely/Definitely/Oh yes ...	No/Absolutely not, I hate ...
What kinds/types of ...?	Give names of flowers/animals/environments	

Chapter 2 Common Topics and Sample Answers
常考话题及答案范例

Frequently Asked Topics

| Study | Answer 1 （★★★） | 🎧 028 |

Examiner: Do you work, or are you a student?

Candidate: I'm student in China. I'm hoping to go to the UK next year.

Examiner: What subject(s) do you study[3]?

Candidate: I have four courses that I learn[3] now. I am a university student, and the most important subject for me is English because I have to go to England in my final year. The others are Maths, PE and Computing.

Examiner: Why did you choose to study that subject?

Candidate: English is important these days and I think that I must speak in English well to get a good job in the future. International Banking is what I want to do.

Examiner: Do you like your subject? Why?/Why not?

Candidate: Absolutely[4]. My favourite is English. Not only because I use it to talk to more people in the world, but as well to learn more about different cultures.

Examiner's Comment	
Grammar	There are mainly simple sentences in this answer; some are incorrect. The article 'a' needs to be added to the first sentence – 'I'm **a** student in China', for example. There's an attempt at a complex structure at the end, but again this is slightly wrong as it uses 'as well' rather than '*also*', but wouldn't necessarily cause 'comprehension problems'.
	Simple ☑ Compound ☒ Complex ☑ Compound-complex ☑
Lexical Resource	There are no less common words or collocations, only one paraphrase(*study→learn*) and only one discourse marker. 'English' is also used a little repetitively.
	Less Common Language[1] ☒ Collocations/Idiomatic[2] ☒ Paraphrasing[3] ☑ Discourse Marker[4] ☑
Fluency	The speaker is speaking a little slowly and pausing quite a lot.
Pronunciation	There's some good use of features, but not all the time, and they can be understood without too much difficulty.

Examiner: Do you work, or are you a student?

Candidate: Currently, I'm a student at University in China. I'm hoping to study in the UK next year.

Examiner: What subject(s) do you study[3]?

Candidate: I have four courses that I'm learning[3] now. I am a university student, and the most important subject for me is English because I have to go to England in my final year. The others are Maths, PE and Computing.

Examiner: Why did you choose to study that subject?

Candidate: English is essential[1] these days and, for me, I figure that if I can communicate[1] in English well enough, I'll have a better chance of getting a good job in the future. International Banking is where I want to end up[2].

Examiner: Do you like your subject? Why?/Why not?

Candidate: Absolutely[4]. My favourite is English. Not only I can use it to talk to more people in the world[3], but also to learn more about different cultures from around the globe[3].

Examiner's Comment

Grammar	There are no mistakes in the simple structure sentences, and multiple different structures of complex structures also have no errors. Simple ☑ Compound ☑ Complex ☑ Compound-complex ☑
Lexical Resource	There are a couple of less common words included as well as a first correct attempt at collocations. The paraphrasing (*study→learning; world→globe*) is good, and we have a first discourse marker. Less Common Language[1] ☑ Collocations/Idiomatic[2] ☑ Paraphrasing[3] ☑ Discourse Marker[4] ☑
Fluency	With this answer, the fluency is much smoother than in the previous example, with minimal pausing except for the last complex sentence.
Pronunciation	Features are used fairly well and mostly sustained. The candidate can be generally understood.

Look at this: *The first and second answers for this topic are VERY similar, and many of the same grammar and vocabulary have been used, BUT the grammar is just a little more correct. Paraphrasing and collocations have been used, and fluency and pronunciation have improved.*

注意：这个话题的两份答案非常相似，还用了很多一样的语法知识和词汇。但是第二份答案的语法准确性更高，还用了同义替换和固定搭配，流畅性和发音也改善了。

Examiner: Do you work or study?

Candidate: I got, I have job, a job.

Examiner: What sort of job do you do?

Candidate: Well[4], bank, in bank.

Examiner: Do you find your work easy? Why/why not?

Candidate: No. It's difficult[3], it's hard[3]. Many to do. No time.

Examiner: Do you think your job will change much in the future? Why/why not?

Candidate: No, I don't think so.

Examiner's Comment	
Grammar	There are only some straightforward sentences given.
	Simple ☑ Compound ☒ Complex ☒ Compound-complex ☒
Lexical Resource	Only basic vocabulary is offered with an incomplete attempt at a paraphrase (***difficult→hard***).
	Less Common Language[1] ☒ Collocations/Idiomatic[2] ☒ Paraphrasing[3] ☑ Discourse Marker[4] ☑
Fluency	Noticeable pausing between every sentence.
Pronunciation	Some features, but it's not easy to assess because there are not really enough words spoken and not particularly fluent.

Examiner: Do you work or study?

Candidate: I've recently started a new job[3], which I'm hoping is actually my new career[3]. I suppose only time will tell.

Examiner: What sort of job do you do?

Candidate: I'm working at the moment for a company called Baidu as I graduated from university a little while ago. Currently[4], I'm at the bottom of the ladder[2] _{底层}, but the work I do is with AI, you know[4], Artificial Intelligence[1], so it's at the cutting edge of computer science and extremely desired as a skill set[1] _{综合技能}, so I don't think I'll be there for long.

Examiner: Do you find your work easy[3]? Why/why not?

Candidate: I wouldn't say it's easy, but it's not that difficult[3] either. It's more that the hours are long and I must sit all day in front of a computer screen, which can be pretty tiring. But I love figuring out the different algorithms[1] _{算法} we need to use and then programming them in.

Examiner: Do you think your job will change much in the future? Why/why not?

Candidate: I hope I can move up the ladder[2] _{晋升} of my company and manage a team one day. So it won't change with respect to my company's products, but my day-to-day[2] role might be very different. I hope to discover something that'll allow us to move to the next level of AI.

Examiner's Comment	
Grammar	There is a good selection of correct complex structures. Simple ☑　　　Compound ☑　　　Complex ☑　　　Compound-complex ☑
Lexical Resource	A good range is given, with some less common and idiomatic language as well as collocations and paraphrases(***job→career; easy→not that difficult***). Less Common Language[1] ☑　　　Collocations/Idiomatic[2] ☑ Paraphrasing[3] ☑　　　Discourse Marker[4] ☑
Fluency	Some good extended answers.
Pronunciation	Good use of a range of features that are used throughout the answers given.

Examiner: Can you describe your hometown?

Candidate: Of course[4]. It's home, isn't it? All my family are there. I still go back for the holidays.

Examiner: How long have you been living there?

Candidate: A long time, since I have … was born. When I came here to study, I suppose, that changed as I live here now. But, like I say earlier, I go back for the holidays.

Examiner: What do you like most[3] about your hometown?

Candidate: My favourite[3] thing about my hometown is the people. They are all very friendly[3] and nice[3]. I also enjoying eating the delicious food.

Examiner: Do you think you will continue living there in the future?

Candidate: Yes, I think I continue living there in the future. After I finish the university, I think I will go back to my hometown to work.

Examiner's Comment	
Grammar	Some of the simple sentences are slightly inaccurate. 'I also enjoying …', for example, should be 'I also *enjoy* …', but they are mostly correct. An attempt is made at complex structures, but they nearly all contain errors. However, they're reasonably easy to understand.
	Simple ☑ Compound ☒ Complex ☑ Compound-complex ☒
Lexical Resource	Only basic vocabulary is offered with one successful and one incomplete paraphrasing attempt(*like most→favourite; friendly→nice*).
	Less Common Language[1] ☒ Collocations/Idiomatic[2] ☒ Paraphrasing[3] ☑ Discourse Marker[4] ☑
Fluency	Some slow speech, but generally keeps going. Only one discourse marker is given in this answer.
Pronunciation	Some features are used, but these are not sustained and are occasionally difficult to understand.

Examiner: Can you describe your hometown?

Candidate: Well[4], my hometown is Beijing, the capital of China. I think maybe it's the largest city in the world; it must be pretty close. From memory, it has about 25 million people living in it.

Examiner: How long have you been living[3] there?

Candidate: Well, I was born and bred[3] in Beijing, so I've lived here all my life. My family's lived here for generations and I can't imagine moving and becoming a resident[1] of another city, but you never know what the future brings.

Examiner: What do you like[3] most about your hometown?

Candidate: Well, like I said[4], Beijing is the capital, so the transportation is very good and much more convenient than in other cities around China. Another thing I really enjoy[3] is the food. There's just such a variety, not just Chinese food but cuisine[1] from all over the world.

Examiner: Do you think you will continue living there in the future?

Candidate: Well, I think so, yes. I'm going to England for a year to finish my studies, but I hope when I come back, I can find a good job and stay here. It's where my forebears[1] come from and I'd like to be able to put down roots[2] too.

Examiner's Comment	
Grammar	A good mix of simple and complex structures that are all correct. Simple ☑ Compound ☑ Complex ☑ Compound-complex ☑
Lexical Resource	A good range was given about this topic with multiple paraphrasing(***living→born and bred; like→enjoy***) and less common, idiomatic, and discourse markers. Less Common Language[1] ☑ Collocations/Idiomatic[2] ☑ Paraphrasing[3] ☑ Discourse Marker[4] ☑
Fluency	Pauses sometimes but not too much. Uses 'Well' in every answer, which is repetitive.
Pronunciation	Some features and range are used, but this is not kept up, and some lapses are obvious.

Examiner: What kind of housing/accommodation do you live in?

Candidate: I live in an apartment downtown[3], you know[4], in the city centre[3], so it's easy[3] and convenient[3] to get anywhere I want to go or get anything I need to buy. It's a newly built compound, which is rare[1] considering where it is, and it has many mod cons[2], like a gym and lots of shops.

现代化的生活设备

Examiner: Have you lived there for a long time?

Candidate: Quite a long time. Because my father is in the army, we used to move around a lot, but at the moment, we don't have plans to move again anytime soon. At least, I certainly hope not.

Examiner: What's the difference between where you are living now and where you have lived in the past?

Candidate: Well[4], the main difference for me is that we moved to the centre of town from where we were in the countryside. I much prefer where we are now because there's a lot more to do. It was a bit boring in where we were.

Examiner: Can you describe the place where you live?

Candidate: It's very nice where I live. There's a small park nearby, maybe a five-minute walk, and the community is very peaceful[3] and quiet[3]. After the flowers and trees bloom in the summer, the colours are just incredible, making it quite beautiful.

	Examiner's Comment			
Grammar	Some very minor mistakes in the grammar – '… in where we were' should be '… where we were' – but that doesn't cause any absolute misunderstanding. A good mix of simple and complex grammar.			
	Simple ☑	Compound ☑	Complex ☑	Compound-complex ☑
Lexical Resource	One less common word is used, and a good amount of paraphrasing(*downtown→city centre; easy→convenient; peaceful→quiet*). Multiple discourse markers are also used.			
	Less Common Language[1] ☑ Paraphrasing[3] ☑		Collocations/Idiomatic[2] ☑ Discourse Marker[4] ☑	
Fluency	Some good use of features, mostly, but not always sustained.			
Pronunciation	There is some mispronunciation of the longer words, 'community', for example.			

Examiner: What kind of housing/accommodation do you live in?

Candidate: I live in an apartment downtown[3], you know[4], in the city centre[3], so it's easy[3] and convenient[3] to get anywhere I want to go, or get anything I need to buy. It's a newly built compound, which is rare[1] considering where it is, and it has many mod cons[2], like a gym and lots of shops.

Examiner: Have you lived there for a long time?

Candidate: What feels like donkey's years[2] 很久, but is probably only about five. Because my father is in the army, we used to move around a lot, but at the moment, we don't have plans to move again anytime soon. At least, I certainly hope not.

Examiner: What's the difference between where you are living now and where you have lived in the past?

Candidate: Well[4], the main difference for me is that we moved to the centre of town from where we were in the countryside. I much prefer where we are now because there's a lot more to do. It was a bit boring where we were.

Examiner: Can you describe the place where you live?

Candidate: It's very pretty[1] where I live. There's a small park nearby, maybe a five-minute walk, and the community is very peaceful and quiet. After the flowers and trees bloom in the summer, the colours are just incredible, making it quite picturesque[1].

	Examiner's Comment
Grammar	Some very minor mistakes in the grammar that don't cause any misunderstanding. More complex structures than simple ones. Simple ☑ Compound ☑ Complex ☑ Compound-complex ☑
Lexical Resource	Multiple less common words are used, and a good amount of paraphrasing (*downtown→city centre; easy→convenient; peaceful→quiet*). Multiple discourse markers are also used. Less Common Language[1] ☑ Collocations/Idiomatic[2] ☑ Paraphrasing[3] ☑ Discourse Marker[4] ☑
Fluency	No effort is needed to maintain fluency, and it has the beginnings of a range of discourse markers.
Pronunciation	Some minor pronunciation issues with the first language – the 'th' sound, but understandable throughout and has good, sustained use of features.

Maths	*Answer 1*（★★☆）	🎧 036

Examiner: Do you think Mathematics is important?

Candidate: Well[4], yes. I think Maths is very important. When we are at a school, we must all study Maths. I don't like it very much, and I think it's too difficult.

Examiner: Do you think it's difficult to learn Mathematics?

Candidate: Yes, I do. Maths is very difficult. Calculus[1] is the worst, and I often don't understand it. I have to study late to the night and often ask my friends to help me because they're better at it than me.

Examiner: How often do you use a calculator?

Candidate: Every day. When I have to do complex calculation like square root[1] calculation, I can't do it without one. It's a necessary thing for me to use. I use the calcualtor on my phone as it has scientific mode too.

Examiner: Do you think girls are generally better at Mathematics than boys?

Candidate: No, there are many more boys that are better at Maths than girls in my class. Some girls are good at Maths, even better than me, but I would say, in general[4], boys are better than girls at Maths.

<table>
<tr><td colspan="2" align="center">**Examiner's Comment**</td></tr>
<tr>
<td>**Grammar**</td>
<td>A reasonable mix of simple and complex grammar, but some mistakes in both types of sentences. 'When we are at a school …' should be 'When we are at school …'; 'study late to the night' should be 'study late ***into*** the night', or even 'study late ***at*** night'.

Simple ☑   Compound ☑   Complex ☑   Compound-complex ☑</td>
</tr>
<tr>
<td>**Lexical Resource**</td>
<td>Some minor errors in the formation of words as well as being a little repetitive – 'complex calculations like square root calculation***s*** – with the 's' missing on the same word. No paraphrasing or idiomatic language is offered. There is a beginning of discourse marker range. Some good examples of less common vocabulary.

Less Common Language[1] ☑   Collocations/Idiomatic[2] ☒
Paraphrasing[3] ☒   Discourse Marker[4] ☑</td>
</tr>
<tr>
<td>**Fluency**</td>
<td>Good extended answers and discourse markers with little in the way of pausing.</td>
</tr>
<tr>
<td>**Pronunciation**</td>
<td>Some mispronunciations of the longer words, but good range and use of features.</td>
</tr>
</table>

Examiner: Do you think Mathematics is important[3]?

Candidate: Oh, not just important, absolutely crucial[3]. Without Maths, we wouldn't really be able to do anything. Everything from basic Numeracy[1] (计算) to Geometry[1] (几何学) to Calculus is used by everyone daily, even if they don't actually know about it. The world wouldn't stop functioning without Maths, but we surely would be able to understand or measure anything anymore.

Examiner: Do you think it's difficult[3] to learn[3] Mathematics?

Candidate: Some find it challenging[3] to study[3], but in my view, it's worth the effort and not THAT hard[3]. When you really start to understand some of the more advanced techniques, you really begin to see the beauty in it. Not only that, but you start to appreciate everything around you in a different way, and if you want to, you can figure out[2] how it works.

Examiner: How often do you use a calculator?

Candidate: Well[4], for some of the formulas I need to do, it would be almost impossible without one. Well, at least it would take me a very long time and take up several pages of A4 paper. For most numeracy things like addition[1] (加法) and multiplication[1] (乘法), though, no, I don't. I can probably do faster in my head rather than opening the app in my phone and then doing the typing.

Examiner: Do you think girls are generally better at Mathematics than boys?

Candidate: As a girl, I'd say 'Definitely yes'. Seriously though, I really couldn't say. There's about an even split[2] (平均分布) in my Maths class, slightly tilted towards[2] (偏向于) the boys, so my thinking is if all women were better at Maths than men, why don't more of us take it? But that's a different question and probably a very long answer.

Examiner's Comment	
Grammar	A good range of simple and complex structures with very few errors. Simple ☑ Compound ☑ Complex ☑ Compound-complex ☑
Lexical Resource	Some good use of less common vocab, collocations, idioms and paraphrasing (***important→crucial; difficult→challenging/hard; learn→study***). Less Common Language[1] ☑ Collocations/Idiomatic[2] ☑ Paraphrasing[3] ☑ Discourse Marker[4] ☑
Fluency	Good extended answers and discourse markers with little in the way of pausing or self-correction.
Pronunciation	Excellent and sustained use of all pronunciation features and was easy to understand throughout.

Examiner: Did you like history as a subject at school?

Candidate: No, I don't like history at school. I find it bor … boring, so I don't pay attention[1] to it. I like Maths, because I'm good at Maths.

Examiner: Have you visited any historical museums?

Candidate: Not really. I think one time I went with my school, but I would not go to a museum on my own.

Examiner: When was the last time you read a book about history[3]?

Candidate: Maybe[4], at school. You know, I don't like read … reading books about the past[3].

Examiner: Do you think history is important?

Candidate: Well[4], I don't think history is important, but maybe some other people do.

Examiner's Comment	
Grammar	Only simple sentences are used, and there are some errors in them, but these don't cause communication problems.
	Simple ☑ Compound ☑ Complex ☑ Compound-complex ☑
Lexical Resource	No idiomatic language or use of colocations, and limited use of paraphrasing (*history→the past*) and discourse markers.
	Less Common Language[1] ☑ Collocations/Idiomatic[2] ☒ Paraphrasing[3] ☑ Discourse Marker[4] ☑
Fluency	A few small pauses and repetitions, but nothing that causes difficulty.
Pronunciation	Occasional good use of features.

Examiner: Do you like history as a subject at school?

Candidate: Well[4], if I'm going to be brutally honest[2]（直言不讳的）, no. Like is not a word I would associate with history. Hate[3], loathe[3], and maybe detest[1] would be the words I'd choose. I'm very glad that I don't need to bother with it anymore.

Examiner: Have you visited any historical museums?

Candidate: Only when I've been dragged around them by my mother or maybe on a compulsory school trip. It's certainly not somewhere I'd go by choice. I'd rather have my teeth pulled[2].

Examiner: When was the last time you read a book about history?

Candidate: Probably in high school. It's compulsory[3] then, so we have to[3] learn it. As I've already said, I'm not a history fan, and I binned it[2]（扔掉）as soon as I could.

Examiner: Do you think history is important?

Candidate: Actually[4], yes I do. Even though I don't like studying it myself, I do believe building on previous knowledge is a good idea. Understanding the past helps us plan our future.

	Examiner's Comment
Grammar	A good range of complex and simple structures, with complex structures being the majority. Only a minor grammatical mistake: 'have' in 'so we have to learn it' should be '**had**' (past tense). Simple ☑ Compound ☑ Complex ☑ Compound-complex ☑
Lexical Resource	A good range of less common vocabulary, collocations, idioms and paraphrasing (***hate→loath; compulsory→have to***). Less Common Language[1] ☑ Collocations/Idiomatic[2] ☑ Paraphrasing[3] ☑ Discourse Marker[4] ☑
Fluency	No noticeable effort that can be detected, and the beginnings of a range of discourse markers.
Pronunciation	Good, effective and sustained use of all features and the accent doesn't affect understanding.

■ Places

Examiner: Did you usually go to the cinema when you were a kid?

Candidate: No. My parents were busy, so they didn't have time. The cinema is far, either.

Examiner: Do you usually go to the cinema with your friends?

Candidate: No, I would choose the one attracting me a lot to go to the cinema.

Examiner: Do you still enjoy watching the movies you loved as a child?

Candidate: No. When I was a child, I watch movies just for fun. But now, I watch not only for fun, but for digging out[2] the deep thoughts implied by the movies.

Examiner: Do you prefer watching movies at home or in the cinema?

Candidate: At cinema. It has a huge screen, which make me more enjoyable. Also, some 3D or 4D are only available in the cinema.

<table>
<tr><th colspan="2">Examiner's Comment</th></tr>
<tr>
<td rowspan="2">Grammar</td>
<td>Attempts at complex structures, but with small errors. For example, 'When I was … I watch movies …' should be 'When I was … I watched movies …'; 'It has a huge screen, which make me …' should be 'It has a huge screen, which makes me …'. Quite a few mistakes in the simple sentences too – 'The cinema is far, either.' should change to 'The cinema was far as well.'.</td>
</tr>
<tr>
<td>Simple ☑   Compound ☑   Complex ☑   Compound-complex ☒</td>
</tr>
<tr>
<td rowspan="2">Lexical Resource</td>
<td>Mostly simple language is given with a single piece of idiomatic language.</td>
</tr>
<tr>
<td>Less Common Language[1] ☒   Collocations/Idiomatic[2] ☑
Paraphrasing[3] ☒   Discourse Marker[4] ☒</td>
</tr>
<tr>
<td>Fluency</td>
<td>Multiple pauses within and between sentences and no discourse markers given.</td>
</tr>
<tr>
<td>Pronunciation</td>
<td>Some features used, but neither consistent nor sustained.</td>
</tr>
</table>

Examiner: Did you usually go to the cinema[3] when you were a child[3]?

Candidate: Actually[4], yes. When I was much younger[3], I used to go to the pictures[3] every other weekend. Mostly, I went with my friends, but sometimes I went with my parents too. I still love going to the movies, just can't so much because of my studies.

Examiner: Do you usually go to the cinema with your friends?

Candidate: Like I just said[4], yes. I think it was because I was a little embarrassed[1] to go with my 漫威电影 folks. I'm kinda over that now, though, and enjoy going with my Dad to see the Marvel Movies[2]. Mum's not much of a movie fan.

Examiner: Do you still enjoy watching the movies you loved as a child?

Candidate: Absolutely[4]. With the streaming sites available here, I often watch some of my old 怀旧 favourites. Sometimes nostalgia[1] is a beautiful thing. I find it interesting how movies have changed over the last few years.

Examiner: Do you prefer watching movies at home or in the cinema?

Candidate: Well[4], I suppose these days I have gotten used to watching movies at home. I recently 而且 bought a 75-inch TV with a surround sound system to boot[2]. I adore it. To be honest[4], when I'm on holidays, my parents has great difficulty in getting me out of my room. I 遁世者 turn into a hermit[1] and only come out for food.

	Examiner's Comment
Grammar	A good range of complex structures with very few errors and certainly none that cause communication problems – 'my parents has great difficulty' should be 'my parents ***have*** great difficulty'. Simple ☑ Compound ☑ Complex ☑ Compound-complex ☒
Lexical Resource	A good range is given with some less common, idiomatic language and paraphrasing (***cinema→pictures; child→much younger***). Less Common Language[1] ☑ Collocations/Idiomatic[2] ☑ Paraphrasing[3] ☑ Discourse Marker[4] ☑
Fluency	A range of discourse markers and only minor pausing.
Pronunciation	Reasonable control of pronunciation features with only minor lapses.

Examiner: Have you ever seen some old buildings in the city?

Candidate: Yes. Their walls looked broken and dusty. Often old people will live in them.

Examiner: Do you think we should preserve[3] old buildings in cities?

Candidate: It depends. If these old buildings are cultural relics[1], they should be looked after[3]. And if it is personal and block the traffic, it should be tear down.

Examiner: Do you prefer living in an old building or a modern house?

Candidate: A modern house because it has a lot of facilities, which give me convenience, while the old building cannot.

Examiner: Are there any old buildings you want to see in the future?

Candidate: Yes. I like to see old buildings like the Forbidden City and so on.

Examiner's Comment	
Grammar	Simple sentences are reasonably accurate, and there is a limited range of complex structures with some mistakes. For example, 'And if it … block the traffic, it should be tear down.' should change to 'And if it … **blocks** the traffic, it should be **torn** down.'.
	Simple ☑ Compound ☒ Complex ☑ Compound-complex ☑
Lexical Resource	The words used are often used in the questions, which doesn't allow for much in the way of range except for 'relics', which could be classed as less common. A beginning of paraphrasing (**preserve→looked after**) is given too.
	Less Common Language[1] ☑ Collocations/Idiomatic[2] ☒ Paraphrasing[3] ☑ Discourse Marker[4] ☒
Fluency	Noticeable pausing when giving answers. No discourse markers are provided.
Pronunciation	Limited range of pronunciation features. No intonation throughout the entire topic, and chunking is ineffective due to the pausing.

Examiner: Have you ever seen some old buildings in the city?

Candidate: Yes, I have and my city is quite historical in some parts, so we do have things like old temples and palaces that date back thousands of years. Old buildings are good way of remembering the past and what life was like long ago.

Examiner: Do you think we should preserve[3] old buildings in cities?

Candidate: I think we should save[3] some. If they show or represent a particular era[1] or event, then they should be preserved. But on the other hand[4], some are too old and perhaps need to be renovated[1] so people can see what it once looked like.

Examiner: Do you prefer living in an old building or a modern house?

Candidate: For me, a modern house. I think that in terms of the design and quality and also utilities, it is much more comfortable to live in a modern-day[2] house certainly for folks living in the city. I'd be worried about the quality and safety of an old building in a modern-day city.

Examiner: Are there any old buildings you want to see in the future?

Candidate: That's a good question because the world is full of different buildings. If I picked one or two, then I'd go for Big Ben in London because it is so iconic and then probably the Palace Museum in Beijing as it's part of my country's heritage and it's so vast that we can spend ages[2] walking around it.

Examiner's Comment

Grammar	Some use of complex structures with some minor errors – 'Old buildings are good way ...' missing article '*a*' before 'good', as an example. Simple ☑ Compound ☑ Complex ☑ Compound-complex ☑
Lexical Resource	Some beginnings of paraphrasing(***preserve→save***) and less common words. Some words are just taken from the question and used repetitively – 'modern' – for example. Less Common Language[1] ☑ Collocations/Idiomatic[2] ☑ Paraphrasing[3] ☑ Discourse Marker[4] ☑
Fluency	Willing to speak at length, but there's just a little too much noticeable effort. An unusual discourse marker.
Pronunciation	A range and some effective use of features but not sustained. Some occasional slight mispronunciations.

Examiner: Have you visited a farm?

Candidate: Yes. When I was a kid, my grandfather led me to a local farm.

Examiner: What kind of farm do you like?

Candidate: I like the farm where cute mammals are raised, like rabbits. These animals are harmless and fluffy.

Examiner: Do you think farming is important?

Candidate: Yes. If it raises the cow, it produces milk, which is a necessity in our life. The beef is also important in our food.

Examiner: Did you do farm work when you were young?

Candidate: Yes. I fed the rabbits with grass and I helped to do some cleaning to their houses.

Examiner's Comment	
Grammar	A mix of simple and complex sentence structures. Both styles have small errors – 'If it raises the cow, it produces milk', these '***it***'s refer to different things, which could be confusing.
	Simple ☑　　　Compound ☑　　　Complex ☑　　　Compound-complex ☒
Lexical Resource	Some of the choices of words are incorrect – 'my grandfather led me ...', 'led' should be '***took***' – and no paraphrasing is given. No less common words are given, nor are collocations or idiomatic language.
	Less Common Language[1] ☒　　　　Collocations/Idiomatic[2] ☒ Paraphrasing[3] ☒　　　　Discourse Marker[4] ☒
Fluency	Occasionally slow and repetitive speech. Simple speech is relatively fluent.
Pronunciation	Features like chunking are challenging to measure due to the pausing and the fact that there's not enough speech given.

Examiner: Have you visited a farm?

Candidate: Yes, I have because I think it's the best place to pick up some organic[1] produce such as fresh milk[2] or free-range eggs[2] _{散养鸡蛋} and that kind of thing. Maybe it is cheaper than the supermarkets too!

Examiner: What kind of farm do you like?

Candidate: I quite like the farms that involve different animals too. A real working farm is more interesting because you might get to feed animals or even pick your own veg[1] _{蔬菜}, which is good fun.

Examiner: Do you think farming[3] is important?

Candidate: Oh, without a doubt[4]. Where would we be if we didn't have any farming? It's important because we need people who know about growing and planting[3] vegetables so we can eat them to keep health.

Examiner: Did you do farm work when you were young?

Candidate: No, I mean, my grandparents would grow their own vegetables and work a lot in the fields, but as for me, I don't really have green fingers[2] _{有高超的园艺技能}, so I stayed out of their way!

Examiner's Comment

Grammar	Mostly complex structures are correctly used. Only one minimal error – 'keep health' *should change to* 'keep ***healthy***'. This wouldn't cause any misunderstanding. Simple ☑　　Compound ☑　　Complex ☑　　Compound-complex ☑
Lexical Resource	Some good use of native terms – 'veg', rather than vegetables, and some use of paraphrasing (***farming→growing and planting***) and idiomatic language. Less Common Language[1] ☑　　Collocations/Idiomatic[2] ☑ Paraphrasing[3] ☑　　Discourse Marker[4] ☑
Fluency	No noticeable effort and has started by using a more unusual discourse marker.
Pronunciation	Good, sustained use of features and can generally be understood.

Habits

Examiner: How do you plan your time in a day?

Candidate: I plan to get up early, do some sports, study, make my lunch, do some work, play online games and go to bed early. This is ideal.

Examiner: Is it easy to manage time?

Candidate: Definitely[4] not. I think it is extremely[1] difficult. Every time I make a plan, I seem to never finish it. Or I just keep to the morning plan.

Examiner: When do you find it hard to allocate time?

Candidate: In the morning and in the evening[3]. In the morning I find it hard to get up early. And at night[3], I usually spend a lot of time play the phone and I cannot resist it.

Examiner: Do you like being busy?

Candidate: Yes. Especially[4] when I am busy with courses or task, I feel fulfilled[1] (满足的). I won't be distracted[1] by other things because I am devoted to[2] it. After I finish, I will be excited.

	Examiner's Comment		
Grammar	A mix of simple and complex structures with a few inaccuracies – 'play' should change to '***playing***' in 'I usually spend a lot of time play the phone'– but with a limited range.		
	Simple ☑ Compound ☑ Complex ☑ Compound-complex ☒		
Lexical Resource	Some good paraphrasing(***evening→night***) and collocations. Can be mostly understood but has some inappropriacies.		
	Less Common Language[1] ☑ Collocations/Idiomatic[2] ☑ Paraphrasing[3] ☑ Discourse Marker[4] ☑		
Fluency	Willing to give extended answers and speak at length.		
Pronunciation	Some effective use of features, but not sustained.		

Examiner: How do you plan your time in a day?

Candidate: My day is quite easy to plan. My routine is dictated by my class timetable, which is fixed so I can plan other things around the lessons. Going shopping, playing sports and seeing friends can be done around my school schedule and then just take it from there.

Examiner: Is it easy to manage time?

Candidate: I think it is when you have a fixed routine because you know what you need to do and where you need to go etc., but sometimes if I am at a loose end² 无所事事 then I don't manage my time well. So I'd say if you can prioritize¹ your things on your to-do list then it's much easier to manage.

Examiner: When do you find it hard to allocate time?

Candidate: Probably in the evening. That's usually when I have got chores¹ to do or homework to do and even just have some me-time² 私人专属时间, and I value that time when I can be away from everyone and everything and just focus on myself and relax. I tend to procrastinate¹ more in the evenings!

Examiner: Do you like being busy³?

Candidate: I do because, for me, it makes the day go quicker. But with that said⁴ 尽管如此, I hate being busy 24/7 and being rushed off my feet³ 奔忙 all the time is exhausting¹ 使人疲惫不堪的. Keeping busy in the daytime is fine but after 6 or 7 pm I just want to chill¹ 放松.

	Examiner's Comment
Grammar	Some good, correct use of complex structures, which is beginning to show range. Simple ☑ Compound ☑ Complex ☑ Compound-complex ☑
Lexical Resource	Good use of idiomatic language, less common language and paraphrasing (***busy→rushed off my feet***). Showing a good range of vocabulary. Less Common Language¹ ☑ Collocations/Idiomatic² ☑ Paraphrasing³ ☑ Discourse Marker⁴ ☑
Fluency	No noticeable effort, but using the connective 'and' a little too much, especially in the third answer.
Pronunciation	Easy to understand throughout and no issues with L1 accent.

Examiner: Do you often read books?

Candidate: Seldom[1]. I think playing the phone is my habit.

Examiner: Are your reading habits now different than before?

Candidate: Yes, as for the kind of materials of reading. When I was a kid, I preferred stories but now literature[1] work suits me better.

Examiner: Have you ever read a novel[3] that has been adapted into a film?

Candidate: Yes. Like the first book[3] of *Harry Potter*. But I didn't read it carefully because I saw the film and then read the book.

Examiner: Which do you prefer[3], reading books or watching movies?

Candidate: Actually[4], I like[3] them both. When I want a quiet environment, I prefer read a book. When I feel bored, I prefer to watch movies which is more vivid[1].

Examiner's Comment			
Grammar	Limited range of complex structures and some may lead to misunderstanding –'Yes, as for the kind of materials of reading.', as an answer to this question, this isn't very clear. Some of the simple sentences also have minor errors – 'playing the phone is my habit' should be 'I habitually play with my phone' or 'I have a habit of playing with my phone'.		
	Simple ☑	Compound ☒	Complex ☑	Compound-complex ☑
Lexical Resource	Some good paraphrasing (***novel→book; prefer→like***) and the beginnings of a range, but no idiomatic language, which prohibits the allocation of higher scores.		
	Less Common Language[1] ☑ Paraphrasing[3] ☑	Collocations/Idiomatic[2] ☒ Discourse Marker[4] ☑	
Fluency	Some repetition and self-correction. Some of the sentences are a little short.		
Pronunciation	Limited range of pronunciation features, but can generally be understood.		

Examiner:　Do you often read books?

Candidate:　I wouldn't say I'm a bookworm[2], but I might read a couple novels each year, perhaps during the holidays. A good novel is a good way to escape reality[2] and get lost in a story, but, to be honest, the only books I might read often are just for my studies, and they are all online nowadays.

Examiner:　Are your reading habits[3] now different than before?

Candidate:　Well[4], my behaviours[3] are a bit different now because I certainly don't read as much as I did when I was 10 or 11, for example, but I read more current affairs[2] and academic journals[2] etc. So while I don't read much fiction these days, I still read plenty of factual books and articles to learn more.

Examiner:　Have you ever read a novel that has been adapted into a film[3]?

Candidate:　Indeed[4] I have, and it's very popular. It's called *Harry Potter and the philosopher's stone*. I remember reading the book, and when I heard they were going to adapt[1] it into a movie[3], I was really excited. The book was a real page-turner[2], and the films were so much fun.

Examiner:　Which do you prefer, reading books or watching movies?

Candidate:　Movies. You know[4], with movies you don't have to think as much as everything is shown in front of you on the screen, and as English is not my native[1] language, I'm a little slower with books, so I prefer to watch movies.

	Examiner's Comment
Grammar	A good mix of simple and complex structures. Most sentences are correct with only minor mistakes – 'read a couple novels' should be 'read a couple *of* novels'. Simple ☑　　　Compound ☑　　　Complex ☑　　　Compound-complex ☑
Lexical Resource	Paraphrases well (***habits→behaviours; film→movie***) and uses some good less common vocabulary with some idiomatic language and collocations added too. Mostly flexible use of vocab. Less Common Language[1] ☑　　　　　Collocations/Idiomatic[2] ☑ Paraphrasing[3] ☑　　　　　　　　　　Discourse Marker[4] ☑
Fluency	A range of discourse markers, good extended answers, no noticeable effort.
Pronunciation	Good use of features. Only minor mistakes and easy to understand.

Examiner:　How do you usually spend your time by yourself?

Candidate:　Play online games or surf[1] on social media.

Examiner:　Do you like spending time by yourself?

Candidate:　Yes, to some degree. I think everyone need solitary[1] time to quiet themselves down. They can do anything they want, and other' feelings are not my consideration.

Examiner:　What did you do last time you were by yourself?

Candidate:　Looking through TikTok to kill the time[2] while having snacks.

Examiner:　Do you usually spend time by yourself?

Candidate:　Yes. I think to be alone don't necessary means to be lonely. Solitary provides me a chance to introspect[1] myself and focus myself on the things to be done.

	Examiner's Comment
Grammar	Few complex structures offered, and some errors could cause misunderstanding – 'to be alone don't necessary means to be lonely' should be '**being** alone **doesn't necessarily** mean **being** lonely'. Also, 'everyone need solitary time' and 'other' feelings' should change to 'everyone **needs** solitary time' and '**others'** feelings' respectively.
	Simple ☑　　　Compound ☑　　　Complex ☑　　　Compound-complex ☑
Lexical Resource	Some good less common language and attempts at idioms, but these are not always correct – 'kill the time' should be 'kill time'. No attempts at paraphrasing.
	Less Common Language[1] ☑　　　Collocations/Idiomatic[2] ☑ Paraphrasing[3] ☒　　　Discourse Marker[4] ☒
Fluency	Generally quite slow and often hesitates between sentences. No discourse markers given.
Pronunciation	Some control of features, but poor enunciation and intonation.

Answer 2（★★★）　　　　　　　　　　　🎧 051

Examiner: How do you usually spend your time by yourself?

Candidate: If I'm alone at home, then I'll do some household chores if they need doing, but if not, then I'll watch³ TV shows. I'll watch the ones I want to watch and not the ones my family always want to see³. If I have time to kill² outside by myself, then I might do a spot of window shopping² or just wander around a local park and gather my thoughts² and maybe make a few plans for the coming weeks.

Examiner: Do you like spending time by yourself?

Candidate: I do. It's nice to be around friends and family, but you don't always have time to think by yourself and focus on your own things that you want to do. That could be anything, but having time alone is a good thing. You get some time to chill out² and just get out of everyone's way for a while.

Examiner: What did you do last time you were by yourself?

Candidate: I went to the park. The weather wasn't great, but it was nice to just feel the wind in my hair for a while and enjoy the tranquil¹ environment of the park. So the last time I was alone, I just had a good walk to clear my head² and forget about things for a while. I even switched off my phone for an hour!

Examiner: Do you usually spend time by yourself?

Candidate: At school, no. But at home, yes. You know⁴, at school there are always people there so you can't usually walk down the corridor without bumping into someone you know and the same goes for sitting in class. But at home, my parents work 9-5, so when they are at work, I've got the house to myself which is nice, even if it's only for an hour.

Examiner's Comment

Grammar	A good range and mix of simple and complex structures with few errors. Simple ☑　　Compound ☑　　Complex ☑　　Compound-complex ☑
Lexical Resource	Some good idioms and paraphrases(***watch→see***) coupled with the beginning of a range of less common language. Less Common Language¹ ☑　　　Collocations/Idiomatic² ☑ Paraphrasing³ ☑　　　　　　　Discourse Marker⁴ ☑
Fluency	A little slow at times with occasional hesitation. Only one discourse marker given.
Pronunciation	Some good intonation and chunking, but doesn't finish some of the words.

Examiner: Are you a tidy person?

Candidate: To some degree, I am.

Examiner: How do you keep things tidy?

Candidate: I will sort out my room on a irregular[1] time. When I feel boring or want to fresh myself, I will clean up[2] my room.

Examiner: Do you think people should be tidy all the time?

Candidate: Er … No. At home, people can be relative free because nobody will see you.

Examiner: Are you tidier at work (school) or at home?

Candidate: Yes. In the dormitory, I am the one who clean[3] the room. At home, I will tidy up[3] my own room.

Examiner's Comment	
Grammar	Simple sentences are mostly correct with some minor errors. For example, 'on a irregular time' should be 'on **an** irregular time'. Attempts at complex structures are given. These are incorrect though. For example, 'When I feel boring … fresh myself …' should be 'When I feel **bored … refresh** myself …'; 'relative free' needs to change to '**relatively** free'.
	Simple ☑ Compound ☒ Complex ☑ Compound-complex ☑
Lexical Resource	Minimal less common language and paraphrases(**clean→ tidy up**). No actual range of vocabulary is offered.
	Less Common Language[1] ☑ Collocations/Idiomatic[2] ☑ Paraphrasing[3] ☑ Discourse Marker[4] ☒
Fluency	Some slow speech and the answers are very short so not speaking at length.
Pronunciation	Some range of features, but not sustained. Can be understood mostly.

Answer 2（★★★☆） 　　　　　　　　　　　　　　　　　　　　🎧 053

Examiner: Are you a tidy[3] person?

Candidate: Absolutely[4], I am a neat freak[2], especially at home. I've got so many books and things scattered[1] all over my desk, and it's not easy to keep everything in its place[3], but I do my best! I think I'm a tidy person but if you ask my mum that question, she might disagree with me!

Examiner: How do you keep things tidy?

Candidate: I've got drawers where I allocate all my belongings and separate the things I use on a daily basis to the items that I don't use so often. As for my clothes, I have a pretty big wardrobe and can easily organize the things I wear.

Examiner: Do you think people should be tidy all the time?

Candidate: I would say it's good to be tidy all the time, especially at work, because if your workspace looks like a bomb has hit it[2], you may not work efficiently, and the boss may have a word with you about cleaning up!

Examiner: Are you tidier at work (school) or at home?

Candidate: Well[4], I'm not that tidy at home. I try to tidy my desk at school because of all the books and notepads, and if it isn't neat, then I might lose things, and then I'll panic[1] about where I may have put it. But at home, I tend to just leave stuff all over my room!

	Examiner's Comment
Grammar	A good mix of simple and complex structures, most of which are error-free. The errors are very minor and don't cause misunderstandings – in 'separate the things … to the items', '**to**' should change to '**from**'.
	Simple ☑　　Compound ☑　　Complex ☑　　Compound-complex ☑
Lexical Resource	The beginnings of a good range with some good paraphrases (**tidy→keep everything in its place**), discourse markers and idiomatic language.
	Less Common Language[1] ☑　　　　Collocations/Idiomatic[2] ☑ Paraphrasing[3] ☑　　　　　　　　Discourse Marker[4] ☑
Fluency	Some noticeable effort during the answers, but generally able to keep going.
Pronunciation	Good, sustained use of a range of features and easy to understand.

Look at this: *In this answer, contradictory information is given – 'Absolutely, I am a neat freak, especially at home.' and 'Well, I'm not that tidy at home.'. Be careful of this, as it can signal to the examiner that you've memorized an answer. It's much better if you stick to one position in your answers rather than have opposites like in the example here.*

注意： 这个答案中有前后矛盾的信息——"当然，我有洁癖，特别是在家时。"和"嗯，在家时我没那么爱整洁。"。小心这种情况，因为这会让考官认为你在背诵答案。在回答中坚持同样的立场更好，不要像这份答案这样包含矛盾的信息。

Examiner: What will you do if you find something lost by others?

Candidate: First[4], I will try to find if there is information to contact the owner. If there is no, I will call the police and let them to deal with it. If there is, I will call the owner directly.

Examiner: Do you report to the police when finding something lost by others?

Candidate: Yes. If I am busy or not able to find the owner, I am bound[1] to report to the police.

Examiner: Have you ever lost anything?

Candidate: Yes, definitely. Once I am on a travel, I lost my wallet where I had money and important cards. Luckily, I called the police and found it back.

Examiner: Will you post on social media if you lose your item?

Candidate: Yes. Especially on campus. Other students will also post my loss to help me. This really helps me a lot because it makes more people to know it.

	Examiner's Comment
Grammar	A good mix of simple and complex structures, but there are minor errors in nearly every sentence given. For example, 'If there is no … let them to deal with it.' should be 'If there is **none** … let them deal with it.'. '… I am bound to report to the police …' should have an '*it*' after 'report'. 'Once I am on a travel …' should change to 'Once I **was** on travel'. They don't affect understanding, but the quantity of errors is problematic.
	Simple ☑ Compound ☑ Complex ☑ Compound-complex ☑
Lexical Resource	Most of the language is copied from the questions, and no paraphrasing is given.
	Less Common Language[1] ☑ Collocations/Idiomatic[2] ☒ Paraphrasing[3] ☒ Discourse Marker[4] ☑
Fluency	The answers are a little bit short, but a good flow of speech. Only one discourse marker is given, and I hope that more and different ones are given later in the test.
Pronunciation	Some range, and sustained use of features with only minor mispronunciations.

Answer 2 (★★★★) 🎧 055

Examiner: What will you do if you find something lost by others?

Candidate: If I found something that belongs to someone else, I would not keep it, that's for sure. I would hand it in[2] somewhere or try to contact the person who has lost it, as I believe that's the right thing to do. And you might feel good by doing a good deed[1] and returning an item to someone who has lost[3] or misplaced[3] it.

Examiner: Do you report to the police when finding[3] something lost by others?

Candidate: Maybe[4], it might depend on where I am. If I discover[3] something like a phone or a wallet outside, I would maybe try and take it to the local police station, but if someone leaves their phone on a bus, then I may just hand it over to the driver and hope they can keep it safe until the owner contacts them about the lost item.

Examiner: Have you ever lost anything?

Candidate: Certainly[4], but only once, and it was my phone. I was gutted[2] ^(伤心透了). I had just used it on the shop and must have left it in the shop and then walked out. It wasn't until later that I realized I had lost it and searched high and low[2] ^(到处) for it and had to retrace my steps back to the shop. Thankfully the shop assistant found it and gave it back to me.

Examiner: Will you post on social media if you lose your item?

Candidate: I might do, but the chances are small of getting a reply from someone that might know of the item's whereabouts[1] ^(下落). It's a long shot[2] ^(希望不大), but maybe if you did post on social media that you lost something, you might get lucky, and someone has found it and can return it to you.

	Examiner's Comment
Grammar	A good mix of simple and complex structures with only minor errors in the complex structures that wouldn't cause misunderstanding – 'I had just used it on the shop', 'on' should be '***in***'. Simple ☑ Compound ☑ Complex ☑ Compound-complex ☑
Lexical Resource	A good range of vocabulary is used, with multiple idioms and paraphrases (***lost→misplaced; finding→discover***) used. Some effective less common language is also used. Less Common Language[1] ☑ Collocations/Idiomatic[2] ☑ Paraphrasing[3] ☑ Discourse Marker[4] ☑
Fluency	Good discourse markers are used as well, with very little pausing. Pauses are content-related rather than language-related.
Pronunciation	A good range and sustained effective use of features. The Chinese accent has a minimal effect on understanding.

Examiner: What kind of public transportation do you usually take?

Candidate: Erm ... Subway.

Examiner: When do you usually take public transportation, in your everyday life or when you are travelling?

Candidate: When I am travelling. It is cheaper and safer. In my everyday life, I usually ride my bike.

Examiner: Do most people prefer public transportation in your country?

Candidate: Yes, I think. First[4], the price is low. Second[4], when it is peak time[2] (高峰期) for traffic, public transportation may be quicker than a personal car.

Examiner: Will there be more people taking public transportation in the future?

Candidate: Yes. It is more environmentally friendly[2]. And it will be upgraded according to the time, I think.

	Examiner's Comment		
Grammar	A very limited offering of complex structures. What is given, though, is correct.		
	Simple ☑ Compound ☒ Complex ☑ Compound-complex ☒		
Lexical Resource	Mainly simple vocabulary is used, but there are some good, albeit reasonably common, collocations used.		
	Less Common Language[1] ☒ Collocations/Idiomatic[2] ☑ Paraphrasing[3] ☒ Discourse Marker[4] ☑		
Fluency	Some slow speech during the longer sentences and occasional pausing.		
Pronunciation	Difficult to assess properly as there isn't much language given. As there are a few pauses and the whole speech is slow, there are very few features that can be measured.		

Examiner: What kind of public transportation do you usually take?

Candidate: I take the bus on a daily basis². My place is not too far from school, but it's a fair walk, so I'll jump on the bus² to save time. If I'm going to a different part of the city, then I'll take the subway³, but most of the time, for me⁴, it's the bus.

Examiner: When do you usually take public transportation, in your everyday life or when you are travelling?

Candidate: For me, everyday life. It's convenient, and it's the quickest way for me to get from A to B¹, but taking public transport in a new city can be quite an adventure! A lot of cities now in China have a much-improved public transport network, and the cost is not high³, so I'm OK with that.

Examiner: Do most people prefer public transportation in your country?

Candidate: I think so, partly because it's developed a lot over the years and also it's quite cheap³, certainly compared to other major cities. It's cheaper to get the bus or the metro³ to work and back on a daily basis than it is to drive a car and then spend a lot of time in rush hour¹ traffic.

Examiner: Will there be more people taking public transportation in the future?

Candidate: I can't speak for everyone⁴, but in my opinion, people will always take public transport, especially in Beijing, because of its low cost and efficiency. The metro trains run from very early in the morning to late at night, and that goes for a lot of buses too. As long as it saves people money to get around² (四处走动) on public transport, I can't see people not using it anytime soon.

Examiner's Comment	
Grammar	A mix of simple and complex structures that are mostly error-free. Simple ☑ Compound ☑ Complex ☑ Compound-complex ☑
Lexical Resource	Some good use of collocations and idiomatic language, as well as some less common vocabulary and paraphrasing(***subway→metro; cost not so high→cheap***). 'public transport' is used a little repetitively, though. Less Common Language¹ ☑ Collocations/Idiomatic² ☑ Paraphrasing³ ☑ Discourse Marker⁴ ☑
Fluency	No noticeable effort when speaking and the beginnings of a range of connectives.
Pronunciation	Good, flexible use of language throughout and is easy to understand.

■ Rest & Diet

Examiner: Do you prefer a long break or several short breaks?

Candidate: A long break definitely[4]. In a long break, I can relax more thoroughly.

Examiner: What do you usually do during a break?

Candidate: I usually play online games like *League of Legends* or play on the Tiktok. I will go to the street as well.

Examiner: Why do you need to take a break?

Candidate: I hopes there are two reasons. First[4], if I work too long, I can't focus on the work. Second[4], I need a break to get inspiration[1].

Examiner: How often do you take a break?

Candidate: I usually work for one hour and take a break for 20 to 30 seconds … minutes. And I tend to travel for 4–5 days during a long vocation[1].

	Examiner's Comment
Grammar	An effort at complex structures and the one given is correct. Many of the simple structures are incorrect though, and may lead to comprehension problems – 'I hopes … reasons.' should be 'I ***think*** … reasons.'.
	Simple ☑ Compound ☑ Complex ☑ Compound-complex ☒
Lexical Resource	'Long' is used repetitively, and no range of vocabulary is given. Some words are incorrect and may lead to misunderstanding. For example, 'during a long vocation' should be 'during a long ***vacation***'.
	Less Common Language[1] ☑ Collocations/Idiomatic[2] ☒ Paraphrasing[3] ☒ Discourse Marker[4] ☑
Fluency	Some pausing and repetition to keep going. A good beginning of a range of discourse markers. Answers are a little short to be considered at length.
Pronunciation	Some control of features but lapses are frequent, and some mispronunciations may reduce clarity.

Examiner: Do you prefer a long break or several short[3] breaks?

Candidate: I would prefer several mini[3] breaks. If a break is too long, I might be tempted to take a nap[2], and if I do that, then I will sleep for ages! As long as I have enough time to use the bathroom, maybe make a coffee and stretch my legs[2] 活动身体，走一走 for a moment, that's good enough for me.

Examiner: What do you usually do during a break[3] 短暂休息?

Candidate: During a breather[1/3], I'll check my phone for messages, maybe also just check my schedule and to-do list for the day. I may go on the social media and see who has posted, but that's about it. If it's not raining cats and dogs[2] 倾盆大雨, then I'll go outside for a moment and get some fresh air.

Examiner: Why do you need to take a break?

Candidate: For me[4], I need a break to give my eyes a rest[3] from reading and studying all the time. I can't concentrate for hours on end, so I like to have a break at least once an hour to digest[1] 理解，消化 what I've learnt and just to freshen up for a moment.

Examiner: How often do you take a break?

Candidate: Probably once every hour, I'll take a short rest just to take my mind off of what I'm doing for a while. I might go for a quick walk around the local park and listen to music, or I'll grab[1] a snack and a drink just to charge up the batteries[2] 休息以恢复精力 a little.

Examiner's Comment

Grammar	A mix of simple and complex structures with only minor errors – in 'I may go on the social media', there is no need for '***the***'. This would cause comprehension problems. Simple ☑ Compound ☑ Complex ☑ Compound-complex ☑
Lexical Resource	A good range of vocabulary is shown through multiple synonyms of the same word (***short→mini; break→breather/rest***) and some very native language used as well – 'grab' and 'breather'. Less Common Language[1] ☑ Collocations/Idiomatic[2] ☑ Paraphrasing[3] ☑ Discourse Marker[4] ☑
Fluency	A limited number of discourse markers, but this may change later in the test, with no noticeable effort in the answers.
Pronunciation	Mixed control that isn't sustained throughout the answers. Can be generally understood throughout.

Examiner: Do you often stay up late?

Candidate: Yes, especially during the holiday. When at home, I almost stay up every night.

Examiner: What do you do when you stay up late?

Candidate: I just immerse[1] myself in TikTok or other social media, and I cannot stop. Or sometimes, I will play online games with my friends.

Examiner: How do you feel when you have stayed up late the night before?

Candidate: First[4], I feel pain in my eyes. Second[4], I will often feel sleepy when I am working. And sometimes I feel my mind is in a mess.

Examiner: What are the bad effects of staying up late?

Candidate: In the short run[2], it cause pain in some parts of our body or sleepiness, which decrease the efficiency. In the long run[2], it will impair[1] the function of our body and make us weak and ill.

	Examiner's Comment
Grammar	An effort at complex structures, but some of the simple structures are incorrect in a fundamental way – 'it cause pain' rather than '***causes***'; '... which decrease the efficiency' should be '... which ***decreases*** the efficiency'. Also, the change from the first person to third person (in the last answer) is a little strange.
	Simple ☑ Compound ☑ Complex ☑ Compound-complex ☒
Lexical Resource	Some attempts at less common language and collocations, but paraphrasing is non-existent.
	Less Common Language[1] ☑ Collocations/Idiomatic[2] ☑ Paraphrasing[3] ☒ Discourse Marker[4] ☑
Fluency	Some slow speech and a limited range of discourse markers.
Pronunciation	Some range demonstrated but not sustained. Can be generally understood though throughout the answers.

Examiner: Do you often stay up late?

Candidate: Actually[4], I don't stay up late often, so I wouldn't say I'm a night owl[2]. I'm definitely more of a morning person. My classes begin early in the morning, so if I don't get a good night's sleep the night before, I feel drowsy[1] in class! <small>昏昏欲睡的</small>

Examiner: What do you do when you stay up late?

Candidate: I usually watching a film or some TV shows. Maybe I can't sleep, or I just don't feel tired. Quite often, my friends do stay up late, so I might chat with them for a while online, but if I'm up late, I'm not doing any studies, that's for sure!

Examiner: How do you feel when you have stayed up late the night before?

Candidate: To be honest[4], I might feel OK in the morning, but the tiredness might catch up with me just after lunch, and I'll feel sleepy pretty quick! If I feel like that, I'll get more sugary drinks and snacks for some energy just to get me through my afternoon classes!

Examiner: What are the negative effects of staying up late?

Candidate: It can affect our appearance and also how we function[1] during the day as it can make us less focused, sleepy[3] and often lethargic[1/3]. <small>没精打采的</small> If you stay up late just once in a while, I'd say it doesn't matter too much, but if you make a regular habit out of it, you might want to think about making a change and don't burn the candle at both ends[2]. <small>起早贪黑而疲惫不堪</small>

Examiner's Comment

Grammar	Many error-free sentences and the errors given wouldn't cause comprehension problems – 'I usually watching a film' and 'I'll feel sleepy pretty quick'. **'watch'** and **'quickly'** would be the correct versions of these words. Simple ☑ Compound ☑ Complex ☑ Compound-complex ☑
Lexical Resource	A good range of less common language with some effective use of collocations, idiomatic language and paraphrasing(**sleepy→lethargic**). Less Common Language[1] ☑ Collocations/Idiomatic[2] ☑ Paraphrasing[3] ☑ Discourse Marker[4] ☑
Fluency	These answers are definitely extended and show an ability to speak at length. No noticeable effort during the answers and the beginnings of a range of discourse markers.
Pronunciation	Easy to understand throughout with a good range of features that are sustained.

Examiner: What snacks do you like to eat?

Candidate: Um … preserved fruit[2] (果脯), cake, and hot snacks.

Examiner: Did you often eat snacks when you were young?

Candidate: Er … No, because my mother forbade[1] me from eating them.

Examiner: When do you usually eat snacks now?

Candidate: When I am hungry or when I find a new kind which attracts me and I have never tried before.

Examiner: Do you think it is healthy for you to eat snacks?

Candidate: It hard to say because it depends on the amount I eat. On one hand[4], snacks bring me a happy mood. On the other hand[4], some chemical ingredients may do harm to my body.

	Examiner's Comment
Grammar	Both simple and complex structures are correct, but only one complex structure is used – not indicating a mix of structures.
	Simple ☑ Compound ☒ Complex ☑ Compound-complex ☑
Lexical Resource	Mostly simple vocabulary used with little range offered.
	Less Common Language[1] ☑ Collocations/Idiomatic[2] ☑ Paraphrasing[3] ☒ Discourse Marker[4] ☑
Fluency	Can't speak with pausing and has frequent repetition.
Pronunciation	Frequent mispronunciations that cause difficulty in understanding.

Examiner: What snacks do you like to eat?

Candidate: Too many to choose from! But I would say I prefer to eat some fruit as a snack. It's tasty and healthy and not overly expensive. As for a drink, usually just some water, tea or coffee during the day. I try to cut out the drinks with too much sugar.

Examiner: Did you often eat snacks when you were young?

Candidate: I was spoilt[1] for snacks when I was a kid. I'd eat them quite a lot, but it was my parents that had to get me to change my habits. I would probably eat more unhealthier snacks during the day, and then I wouldn't eat my dinner that my mom had cooked, and she would get really wound up[2] if I didn't eat her dinner.

担忧

Examiner: When do you usually eat snacks now?

Candidate: Now, I would say it's just between classes that I'll snack the most. I certainly won't snack before I'm going to have a meal. But as I said, I'm more likely to snack between classes.

Examiner: Do you think it is healthy for you to eat snacks?

Candidate: Not all the time, and it probably depends on what the snack is, but I don't think it's too bad. More fruit-based snacks are better for our health, and to be honest, they do give me a lift when I feel tired and sleepy so I would say snacks are fine but just be careful what you put in your mouth!

	Examiner's Comment
Grammar	A decent mix of structures with a few small errors that don't cause any real misunderstanding. Simple ☑ Compound ☑ Complex ☑ Compound-complex ☑
Lexical Resource	Little in the way of paraphrasing and is somewhat repetitive. 'Snack' is used nine times and taken directly from the questions. It is used as both a verb and a noun, though. Less Common Language[1] ☑ Collocations/Idiomatic[2] ☑ Paraphrasing[3] ☒ Discourse Marker[4] ☒
Fluency	Good extended answers, but for higher scores, it would be good to include some discourse markers.
Pronunciation	Some control of features but not sustained. The chunking is wrong in places.

Taking photos	*Answer 1*（★★）	🎧 064

Examiner: Do you like taking photos?

Candidate: Yes. I think it is a good way to keep a memory.

Examiner: Do you like taking selfies?

Candidate: No. I seldom[1] take selfies because I am not satisfied with my face in some parts.

Examiner: What is your favourite family photo?

Candidate: To be honest[4], my family don't have a formal family photo. But I like the one taken when we were having the dinner because everyone seems to be happy and hopeful.

Examiner: Do you want to improve your photography skills?

Candidate: Yes. I always find the photos I've taken is much far away from beautiful. So I have to take many times and select the best one, which costs me too much time.

<table>
<tr><th colspan="2">Examiner's Comment</th></tr>
<tr>
<td rowspan="2">Grammar</td>
<td>Some basic subject-verb agreement errors – 'my family don't …' should be 'my family doesn't …' – and some errors with articles – 'having the dinner' should be 'having dinner'. The sentences are still understandable though.</td>
</tr>
<tr>
<td>Simple ☑   Compound ☒   Complex ☑   Compound-complex ☑</td>
</tr>
<tr>
<td rowspan="2">Lexical Resource</td>
<td>Only simple vocabulary is used and is mainly copied from the questions.</td>
</tr>
<tr>
<td>Less Common Language[1] ☑   Collocations/Idiomatic[2] ☒
Paraphrasing[3] ☒   Discourse Marker[4] ☑</td>
</tr>
<tr>
<td>Fluency</td>
<td>Mostly quite short anwers, and the speech rate is a little slow.</td>
</tr>
<tr>
<td>Pronunciation</td>
<td>Mostly able to keep going, but speaks a little slowly with occasional repetition.</td>
</tr>
</table>

Examiner: Do you like taking photos[3]?

Candidate: Definitely[4], I do enjoy taking snaps[3] when I'm out visiting new places. It's a good way of keeping the memories fresh, and you can look back on[2] them in years to come. On the normal day, I don't take many pictures, but if there is a special event or a party, then I'm all for taking pics!
追忆

Examiner: Do you like taking selfies?

Candidate: Not often. I don't feel like I'm very photogenic[1], but I will take some selfies with friends if we are hanging out together, but that's more about 'capturing the special moment' than anything else.
上镜的

Examiner: What is your favourite[3] family photo?

Candidate: The photo I like best[3] would be a photo taken when I was maybe 4 or 5 years old. My whole family is in that photo, and we don't have any others like it. It's certainly a photo that I cherish[1], and I might look at it once in a while if I miss my home and my relatives.

Examiner: Do you want to improve[3] your photography skills?

Candidate: I don't think I need to better[3] my skills. In my opinion, the modern-day cameras already make your photos look good from a technical viewpoint[1]. With that said[4], there can always be room for improvement, and maybe I should pay more attention to photo composition and setting up the shot sometimes, so that could be an area that I might like to improve.
话虽如此

Examiner's Comment	
Grammar	Some small issues with articles – in 'On the normal day', 'the' should be '*a*' – and a mix of simple and complex structures. Simple ☑ Compound ☑ Complex ☑ Compound-complex ☑
Lexical Resource	A good range of vocab with a selection of less common words. Some good paraphrasing (*photos→snaps; favourite→like best; improve→better*) is used too. Less Common Language[1] ☑ Collocations/Idiomatic[2] ☑ Paraphrasing[3] ☑ Discourse Marker[4] ☑
Fluency	The answers are a good length with only occasional hesitation.
Pronunciation	Uses a range of features, but not all the way through. There are times when it's quite monotonous.

Examiner:　Are you good at telling jokes?

Candidate:　No. I am a silent and serious person.

Examiner:　Do your friends like to tell jokes?

Candidate:　Yes. Some of them is really good at light the atmosphere[1] and make others laugh.

Examiner:　Do you like to watch comedies?

Candidate:　No. I think constant laugh is a little bit stupid. I prefer tragedies[1].

Examiner:　Have you ever watched a live show?

Candidate:　Yes. I think the per … performance in the show is closer to our daily life. And sometimes the opinions shared by the host are really interesting and inspiring[1].

	Examiner's Comment
Grammar	Only basic grammar is used, and most of the sentences have small errors. For example, 'Some of them … is really good at light the atmosphere …' should be 'Some of them … *are* really good at *lightening* the atmosphere …'.
	Simple ☑　　　Compound ☑　　　Complex ☑　　　Compound-complex ☒
Lexical Resource	Some less common language is used, but no paraphrasing and only a limited range.
	Less Common Language[1] ☑　　　Collocations/Idiomatic[2] ☒ Paraphrasing[3] ☒　　　Discourse Marker[4] ☒
Fluency	No discourse markers are given, noticeable pausing, and the answers are a little short.
Pronunciation	It isn't easy to measure the pronunciation as there are so many pauses during the answers. This means that there is limited control over the features being measured.

Examiner: Are you good at telling jokes?

Candidate: Sometimes, I think if the joke makes me laugh, then I can tell others the joke, and with a bit of enthusiasm[1] and body language it can add more of an impact to the punch line[2] ^{笑点}, which will make others laugh[3] or at least make them chuckle[3]!

Examiner: Do your friends like to tell jokes?

Candidate: Well[4], I've got one friend, and he is always telling jokes. He tells jokes at inappropriate[1] times, like in classes, or on a crowded subway! He only tells them to me, but I think he wants to tell a new joke whenever he feels bored!

Examiner: Do you like to watch comedies?

Candidate: I do. What I want to watch might depend on[2] my mood, but comedy is a popular genre[1] for me. You know[4], classes and the daily life takes quite a lot of energy and can be tiring, but if I want to relax and feel like having a good laugh, I'll watch a comedy show or movie.

Examiner: Have you ever watched a live[3] show?

Candidate: I haven't watched a show on stage[3], but I've seen them on TV. I think it must be a much better experience and a lively atmosphere to go and be part of the audience at a live show, but I haven't had the chance. Not yet anyway!

	Examiner's Comment
Grammar	A good mix of structures with only some tiny errors – '… classes and the daily life takes quite a lot …' should be 'classes and daily life ***take*** quite a lot …'. Simple ☑ Compound ☑ Complex ☑ Compound-complex ☑
Lexical Resource	A good range of vocabulary with some paraphrasing(***laugh→chuckle; live→on stage***), some good less common language together with some collocations. Less Common Language[1] ☑ Collocations/Idiomatic[2] ☑ Paraphrasing[3] ☑ Discourse Marker[4] ☑
Fluency	A couple of basic discourse markers are given, and the answers are a good length. 'But' is used a little repetitively as is 'and'. Some small hesitations throughout, but doesn't lose coherence.
Pronunciation	A good flow of language, but with some control and sustainability issues.

Examiner: Do you like singing? Why?

Candidate: Yes. I think singing is a good way to express my happiness. And when I am bored, singing can excite me.

Examiner: Have you ever learnt how to sing?

Candidate: No. I am an amateur in singing. I think I am lacking in judging the rhythm and notes. They are complicated.

Examiner: Who do you want to sing for?

Candidate: Myself. I think my singing is not so good. Others may feel uncomfortable when listening to me.

Examiner: Do you think singing can bring happiness[3] to people?

Candidate: Yes. And not only the sound but also the content may make people amuse[3].

Examiner's Comment	
Grammar	A decent mix of simple and complex structures with some minor errors that wouldn't impede communication – 'my singing is not so good' can change to 'I'm not good at singing/I'm not a good singer'.
	Simple ☑ Compound ☒ Complex ☑ Compound-complex ☒
Lexical Resource	No less common language, although 'lack' ad 'amateur' are probably borderline, and some of the word choices are wrong – 'amuse' in the last sentence should be '*laugh*'. No collocations or Idioms are offered with a little bit of paraphrasing(*happiness→amuse*).
	Less Common Language[1] ☒ Collocations/Idiomatic[2] ☒ Paraphrasing[3] ☑ Discourse Marker[4] ☒
Fluency	No discourse markers are given, and the speech is a little slow overall. The answers are also a little short.
Pronunciation	A limited range of features, but can generally be understood. It's difficult to measure due to the speed of the speech.

Examiner: Do you like singing? Why?

Candidate: Actually[4], I love it. I'm not as good as a professional, but I think I can hold my own in KTV. I think it's because my mum is a good singer, and always sang to me when I was younger.

Examiner: Have you ever learnt how to sing?

Candidate: Not beyond in some music classes at school. I never joined a singing club or anything like that. I have though thought about it more than once. I suppose I've just never gotten around to doing it.

Examiner: Who do you want to sing for?

Candidate: I think I would sing for friends if there is a special occasion like a birthday or a wedding, but I'd prefer to sing in a duet[1]（二重唱）with a pal[1] of mine instead of singing solo[1]! I'm not confident enough to get on stage and sing when it's just me!

Examiner: Do you think singing can bring happiness to people?

Candidate: Oh, without a doubt[4]. It can bring happiness, and in my opinion, that's why we listen to it. Songs can affect our mood, but upbeat[3]（积极向上的）and lively[3] songs can certainly make us feel more cheerful if we are a bit down in the dumps[2]（郁闷的，低落的）.

	Examiner's Comment
Grammar	A good mix of simple and complex grammar structures that are error-free.
	Simple ☑ Compound ☒ Complex ☑ Compound-complex ☑
Lexical Resource	Some good less common language and paraphrasing(*upbeat→lively*). A good beginning for idiomatic language too.
	Less Common Language[1] ☑ Collocations/Idiomatic[2] ☑ Paraphrasing[3] ☑ Discourse Marker[4] ☑
Fluency	A good flow of language with extended answers with no noticeable effort. Beginning of a good range of discourse markers.
Pronunciation	Easy to understand and has control, mostly, of all the features.

| Barbecue | *Answer 1*（★☆） | 🎧 070 |

Examiner: Do Chinese people like barbecues?

Candidate: Yes. Especially during the young generation.

Examiner: What kind of food do you like to eat at a barbecue?

Candidate: Wings of chicken, potatoes, beef and squid.

Examiner: Would you like to have a barbecue with your family or your friends?

Candidate: Yes, I'd like to have a barbecue with my friends. Because when we are eating, we talk a lot from past to present while I have nothing to talk with my family.

Examiner: Did you have a barbecue when you were a child?

Candidate: No, my mother think it's unhealthy. She never allow me to have a barbecue.

<table>
<tr><td colspan="2" align="center">Examiner's Comment</td></tr>
<tr>
<td>Grammar</td>
<td>Most sentences, even the simple structures, have some errors in them. For example, 'during the young generation' should be '*among* the young generation'. There are also multiple subject-verb agreement errors – 'my mother think' should be 'my mother *thinks*'; 'She never allow me …' should be 'She never *allows* me …'.

Simple ☑   Compound ☒   Complex ☑   Compound-complex ☒</td>
</tr>
<tr>
<td>Lexical Resource</td>
<td>There are no attempts at paraphrasing, less common or idiomatic language.

Less Common Language[1] ☒   Collocations/Idiomatic[2] ☒
Paraphrasing[3] ☒   Discourse Marker[4] ☒</td>
</tr>
<tr>
<td>Fluency</td>
<td>Usually keeps going, but the speech is slow, and no discourse markers are used. The answers are also very short.</td>
</tr>
<tr>
<td>Pronunciation</td>
<td>Multiple mispronunciations of even simple language.</td>
</tr>
</table>

Examiner: Do Chinese people like barbecues?

Candidate: Yes, they do. It's very popular to have a barbecue when the weather is good and grill[1] _{烧烤} some different foods. It wasn't too long ago that me and some buddies[1] went out for a picnic, but instead of preparing things like sandwiches and salads, we took a barbecue with some coal to burn and cook by ourselves.

Examiner: What kind of food do you like to eat at a barbecue?

Candidate: A lot of people prefer to barbecue meat, especially red meat like lamb and beef, but I really enjoy barbecued fish and also some tofu and vegetables. Come to think of it[2] _{细想一下}, it seems I prefer the healthier option[1] with barbecues.

Examiner: Would you like to have a barbecue with your family or your friends?

Candidate: I'd love to have a barbecue with my friends! You know[4], with family, we are different generations, and family is family, but with friends, we just have more in common. It's really nice to get out and about[2] _{外出} with friends and family in the springtime because we spend the winter cooped up[2] _{被禁锢} indoors.

Examiner: Did you have a barbecue when you were a child[3]?

Candidate: I can't recall from memory about my family owning a barbecue, but I do remember going to some friends' houses when I was young[3] with my parents, and people would be barbecuing there, but I don't recall my family ever owning a barbecue.

	Examiner's Comment
Grammar	A decent mix of simple and complex structures with only some minor errors that wouldn't cause comprehension problems – 'me and some buddies went out' should be 'some buddies and I went out'. Simple ☑　　Compound ☑　　Complex ☑　　Compound-complex ☑
Lexical Resource	Repeats 'barbeque' quite a lot, but it's difficult to avoid that in this instance – namely it's both a verb and a noun, and is quite specific. Otherwise, a good range is offered with some good idioms, collocations and paraphrasing (***child→young***). Less Common Language[1] ☑　　　Collocations/Idiomatic[2] ☑ Paraphrasing[3] ☑　　　　　　Discourse Marker[4] ☑
Fluency	Occasional hesitation and some noticeable effort, but generally able to keep going.
Pronunciation	Good range of features but quite often doesn't finish the words, which can reduce clarity sometimes.

Examiner:　Do you like to travel by car?

Candidate:　Yes. And this way of travelling is free, and I can go everywhere I want.

Examiner:　When do you travel by car?

Candidate:　When I am in university. My friends drive me to a park during the holiday.

Examiner:　Where is the farthest place you have travelled to by car?

Candidate:　Erm … Beijing. It take us for more than 8 hours to arrive there. Two of my friends take turns to drive the car.

Examiner:　Do you like to sit in the front or back when travelling by car?

Candidate:　In the front. Because not only I can see the scenery ahead but also asides.

	Examiner's Comment
Grammar	Mostly simple structures are used with some simple errors appearing – 'It take us for more than …' should be 'it ***takes*** us more than …'.
	Simple ☑　　　Compound ☑　　　Complex ☒　　　Compound-complex ☑
Lexical Resource	Only very basic vocabulary is used with some inappropriacies – '8 hours to arrive there' should change to '8 hours to ***get*** there'.
	Less Common Language[1] ☒　　　　　Collocations/Idiomatic[2] ☒ Paraphrasing[3] ☒　　　　　　　　　Discourse Marker[4] ☒
Fluency	Noticeable pausing and repetition of some words. No discourse markers given. The answers are also very short.
Pronunciation	It's very challenging to measure any of the pronunciation features due to the pausing, repetition and mispronunciations, but at least attempts are made.

Answer 2（★★★★） 6♪ 073

Examiner: Do you like to travel by car³?

Candidate: Well⁴, I do like to travel by car, but it all comes down to the length of the journey. Maybe I'm more likely to enjoy a car journey³ if we take the scenic route but driving for hours on end² on the motorway with much countryside to enjoy might be pretty dull.
连续地

Examiner: When do you travel by car?

Candidate: These days it's usually just taking taxis around to different places in the city. If I go a longer distance, I might jump in a cab²′³. Or if it's late at night I'll take a taxi³ or a car, but other than that, I'll stick to² public transport most of the time.
继续使用

Examiner: Where is the farthest place you have travelled to by car?

Candidate: Years ago, my dad drove from Beijing to WeiHai, and it took most of the day and night. I forget how many hours exactly, but it was a few hundred miles between the two locations. My mum wanted to fly, but dad said by car is cheaper!

Examiner: Do you like to sit in the front or back when travelling by car?

Candidate: I don't mind. I think I'm more likely to fall asleep or just mind my own business if I sit in the back, but I am vulnerable¹ to getting carsick¹ if I sit in the back for a long time. So, with that said⁴, I think if I sit in the front, it's more comfortable, and also I can keep an eye on² where we are going.

	Examiner's Comment
Grammar	Most sentences are error-free and show some flexibility in structures. Simple ☑ Compound ☑ Complex ☑ Compound-complex ☑
Lexical Resource	Some flexible use of vocabulary with a good range. Some good efforts at collocations, less common language and paraphrasing(***travel by car→car journey; cab→taxi***). Less Common Language¹ ☑ Collocations/Idiomatic² ☑ Paraphrasing³ ☑ Discourse Marker⁴ ☑
Fluency	Beginnings of a range of discourse markers and no noticeable effort when speaking.
Pronunciation	Not quite a wide range of features, but good sustained use, with only minor lapses.

Examiner: Are water sports popular in China?

Candidate: Er … yes. China has many waters. So people have close relationship with water … and Chinese athletes are world top as for diving and swimming.

Examiner: Have you done water sports?

Candidate: Er … not really. I just tried one sport on a water-themed park. Um … To be honest⁴, I am a little afraid of it. So I don't like giving it a try.

Examiner: What water sports do you like doing?

Candidate: Er … cycling on the sea. I thinks it would be more safer while interesting.

Examiner: What kind of water sports do you want to try?

Candidate: Er … swim. I have never tried it before. Um … I am expecting the feeling of floating on the water.

Examiner's Comment	
Grammar	Most sentences have errors in them, with some of the errors being very basic. For example, 'on a water-themed park' should be '***in*** a water-themed park'. 'I thinks it would be more safer' should change to 'I ***think*** it would be ***safer***'.
	Simple ☑ Compound ☑ Complex ☑ Compound-complex ☒
Lexical Resource	No range of vocabulary is given, and only elementary words are used, some of which aren't formulated correctly – 'swim', rather than 'swimming'.
	Less Common Language¹ ☒ Collocations/Idiomatic² ☒ Paraphrasing³ ☒ Discourse Marker⁴ ☑
Fluency	Noticeable pausing, certainly at the beginning of nearly every sentence.
Pronunciation	Difficult to measure the use of features due to the constant pausing. Doesn't pronounce the ends of words correctly.

Examiner: Are water sports popular in China?

Candidate: In my opinion, not many water sports are popular, but the main ones are swimming and diving. Over the years, China has racked up² 取得 quite a few medals, and a few of the swimmers have become famous and gotten public recognition for their achievements.

Examiner: Have you done water sports?

Candidate: Only swimming. I think I'd like to try others, but my home is not close to any places where you'll find more water sport activities, but I know coastal¹ cities have sailing events, and that would be fun to try.

Examiner: What water sports do you like doing³?

Candidate: Like I just said⁴, I do like to go for a dip² 游一会泳 sometimes as it's fun to do³ and also quite relaxing. Not to mention it's a great form of exercise.

Examiner: What kind of water sports do you want to try?

Candidate: I think surfing would be cool to try. It takes some practice, but if you are dedicated to it, then you can really enjoy the surfing experience. I've seen surfing on TV, and in a few films, it always looks so cool, so I'd like to have a crack at² 尝试 that one day. I better conquer¹ my fear of the deep blue sea first!

	Examiner's Comment
Grammar	Mostly simple sentences. Not really enough complex structures to be defined as a mix. Some minor errors that wouldn't cause misunderstanding. Simple ☑ Compound ☑ Complex ☑ Compound-complex ☑
Lexical Resource	Some flexible use of words and some good collocations and idiomatic language. Some paraphrasing(*like doing*→*fun to do*) and discourse markers are used, which indicates the beginning of range. Less Common Language¹ ☑ Collocations/Idiomatic² ☑ Paraphrasing³ ☑ Discourse Marker⁴ ☑
Fluency	The answers are a good length and there is only some pausing between the sentences.
Pronunciation	An effort at sustaining features, but lapses are frequent.

Examiner: Do you like watching sports programs on TV?

Candidate: Yes, especially the international competition where Chinese athletes participate.

Examiner: Do you like to watch live sports games?

Candidate: Yes. It is exciting because no one know the result and I like to guess the result ahead.

Examiner: Who do you like to watch sports games with?

Candidate: My friends. They are interested in the games that are being held because we can communicate well and share opinions with each other.

Examiner: What kinds of games do you expect to watch in the future?

Candidate: New items of ping-pong, skiing, diving, skating and so on.

Examiner's Comment			
Grammar	No complex structures are offered. There are some errors in the simple structures – 'no one know …' should be 'no one **knows** …'.		
	Simple ☑	Compound ☒	Complex ☑ Compound-complex ☑
Lexical Resource	Only simple words are given, and no paraphrasing, less common or idioms are attempted.		
	Less Common Language[1] ☒ Paraphrasing[3] ☒	Collocations/Idiomatic[2] ☒ Discourse Marker[4] ☒	
Fluency	Quite slow in places with occasional pausing, but is generally able to keep going.		
Pronunciation	Doesn't enunciate very well, which may occasionally cause difficulty for the listener.		

Examiner: Do you like watching sports programs on TV?

Candidate: Yes, I'm a tennis fan, and I try to watch all the major tennis tournaments[1] ⌐锦标赛 when they are shown live on TV. I can't watch it 24/7[1], but if I miss the action, I'll check out[2] ⌐看一看 the highlights[1] later on in the day.

Examiner: Do you like to watch live sports games?

Candidate: Yes, I do, and I've been to a few basketball matches here in Beijing. It's thrilling[3] to be there, and you really feel part of the atmosphere and excitement[3]. I also like the fact that you can see the basketball stars up close and personal, and it's a whole different feeling than watching on TV.

Examiner: Who do you like to watch sports games with?

Candidate: My friends and I all like basketball, so we sometimes watch them together. Furthermore[4], we all follow the same team, so we experience the highs and lows[2] ⌐起起落落 of the match together. We can discuss any key moments of the game and comment on how well we think our team is doing, and talk about the tactics[1] and how they should have improved. Not that we are professional basketball coaches or anything!

Examiner: What kinds of games do you expect to watch in the future?

Candidate: Well[4], I'm planning on going to the UK later for my studies, and I know football, cricket, and rugby are really popular there, and it would be a dream come true if we can get tickets for the match. I also know the local people are pretty passionate[1] about sports, so I think I can learn a lot more about it and the rivalries[1] ⌐较量 between different teams. Should be fun!

Examiner's Comment	
Grammar	A good mix of simple and complex structures that are mostly error-free. Simple ☑ Compound ☑ Complex ☑ Compound-complex ☑
Lexical Resource	Some flexible use of language with some good less common language and paraphrasing(***thrilling→excitement***). Less Common Language[1] ☑ Collocations/Idiomatic[2] ☑ Paraphrasing[3] ☑ Discourse Marker[4] ☑
Fluency	Good flow of speech overall with just a little bit in the way of pausing. Overuses the connective 'and', though.
Pronunciation	A little monotonous sometimes with occasional chunking issues.

■ Holidays & Festivals

Answer 1（★） 🎧 078

Examiner: Where did you go for your last holiday?

Candidate: Changsha, Hunan province.

Examiner: Do you like holidays? Why?

Candidate: Yes, because it provide me a chance to release me pressure from work and study. Also, travelling in the holiday enables me to experience different cultures.

Examiner: Which public holiday do you like best?

Candidate: The Spring Festival, because it is the most important and grandest holiday in China. The time is relatively long and family will get together.

Examiner: What do you do on holiday?

Candidate: Go out for a travel, or stay at home, studying or cooking.

Examiner's Comment	
Grammar	Only simple sentence structures are used with a limited range. Most of the sentences have some kind of error. For example, 'it provide me … release me pressure' should change to 'it **provides** me … release **my** pressure'.
	Simple ☑ Compound ☑ Complex ☑ Compound-complex ☒
Lexical Resource	Only simple vocabulary is given, with no paraphrasing or more advanced words offered.
	Less Common Language[1] ☒ Collocations/Idiomatic[2] ☒ Paraphrasing[3] ☒ Discourse Marker[4] ☒
Fluency	Some noticeable pauses during the longer sentences, but understandable during the shorter ones.
Pronunciation	Very difficult to judge the amount of language given, but some features are used, but not sustained.

Examiner: Where did you go for your last holiday?

Candidate: That's a good question because it was a long time ago. I went to Shanghai with my parents to visit my aunty and uncle, but we didn't get out and about as much as we hoped. It was good to spend time together nonetheless.

Examiner: Do you like holidays? Why?

Candidate: Absolutely[4]. Travel is quite tiring and often takes a lot of preparation but being in a different place for a change of scene is wonderful. Though, if it's a long holiday, I'm also OK if it's just a staycation[1] (宅度假). Relax at home and just watch movies to my heart's content[2] (尽情地)!

Examiner: Which public holiday do you like best?

Candidate: That's easy[4]. It would be Spring Festival for sure. It's a long holiday, it's the biggest public holiday in China, everyone is with their relatives, and we can hang out together. If my friends[3] are around, then we can catch up[2] (叙旧) too because a lot of my old schoolmates[3] don't go to the same uni as me.

Examiner: What do you do on holiday[3]?

Candidate: So many things to do! If it's a long breather[3] (短暂的休息), I'd like to travel if possible. Go somewhere new, see different places and try different food, do as the Romans do[2], that sort of thing. But if it's a shorter holiday, then I'm more likely to just stay at home and spend time with the family, just eating and catching up with everyone.

	Examiner's Comment
Grammar	Some flexibility in the complex structures, and most of the sentences are error-free. Simple ☑ Compound ☑ Complex ☑ Compound-complex ☑
Lexical Resource	A good range of words is given and less common language, collocations, idioms markers and paraphrases(***friends→schoolmates; holiday→breather***) are all used. Less Common Language[1] ☑ Collocations/Idiomatic[2] ☑ Paraphrasing[3] ☑ Discourse Marker[4] ☑
Fluency	No noticeable effort whilst speaking with flexible use of discourse markers.
Pronunciation	Some minor lapses in some of the features, but can generally be understood throughout.

Examiner: How do you usually celebrate the New Year?

Candidate: I will see the Spring Festival Gala[1]. And later, visiting relatives will be my major activity during the New Year time.

Examiner: Do you still remember a New Year that you celebrated?

Candidate: Yes. I didn't go home one year and I chose to have voluntary work at school. I welcomed the New Year alone in the dormitory. Happily, my friends and family accompanied me online.

Examiner: Do you have any ceremonies to celebrate the New Year in your country?

Candidate: Yes! We will see the Spring Festival Gala and have a reunion dinner. Typically, in my hometown, we will light the firework at 0 o'clock in the first day of the first year.

Examiner: Why do people think New Year is a beginning?

Candidate: In the lunar[1] calendar, New Year lies on the first several days and people will wear new clothes, which means a new start for a better future.

	Examiner's Comment
Grammar	Attempts at complex structures, but these are outnumbered by simple structures. There are also several preposition errors – 'in the first day' should be '***on*** the first day'; 'on the first several days' should be '***in*** the first several days'.
	Simple ☑ Compound ☑ Complex ☒ Compound-complex ☑
Lexical Resource	Mostly simple vocabulary is spoken with some attempts at less common language. No paraphrasing is given.
	Less Common Language[1] ☑ Collocations/Idiomatic[2] ☒ Paraphrasing[3] ☒ Discourse Marker[4] ☒
Fluency	The answers are a good length, and there are only minor pauses. There IS noticeable effort, though, during some of the sentences.
Pronunciation	Some mispronunciations of words. Attempts at the control of features, but this is not sustained and not always controlled properly.

Examiner: How do you usually celebrate the New Year?

Candidate: For Chinese New Year, in my hometown. Usually at either my parents' house or my grandparents' house. We don't go far and wide² ─到处 during New Year. It's better for us to stay at home and try to avoid travelling. Millions of people travel, and it does my head in² ─让我受不了 to travel during Chinese New Year, so I'd rather stay at home and put my feet up.

Examiner: Do you still remember a New Year that you celebrated?

Candidate: Yeah, the last few New Years were quite memorable because we mostly stayed at home. It was nice and peaceful actually, and I must admit that I enjoyed it. Usually, when all the relatives get together, my home is like a mad house² ─乱哄哄的!

Examiner: Do you have any ceremonies³ to celebrate the New Year in your country?

Candidate: There are quite a few, but it does vary between different regions. The most common traditions³ are to stay up to midnight to see in the New Year, and people will make and eat dumplings together. A few years ago, people would set off fireworks² ─放烟花, but that's banned in a lot of places now. Finally⁴, people might also watch the Spring Festival Gala¹ TV show, which is entertaining.

Examiner: Why do people think New Year is a beginning³?

Candidate: I think many people will start³ fresh and maybe even turn over a new leaf² ─重新开始 in the New Year. Maybe try to get rid of bad habits and start doing things better or even in a healthier way! People often make a new year's resolution² ─新年愿望, like a promise to themselves to make their life better. Doesn't always turn out that way, though!

	Examiner's Comment
Grammar	There are just enough complex structures to be classed as a mix of structures. Some minor preposition errors that don't affect comprehension – 'stay up to midnight' should be 'stay up **until** midnight'. Simple ☑ Compound ☑ Complex ☑ Compound-complex ☑
Lexical Resource	Some flexible use of vocabulary and a good collection of less common and idiomatic language as well as paraphrasing(*ceremonies→traditions; beginning→start*). Less Common Language¹ ☑ Collocations/Idiomatic² ☑ Paraphrasing³ ☑ Discourse Marker⁴ ☑
Fluency	Some minor pausing and it would be better if there were more discourse markers.
Pronunciation	Some good use of features, but not all the time. The occasional mispronunciation of words reduces clarity at times.

| Shopping | *Answer 1（★☆）* | 🎧 082 |

Examiner: Do you like shopping?

Candidate: Erm ... Yes, I do. Especially food.

Examiner: Do you think expensive products are always better than cheaper ones?

Candidate: Erm ... Yes. Usually, the material of these products are more expensive. But for some luxuries, I think they are expensive only for their brand.

Examiner: Do you compare prices when you shop? Why?

Candidate: Erm ... Yes. When I am doing the online shopping, I tend to spend a lot of time to compare the prices and find the one with bargain because it saves money for more things.

Examiner: Is it difficult for you to make choices when you shop?

Candidate: Erm ... Yes. When I am doing the online shopping, there are many things to choose.

Examiner's Comment	
Grammar	A very limited number of complex structures, both of which are slightly incorrect. Most sentences have errors. For example, 'spend a lot of time to compare' should be 'spend a lot of time *comparing*'.
	Simple ☑ Compound ☒ Complex ☑ Compound-complex ☑
Lexical Resource	Very limited range given, which is mostly copied from the questions. Some inaccurate words are used ('the one with bargain' should change to 'the one with *a discount*').
	Less Common Language[1] ☒ Collocations/Idiomatic[2] ☒ Paraphrasing[3] ☒ Discourse Marker[4] ☒
Fluency	Some use of features, but difficult to understand sometimes due to frequent mispronunciations.
Pronunciation	Noticeable pausing at the beginning of each answer and slow speech all the way through.

Look at this: *For the last two answers, the opening phrase is EXACTLY the same ('Yes. When I ... shopping'). You must be careful of this as it seems to be a memorised response and it's grammatically incorrect.*

注意： 最后两个问题的答案使用了完全一样的开场白——"是的。当我网上购物时，……"。小心这种情况，因为这样看起来像是背诵的答案，语法也不对，应为"When I shop online, ..."。

Examiner: Do you like[3] shopping?

Candidate: Yeah, I love shopping, and like many others, I'm a huge fan of[3] window shopping! Spending time wandering[1] around the mall after lunch just checking out[2] new styles and clothing trends in the shops is fun for me. I don't always 花钱大手大脚 splash the cash[2], but something nice and new might catch my eye[2]!

Examiner: Do you think expensive products are always better than cheaper ones?

Candidate: Well[4], there is a saying, 'If you buy cheap, you buy twice'. So I do believe that for certain goods, it is better to invest a bit more money and hope the quality of the product is more superior[1] to something which is cheaper and could be poorly made. I'm OK to part with[2] 放弃 my money as long as I'm happy the quality is good.

Examiner: Do you compare prices when you shop? Why?

Candidate: I do. If we take footwear[3] as an example, I will find the style or brand I like and maybe check out a few different shops for the same pair of shoes[3], but after a while, I'll just get them as the prices don't vary much. You know[4], some shops might have a discount so I'll spend some time to compare prices.

Examiner: Is it difficult for you to make choices when you shop?

Candidate: When it comes to electronics, as an example, not so much, because I know precisely[1] what I want and how much it costs, so I will just buy what I want. But with that said[4], I don't buy new phones and electronics regularly, so it's quite easy for me to shop. Buying food, on the other hand[4], is a different story! I can spend ages walking around the supermarket wondering what food to buy!

	Examiner's Comment
Grammar	A good mix of simple and complex structures. A reasonable range of complex structures, but uses '… so …' a little repetitively.
	Simple ☑ Compound ☑ Complex ☑ Compound-complex ☑
Lexical Resource	A good range of vocabulary used with some idioms and paraphrasing(*like→a huge fan of; footwear→shoes*).
	Less Common Language[1] ☑ Collocations/Idiomatic[2] ☑ Paraphrasing[3] ☑ Discourse Marker[4] ☑
Fluency	No noticeable effort while speaking and has a good range of discourse markers.
Pronunciation	Occasional lapses in features, and the occasional mispronounced word.

Examiner: What is your favourite colour of clothes?

Candidate: Black. I think it is easy to match with other clothes.

Examiner: What kind of clothes do you usually wear?

Candidate: I usually wear sport-styled clothes. I think they feel comfortable on my body and it is easy for me to move.

Examiner: What kind of clothes do you never wear?

Candidate: Trousers with many big holes. I think this style is strange[3] and weird[3]. I feel shy to wear them.

Examiner: Do you wear the same style of clothes on weekdays and weekends?

Candidate: Yes. I am a students. So on weekdays I usually choose relatively formal styles of clothes like T-shirt, and on weekends I prefer to wear casual clothes.

Examiner's Comment	
Grammar	Only very basic sentences used with only rare subordinate structures, and these usually contain errors. For example, 'match with other clothes' should be 'match other clothes'; 'I am a students' should change to 'I am a *student'*.
	Simple ☑ Compound ☑ Complex ☑ Compound-complex ☑
Lexical Resource	Only some very simple vocabulary is given with no less common phrases and a little bit of paraphrasing(*strange→weird*).
	Less Common Language[1] ☒ Collocations/Idiomatic[2] ☒ Paraphrasing[3] ☑ Discourse Marker[4] ☒
Fluency	Some noticeable pausing and no discourses markers are given. The answers, in general, are quite short.
Pronunciation	Enunciation is weak and unclear. The chunking is difficult to measure due to the constant pausing. It is sometimes difficult to understand.

Examiner: What is your favourite colour of clothes?

Candidate: For it would have to depend on the mood I'm in. I don't like to wear the same colours all the time, but if take today as an example, I'm wearing a white T-shirt and blue jeans so perhaps I prefer to wear lighter colours most of the time. In terms of actual colour, I think blue suits me the best.

Examiner: What kind of clothes do you usually wear?

Candidate: Casual clothes most of the time. I feel good in just a pair of jeans and a T-shirt most of the time. I've got formal attire[3], but I don't have many reasons to get suited and booted[2/3] 穿着正式 these days. I dress for comfort more than anything else.

Examiner: What kind of clothes do you never wear?

Candidate: I never wear suits or something like tuxedos[1] for any kind of event. I'll admit you can look very dapper[1] 衣冠楚楚 in those kind of clothes but, A) they aren't cheap, and B) I think I'd hardly ever wear something like that because I don't have a reason to.

Examiner: Do you wear the same style of clothes on weekdays and weekends?

Candidate: Yeah, these days I do. You know[4], I'm a student nowadays, and what I wear to class I can also wear on the weekends, and I'll dress appropriately for any kind of weather situations. I like plain colours and nothing too flowery or something to draw attention to[2] my appearance, so I like to keep it plain and simple[2], as they say.

	Examiner's Comment
Grammar	A good mix of simple and complex structures with only some minor errors – 'those kind of clothes' should be 'those **kinds** of clothes'. Simple ☑ Compound ☑ Complex ☑ Compound-complex ☑
Lexical Resource	Some good vocabulary offered with a range of collocations, less common language and paraphrasing(**formal attire→suited and booted**). Less Common Language[1] ☑ Collocations/Idiomatic[2] ☑ Paraphrasing[3] ☑ Discourse Marker[4] ☑
Fluency	Some pausing, especially when using complex structures and, so far, a limited amount of discourse markers.
Pronunciation	Chunking is hard to measure sometimes. Most other features are controlled well but not sustained.

Examiner: Do you like buying shoes?

Candidate: Yes, but not very addicted[1] to it.

Examiner: Have you ever bought shoes online?

Candidate: Yes. Actually[4], I buy all my shoes online in the university because they are cheaper and various in styles.

Examiner: How much money do you usually spend on shoes?

Candidate: Around 700 RMB. I think shoes with this price is a good balance between price and quality.

Examiner: Which do you prefer, fashionable shoes or comfortable shoes?

Candidate: I prefer comfortable ones now. I don't like to be much fashionable. And I like walking, which means a pair of comfortable shoes is essential.

Examiner's Comment	
Grammar	Few complex structures are given in any of the answers, and some of the simple structures have small errors in them – 'shoes with this price *is* …', rather than 'shoes with this price *are* …'. Simple ☑ Compound ☒ Complex ☑ Compound-complex ☑
Lexical Resource	Some examples of less common language, but no paraphrasing or idioms are used. Less Common Language[1] ☑ Collocations/Idiomatic[2] ☒ Paraphrasing[3] ☒ Discourse Marker[4] ☑
Fluency	Occasionally a little slow, and the answers are a little short.
Pronunciation	Some effective use and range of features, but occasional lapses and the quantity of language is challenging to measure.

Examiner: Do you like buying shoes?

Candidate: I can't say that I like buying shoes, but I do buy a few pairs each year for summer and winter or for playing sports. For it's more of a necessity to buy shoes than it is a hobby and that's all I have to say about that.

Examiner: Have you ever bought shoes online[3]?

Candidate: I have got some from the Internet[3] before, but only for some shoes to wear casually when I'm out and about[2]. If I want some smart shoes, or boots or trainers[1], then I better get down the mall and find some shops that have got the brands and styles I like so I can try them on.

Examiner: How much money do you usually spend on shoes?

Candidate: On average[4], I'd say a few thousand RMB each year on shoes, but to be honest[4], I don't keep track of[2] how much I spend on shoes. I'm not a 花钱大手大脚的人 big spender[2], but at the same time, If I find a pair that I really like and they are suitable[1] for a particular purpose, I 花很多钱 wouldn't be afraid to go the extra yard and splash out[2].

Examiner: Which do you prefer[3], fashionable shoes or comfortable shoes?

Candidate: That's a good question. I'm probably leaning more towards[3] comfortable shoes. I do quite a lot of walking on a daily basis, and while I don't want to buy something I really don't like or is not my cup of tea, I pay more attention to how comfortable they are, than I do to how cool I might look.

Examiner's Comment	
Grammar	A good mix of simple and complex structures with most sentences error-free. Simple ☑ Compound ☒ Complex ☑ Compound-complex ☑
Lexical Resource	A good range of flexible language used with some good collocations, paraphrasing(*online→Internet; prefer→leaning more towards*) and less common language. Less Common Language[1] ☑ Collocations/Idiomatic[2] ☑ Paraphrasing[3] ☑ Discourse Marker[4] ☑
Fluency	A couple of unusual discourse markers spoken and maintains the flow of speech with only minor effort.
Pronunciation	A good range of features used, but not all the time. Occasional mispronunciation of words, and the intonation is wrong on some words.

Examiner: Have you ever had an unhappy haircut experience?

Candidate: Yes. The barber didn't understand my requirement and had cut too much from my hair.

Examiner: How long have you had your current haircut?

Candidate: Three days ago. And I even have my hair designed, which means from straight to curly to make it featured.

Examiner: How often do you have a haircut?

Candidate: About two weeks. Because my hair is relatively long for a man, so I have to have it cut more often.

Examiner: Do you like having your hair cut?

Candidate: Yes. I think after having my hair cut, I may look tidy and clean. Also, shorter hair is easier for me to deal with.

Examiner's Comment			
Grammar	Attempts complex structures, but these nearly always contain errors – 'so' should be removed from 'Because my hair is … so I …'.		
	Simple ☑	Compound ☑　　　Complex ☑	Compound-complex ☒
Lexical Resource	No range of vocabulary given, and uses 'hair' in every answer, sometimes twice. Nothing in respect of paraphrasing, collocations or less common language.		
	Less Common Language[1] ☒	Collocations/Idiomatic[2] ☒	
	Paraphrasing[3] ☒	Discourse Marker[4] ☒	
Fluency	Able to keep going, but very slow in places bordering on pausing.		
Pronunciation	Limited range ad use of features but can generally be understood throughout.		

Answer 2（★★★☆） 🎧 089

Examiner: Have you ever had an unhappy haircut[3] experience?

Candidate: Not very unhappy! I mean[4], there have been times where I have thought that maybe I paid too much for such a simple trim[3] on top! Some of the salons[3] provide a good service and treat you well when you are there, but it might be a bit too 'over the top' for what I need most of the time. But, with that said[4], I'm usually happy with how my hair looks at the end.

Examiner: How long have you had your current haircut?

Candidate: Oh[4], I've had this style[3] for years. It's easy to manage and to take care of. Ever since I was young, I've always had short hair, and it's something I'm used to now. I might change it in the future, but I'll worry about then!

Examiner: How often do you have a haircut?

Candidate: I have my haircut once every 3 or 4 months. I usually get a trim before the start of term, then maybe again a few months later, and I usually get a trim at the same place. Maybe If I'm going on a trip or there is a special event coming up[2], then I might think about getting my haircut then just to look a bit smarter!

Examiner: Do you like having your hair cut?

Candidate: I do, actually. I feel better afterwards when all the dead hair has been cut away[2], and it's easier to manage. Also, I'm never in the barbers[3] that long so it doesn't take long for me to get a quick short back and sides[3]. But yes, I like having my haircut, it's quite refreshing[1].

Examiner's Comment	
Grammar	A good mix of structures with only minor errors in the complex ones – 'times where I have thought ...' should be 'times **when** I have thought ...'. Simple ☑ Compound ☑ Complex ☑ Compound-complex ☑
Lexical Resource	Multiple paraphrases of 'haircut' used, which begins to demonstrate a good range of vocabulary(**haircut→trim/style/short back and sides; salons→barbers**). Some use of less common vocab and collocations. Less Common Language[1] ☑ Collocations/Idiomatic[2] ☑ Paraphrasing[3] ☑ Discourse Marker[4] ☑
Fluency	Only very occasional pausing, which points to some noticeable effort. Some simple discourse markers are given too.
Pronunciation	Unsustained use of features, but attempts to show a range.

■ People

Examiner: Does your name have a special meaning?

Candidate: Yes. I was born in a rainy day, so the second character of my Chinese name is the word 'rain'. And the last character is the function[1] of raining.

Examiner: How would you choose names for your next generation?

Candidate: If it is a boy, he will share the same family name with me; instead, she will be named after her mother. I may think of words related to Chinese traditional culture.

Examiner: Are there any differences between how Chinese name their children now and in the past?

Candidate: No. I don't think so. We all use the same way as before. It's like a tradition.

Examiner: Are there any names that are more popular than others in China?

Candidate: Yes, definitely[4]. For girls, words related to flowers are popular, and for boys, words which means handsome or smart are usually used.

Examiner's Comment	
Grammar	A limited number of complex structures and errors in most sentences – in '… words which means handsome …', 'means' should change to '***mean***'.
	Simple ☑ Compound ☑ Complex ☑ Compound-complex ☑
Lexical Resource	Only simple vocabulary is used through this topic. Where the less common word is used, it's not really appropriate.
	Less Common Language[1] ☑ Collocations/Idiomatic[2] ☒ Paraphrasing[3] ☒ Discourse Marker[4] ☑
Fluency	Pausing and repetition throughout as well as multiple instances of self-correction.
Pronunciation	Mostly very monotonous, with only occasional use of features.

Examiner: Does your name have a special meaning?

Candidate: No, my name doesn't have any special meaning. Maybe it's not special according to any Chinese traditions. I was just given this name because it was popular in my family, and also my English name was just given to me by my primary school teacher, and I stuck with[2] it.

Examiner: How would you choose names for your next generation?

Candidate: I think, for example, if I was to have a baby, then I'd pick a name that perhaps had a close connection to my family, but also I'd search online to see what names are popular or unpopular and maybe just see what I like the sound of. Depends on what my other half[2] also thinks!

Examiner: Are there any differences between how Chinese name their children now and in the past?

Candidate: I can't think of any major differences between these days and previously. Typically, they would always take the father's surname[3] and have the first name chosen by the parents, or maybe grandparents. In some more traditional families, first names are chosen by special masters and relate to the zodiac[1].

Examiner: Are there any names that are more popular[3] than others in China?

Candidate: Yes, there are. You know[4], China is a big country, and in different regions, you'll find that some family names[3] are more common[3] than others. As for given names or even English names, then maybe it is more mixed, but I know for a fact[2], because I've seen it myself, that certain surnames are more popular in different places.

	Examiner's Comment
Grammar	A good mix of simple and complex structures, with some simple errors – 'if I was to have a baby' should be 'if I **were** to have a baby'.
	Simple ☑ Compound ☑ Complex ☑ Compound-complex ☑
Lexical Resource	Some less common language, collocations and paraphrasing used (***surname→family names; popular→common***), but occasionally simply repeats the words in the question.
	Less Common Language[1] ☑ Collocations/Idiomatic[2] ☑ Paraphrasing[3] ☑ Discourse Marker[4] ☑
Fluency	Some hesitation and occasional slow speech. The answers are a good length and there's the beginning of a range of discourse markers.
Pronunciation	Can be generally understood, with only a few lapses in control of features.

Examiner: Have you ever met a famous person?

Candidate: No. I think this chance is too scarce[1].

Examiner: Who do you want to interview?

Candidate: Jay Chou. He has been my idol[1] since I was in the primary school. I love every song of him and I want to ask him about his plan to release new albums.

Examiner: Why do you want to meet them?

Candidate: First[4], I have been his fan for a long time and it would be excited for me to meet him in person. Second[4], I am wanting him to give me a signature.

Examiner: Do you want to meet other famous[3] people? Who?

Candidate: Yes. Especially famous hosts in CCTV, like Kang Hui, Sa Beining and so on. They are excellent and really known[3] to every Chinese, I think.

Examiner's Comment	
Grammar	No complex sentences offered, and there are some errors in the simple structures. For example, 'the' should be removed from 'I was in the primary school'; 'excited' should change to '*exciting*' in 'it would be excited for me ...'.
	Simple ☑ Compound ☑ Complex ☑ Compound-complex ☒
Lexical Resource	Some less common language used as well as an attempt at paraphrasing (*famous→really known*), albeit slightly incorrect.
	Less Common Language[1] ☑ Collocations/Idiomatic[2] ☒ Paraphrasing[3] ☑ Discourse Marker[4] ☑
Fluency	Noticeable pausing, especially at the beginning of sentences. Generally speaks quite slowly.
Pronunciation	Some use of some features, but not sustained and sometimes difficult to measure.

Examiner: Have you ever met a famous person³?

Candidate: I haven't actually met a celebrity³. I've been to a few concerts over the last few years, so I have seen some famous people perform onstage but not met them or taken a selfie with them, nothing like that.

Examiner: Who do you want to³ interview?

Candidate: I'd love to³ interview a really charismatic¹ 有超凡魅力的 and perhaps even controversial¹ figure, someone like Mark Zuckerberg! I think his views and opinions are loved by some and hated by others, so to sit down with him and really pick his brains² 向他请教 about his life in business would be mind-blowing²! 给人印象极深的 You never know⁴, 说不定 I might even learn a thing or two!

Examiner: Why do you want to meet them?

Candidate: To meet someone that has achieved so much and experienced so much and been at the top of their game would just be inspiring¹ to me. I know a lot of people don't agree with him, but I would have so many questions for him. I've got so many questions I wouldn't know where to start, but just a few minutes with him would be amazing.

Examiner: Do you want to meet other famous people? Who?

Candidate: There are others I'd like to meet. I'm a bit of a movie fan, and the *Harry Potter* films are so cool, and I grew up watching them, so all of those actors, especially the younger ones, are like role models to me. Of course⁴, Daniel Radcliffe, because he is the star of the show as he plays the lead character³ 演主角 in the films.

	Examiner's Comment
Grammar	Most complex structures are error-free, and those with errors would not cause communication difficulties – 'To meet someone that has …' should be 'To meet someone **who** has …'. Simple ☑ Compound ☑ Complex ☑ Compound-complex ☑
Lexical Resource	Demonstrates a good range of vocabulary with some flexible use of less common language, idioms and paraphrasing (***famous person→celebrity; want to→love to***). Less Common Language¹ ☑ Collocations/Idiomatic² ☑ Paraphrasing³ ☑ Discourse Marker⁴ ☑
Fluency	Good extended answers with the beginnings of a range of discourse markers. No noticeable effort whilst speaking.
Pronunciation	Good use of features with some minor mispronunciations. Mother accent (L1) doesn't affect the level of communication.

Examiner: What do you think makes good friends?

Candidate: I think mutual[1] trust is the most important point. And mutual appreciation[1] and assistance, etc., are keys, too.

Examiner: Do you keep in contact[3] with friends from your childhood?

Candidate: Yes, but I'm only in touch[3] with two friends from my childhood. We live closely while our parents share good relationship with each other.

Examiner: What kinds of people do you like to make friends with?

Candidate: People who make my laugh and share happy feeling with me. People who respect me and give me a hand when I am in need. I think these two kinds are my first choice.

Examiner: Do you think you are a good friend to others?

Candidate: Yes, I do. I will help my true friend willingly[1]. And If I have something good, they are the first who I will share with.

Examiner's Comment	
Grammar	Limited range of complex structures that are incorrect in minor ways. Some errors in pronouns and a lack of articles used – 'who make my laugh and share happy feeling' should be 'who make *me* laugh and share *a* happy feeling'.
	Simple ☑ Compound ☒ Complex ☑ Compound-complex ☒
Lexical Resource	Occasional less common language used and a successful attempt at paraphrasing (*in contact→in touch*). No collocations or idioms are used, though.
	Less Common Language[1] ☑ Collocations/Idiomatic[2] ☒ Paraphrasing[3] ☑ Discourse Marker[4] ☒
Fluency	Generally able to keep going, although a bit slow at times. No discourse markers given.
Pronunciation	Some use of features, but a bit monotonous at times.

Examiner: What do you think makes good friends?

Candidate: Well[4], so many characteristics[3] can make a good friend, but for me[4], it's probably honesty, loyalty and with a sense of humour[3] too. These three are not always important, but I am more drawn to people who have these traits[3]. I might add hard working too. I'm a bit lazy, so a good friend that's hard-working can get me into gear[2] sometimes and encourage me to work harder.

Examiner: Do you keep in contact with friends[3] from your childhood?

Candidate: Yes, I do. Some of my best mates[3] I have today are those I first met way back in primary school. We have all grown up now and chosen different paths to follow, but that hasn't stopped us from keeping in touch and trying to meet up once in a while when we can.

Examiner: What kinds of people do you like to make friends with?

Candidate: For me, people who are smart, funny[3], loyal and honest. Those are some personality traits I can think of off the top of my head[2], but also people that are outgoing and enjoy having a laugh[2]. I'm quite extroverted[1], so I like to meet people who are similar to me.

Examiner: Do you think you are a good friend to others?

Candidate: You should ask my friends that question! But seriously, I'm sure I am a good friend to others. I spend time with them, and that includes picking them up when they feel down and spending time with each other, whether it's just being lazy at home or going out to spend the day somewhere fun. I always look out for my friends, so I've always got their back.

Examiner's Comment

Grammar	A good mix of simple and complex structures that are mostly error-free. Simple ☑ Compound ☑ Complex ☑ Compound-complex ☑
Lexical Resource	A good range is offered with a range of less common vocabulary, idioms and paraphrases (***characteristics→traits; sense of humour→funny; friends→mates***). Less Common Language[1] ☑ Collocations/Idiomatic[2] ☑ Paraphrasing[3] ☑ Discourse Marker[4] ☑
Fluency	Good extended answers given and no noticeable effort when speaking. Some basic discourse markers are also spoken.
Pronunciation	When speaking the idioms used, there's some definite noticeable effort, but otherwise, some reasonable control and extended use of features.

Objects

Answer 1（★☆）   096

Examiner: What is the best present or gift you have ever received?

Candidate: A handwritten card from my best friend in the university. His words are sincere and expressive[1], which really moved me.

Examiner: Do you give expensive gifts?

Candidate: No. As a student, it is unrealistic[1] for me to give others presents with high price.

Examiner: What do you give others as gifts?

Candidate: I will consider their needs primarily. And usually, I will give notebooks, bottles, or even give them a meal.

Examiner: What kinds of gifts are popular in your country?

Candidate: I think wine is the most popular among adults. And flowers, cards, and perfumes are popular in young generation.

Examiner's Comment	
Grammar	Most sentences have some kind of error in them – 'popular in young generation' should be 'popular **with the younger** generation'.
	Simple ☑ Compound ☒ Complex ☑ Compound-complex ☒
Lexical Resource	Mostly simple words are given with a couple of less common words. Some inappropriacies also given – 'presents with high price' should be 'expensive presents'.
	Less Common Language[1] ☑ Collocations/Idiomatic[2] ☒ Paraphrasing[3] ☒ Discourse Marker[4] ☒
Fluency	Many pauses and hesitations between and within the sentences, and no discourse markers are given. Also, the answers are a little short.
Pronunciation	Some correct use of features, but not sustained and some mispronunciations of fairly simple words.

Examiner: What is the best present or gift you have ever received[3]?

Candidate: The best gift I have received has got to be a necklace that has been passed down from my grandmother to my mother and now to me. The sentimental[1] value of this necklace is so significant, and of all the things I have, like a phone, a computer and nice clothes, this necklace is priceless, and I would say it is 独一无二 one of a kind[2]. This is the best gift I have been given[3].

Examiner: Do you give expensive[3] gifts?

Candidate: If I really want to surprise someone with an expensive gift, then I'm not afraid to spend more money on getting something nice and pricey[3] for my 最好的朋友 bestie[1] or even my parents. I don't buy gifts for people based on price as I might usually just get them something that doesn't cost too much, but if there is a special friend and it's a special occasion, then why not spend a bit more money and get them something special?

Examiner: What do you give others as gifts?

Candidate: For me[4], I think it's more of a 人情味 personal touch[2] because you have thought about someone, and by buying them a gift, you recognize the value of friendships more because you know their interests or hobbies, for example, and you can get them something related to that. I might sometimes 事与愿违 backfire[1], and you get the wrong present for them, but as we all know, it's the thought that counts 最终 at the end of the day[2].

Examiner: What kinds of gifts are popular in your country?

Candidate: Well[4], the most traditional thing that people give is the red envelope which contains cash! This is most commonly given during Chinese festivals, and people like getting red envelopes, but if it's buying a gift for someone, then it might be some things that people can eat and drink.

Examiner's Comment			
Grammar	A good range of complex structures and mostly error-free.		
	Simple ☑ Compound ☒ Complex ☑ Compound-complex ☑		
Lexical Resource	Flexible use of vocabulary and a good range of less common language, paraphrasing (*received→been given; expensive→pricey*) and collocations.		
	Less Common Language[1] ☑ Collocations/Idiomatic[2] ☑		
	Paraphrasing[3] ☑ Discourse Marker[4] ☑		
Fluency	Full length, extended answers with no noticeable effort. Only basic discourse markers given, but it's the beginnings of a range.		
Pronunciation	Good use of features throughout with only some minor lapses.		

Examiner: Do you use a wallet?

Candidate: Yes. It can hold all my cards, money and other little things in one area. It provides convenience when I am out.

Examiner: Have you ever lost a wallet?

Candidate: Yes. During a travel, I lost my wallet. But luckily, someone picked it up and gave it to the counter. I regained it, but I had to change my plan to a sight because of this.

Examiner: Have you ever sent a wallet to someone as a gift?

Candidate: Yes, and I gave it to one of my male classmates in high school. It cost me about 100 RMB. I think he lacked a wallet, so I chose it.

Examiner: Do most of your friends use a wallet?

Candidate: Yes. It really makes our life convenient and can store our cards in a safe place. Maybe they buy it themselves, or others gave it to them as a gift, too.

	Examiner's Comment
Grammar	An effort is made at complex structures, and they are error-free, but they are reasonably short and too few.
	Simple ☑ Compound ☑ Complex ☑ Compound-complex ☑
Lexical Resource	No attempt at less common language or paraphrasing, and there are no idioms either. Some words are incorrect for their purpose – 'I regained it' should be 'I got it back'.
	Less Common Language[1] ☒ Collocations/Idiomatic[2] ☒ Paraphrasing[3] ☒ Discourse Marker[4] ☒
Fluency	Can generally keep going, but sometimes slow, with the occasional noticeable pause. No discourse markers are given.
Pronunciation	Some good use of features, but not sustained through the topic.

Answer 2 (★★★) 6∂ 099

Examiner: Do you use a wallet?

Candidate: I do use a wallet. I've got bank cards, my ID card, my transport card, my student card and some cash in my wallet, so if I didn't have one then I'd lose all these things! So, for these small items that I regularly use then, I do keep them all together in a wallet.

Examiner: Have you ever lost a wallet?

Candidate: Absolutely[4], and it was awful. I remember being on the bus, and for some reason, I used my wallet, probably to pay the bus fare, and I guess I put it on the seat next to me instead of back in my pocket! When the bus arrived, I got up[2] off the seat and hopped off[2] the bus. It was only about a minute later when I had a sudden feeling of losing something, and bingo[1], my wallet and everything inside it was gone.

Examiner: Have you ever sent a wallet to someone as a gift?

Candidate: Yes, I have as a gift, and I think it was a pleasant[1] surprise. My friend uses a wallet, and it's ancient[1] and is falling apart, so I got him a nice new wallet for his birthday. He was 心满意足
chuffed to bits[2], and he immediately took everything out of his old wallet and into the one I had given him.

Examiner: Do most of your friends use a wallet?

Candidate: Some of them do, but not many of them carry a lot of cash these days because everyone can pay online these days. As for carrying a few cards, then, some do have a small[3] wallet, but that's all. So, having a little[3] card wallet, I would say yes, most of my friends do, but not many of them carry big, bulky[1] wallets these days as there is no need for it.

Examiner's Comment	
Grammar	A good mix of simple and complex structures, with only a few very minor errors – 'I got up off' should be 'I got up *from*'.
	Simple ☑ Compound ☑ Complex ☑ Compound-complex ☑
Lexical Resource	Flexible use of vocabulary with good use of less common and idiomatic language as well as paraphrasing (*small→little*).
	Less Common Language[1] ☑ Collocations/Idiomatic[2] ☑ Paraphrasing[3] ☑ Discourse Marker[4] ☑
Fluency	Usually keeps going and provides answers of a good length. Only one discourse marker given.
Pronunciation	The occasional mispronunciation and some of the rhythm is off, but can generally be understood.

Examiner: Do you use headphones?

Candidate: Yes, in the public places.

Examiner: What type of headphones do you use?

Candidate: Wireless ones, because the wired one makes my moving a little difficult.

Examiner: When would you use headphones?

Candidate: When I am doing sports, I will use them. In public transportation, too. When I don't want my family to hear the conversation between my friends and me, I will wear them on.

Examiner: In what conditions would you not use headphones?

Candidate: In some formal classes, I won't because it shows disrespect to the teachers. Or when I am alone, I tend to allow the sound out, which can light the atmosphere around.

Examiner's Comment	
Grammar	Some attempts at complex structures, but these usually contain mistakes and occasionally cannot be understood easily – 'allow the sound out, which can light the atmosphere around'. Simple ☑ Compound ☒ Complex ☑ Compound-complex ☑
Lexical Resource	Only very basic vocabulary is used, with some inappropriacies. Less Common Language[1] ☒ Collocations/Idiomatic[2] ☒ Paraphrasing[3] ☒ Discourse Marker[4] ☒
Fluency	Significant pausing at almost all sentence beginnings, and occasionally in the middle.
Pronunciation	Limited range and control of features, with some words that are not understood.

Examiner: Do you use headphones?

Candidate: I do when I am outside. I always take them out with me because it helps to drown out² the noise of the traffic, and also, listening to music during that time can help to keep me relaxed.

Examiner: What type of headphones do you use?

Candidate: I use the Apple AirPods. They're expensive but really good. The noise cancellation¹ feature is amazing. All I can hear is the music being played on my phone, and no background sounds whatsoever. Also, with these, I can get up to about 20 hours of listening without having to charge them, so they are well worth it² for me.

Examiner: When would you use headphones?

Candidate: I'll always use them too if I am on the bus or subway because if I watch some videos on my phone, then the noise won't annoy other people. Apart from that⁴, I may use them also when I'm in a coffee shop or even in the school study area or library because I can listen to music quietly or I can tune into² whatever I want and not have to worry about disturbing¹ others too much.

Examiner: In what conditions would you not³ use headphones?

Candidate: I'm less likely³ to use headphones when I'm in class or in a place where I am hanging out with friends. To be honest⁴, I find it to be rather rude when you are talking with others, and someone has kept their headphones on! I'm not sure if they are listening to me or listening to something else, so because of that, I'm much less likely to use headphones when I am interacting with friends or family.

	Examiner's Comment	
Grammar	A range of complex structures with very few errors. Simple ☑　　Compound ☑　　Complex ☑　　Compound-complex ☑	
Lexical Resource	Flexible use of vocabulary with a variety of idioms, collocations, less common language and paraphrasing (***not→less likely***). Less Common Language¹ ☑　　　Collocations/Idiomatic² ☑ Paraphrasing³ ☑　　　　　　　Discourse Marker⁴ ☑	
Fluency	Speaks at length with minimal hesitation and shows a beginning of a range of discourse markers.	
Pronunciation	Can be understood throughout, with only minor mispronunciations and lapses.	

■ Media & Advertisements

Examiner: What kinds of TV programs do you often watch?

Candidate: Talk shows and sport games.

Examiner: Do you think kids are watching too much television?

Candidate: No. During these days[4], social media like TikTok or some games on phones has become the new trend for kids. They are more attractive than television for kids now, I think.

Examiner: What are the impacts of watching TV programs on children?

Candidate: I think there are two major impacts. First[4], if children watch TV for a long time, their eyesight will be impaired[1]. Second, children are likely to imitate[1] behaviours from the TV programs, but they cannot distinguish[1] the bad and the good.

Examiner: What kinds of TV programs do you think should be broadcast more?

Candidate: Some documentaries on the nature protection[3] and culture preservation[3] which really contributes to broadening our horizon. It is also helpful for raising human's awareness about these.

	Examiner's Comment		
Grammar	Attempts at complex structures, but there are a few of them with errors. 'Which really contributes to' should change to '... contribute to'.		
	Simple ☑	Compound ☑ Complex ☑	Compound-complex ☑
Lexical Resource	Attempts at paraphrasing (***protection→preservation***) and less common language, but not at idioms or collocations.		
	Less Common Language[1] ☑ Paraphrasing[3] ☑	Collocations/Idiomatic[2] ☒ Discourse Marker[4] ☑	
Fluency	Some good extended answers and only some pausing or hesitation. The use of discourse markers shows a good start to being a range.		
Pronunciation	Some difficulties with the longer words, which in turn affects the rhythm of the sentences.		

Examiner: What kinds of TV programs do you often watch?

Candidate: I like a good crime drama type of TV program. I'm not really into the news or watching any current affairs programs because I can catch up with all that stuff online through the apps, but as far as TV programs go, I do like to get submerged in² a TV drama, especially ones in the crime drama.

沉浸

Examiner: Do you think children³ are watching too much television?

Candidate: I don't know if I would say that kids³ are watching too much television these days, but I would say that kids spend a lot more time on video platforms like TikTok and others. As long as the video content is not harmful and their parents keep an eye on the kids while they watch the videos, then maybe it's not too much. Studies must come first!

Examiner: What are the impacts of watching TV programs on children?

Candidate: Well⁴, there are two sides to every coin, and on the plus side² is that a lot of educational TV programs can be useful for kids when they learn about different topics, but on the other hand, it can have a detrimental¹ impact on kids' physical health, especially eyesight if they are glued to² the TV all day. It can make them become more lazy, and they maybe don't have the enthusiasm¹ to do other things or play with friends, so there is this concern.

从好的方面来说

完全吸引

Examiner: What kinds of TV programs do you think should be broadcast more?

Candidate: I'd like to see more news programs that are related to certain topics like environmental change or how to care for our surroundings. I know, we see the news about this, but it's usually just a small segment¹, and it's not enough, so I think the broadcasting companies should cooperate more with governments etc. and ramp up² the amount of programs that can encourage us all to care more for our surroundings and the environment as a whole.

增加

	Examiner's Comment
Grammar	A good mix of structures, with most sentences being error-free. Minor grammatical errors do persist – 'become more lazy' should change to '*lazier*'. Simple ☑ Compound ☑ Complex ☑ Compound-complex ☑
Lexical Resource	A good range of vocabulary with a selection of less common language as well as attempts at collocations and paraphrasing (*children→kids*). Less Common Language¹ ☑ Collocations/Idiomatic² ☑ Paraphrasing³ ☑ Discourse Marker⁴ ☑
Fluency	Little hesitation while speaking, but only minimal discourse markers.
Pronunciation	Good use of features, some slips and occasional mispronunciations.

Examiner: Are you interested in watching TV advertisements or internet advertisements?

Candidate: No, and sometimes, I am even annoyed about them because it waste my time to see the programs or series.

Examiner: What kinds of advertisements do you dislike?

Candidate: On the phones' applications. Especially discounts for some clothes and propaganda[1] for some goods, which is really exaggerating[1] and ridiculous[1].

Examiner: Do you share advertisements with others?

Candidate: No. I seldom look them and often close them the sight I see them. But for the job-offering advertisements, I sometimes will share with others.

Examiner: Do you want to work in advertising in the future?

Candidate: No. I think a strong sense of creativity and bravery is required. Also, I am not good at designing and drawing.

	Examiner's Comment
Grammar	Some attempts at complex structures, but these usually are incorrect in some way. For example, 'it waste my time ' should be 'it **wastes** my time'; 'which is really exaggerating and ridiculous' should be 'which **exaggerate** and **are** ridiculous'. Some sentences are difficult to understand – 'I seldom look them … the sight I see them'.
	Simple ☑ Compound ☒ Complex ☑ Compound-complex ☑
Lexical Resource	Some attempts at less common language, which aren't always appropriate. Offers no paraphrasing or idiomatic language in the answers.
	Less Common Language[1] ☑ Collocations/Idiomatic[2] ☒ Paraphrasing[3] ☒ Discourse Marker[4] ☒
Fluency	Generally able to keep going but does speak slowly occasionally.
Pronunciation	Some use of pronunciation features, but not consistently controlled.

Examiner: Are you interested in watching TV advertisements or internet advertisements?

Candidate: Absolutely[4] not. I don't like[3] them at all. You could even say I completely[3], thoroughly[3] detest[3] them. I mean[4], why? Everything you do these days, you get these totally[3] useless unskippable[1] 无法跳过的 things that just waste my time[2]. Sorry, but I really hate[3] them.

Examiner: What kinds of advertisements do you dislike?

Candidate: Frankly[4], nearly all of them. If I want to buy something, I search online for it. I suppose I don't mind pop-ups[2] 弹出窗口 on shopping sites for offers or new products and such like. But the others that interrupt TV programmes, or those incessant[1] 不停的, repetitive ones online, argh!

Examiner: Do you share advertisements with others?

Candidate: Very, very rarely. Typically[4] what I do is tell my friends about something I've seen, and then let them find it for themselves, rather than sharing the actual advert through WeChat or something like that.

Examiner: Do you want to work in advertising in the future?

Candidate: I think not. I can appreciate[3] the creativity used in developing them, and I'd quite enjoy doing something like that. Still, considering that most people, at least the ones I know, hate adverts, I don't think working in that industry would be a good idea.

Examiner's Comment	
Grammar	Most structures are correct, with only minor errors. Simple ☑ Compound ☑ Complex ☑ Compound-complex ☑
Lexical Resource	A good selection of less common language, collocations and idiomatic language as well as parapheasing(***completely→thoroughly/totally; don't like→detest/hate***). Less Common Language[1] ☑ Collocations/Idiomatic[2] ☑ Paraphrasing[3] ☑ Discourse Marker[4] ☑
Fluency	Maintains flow of speech with no noticeable effort. A range of discourse markers is also given.
Pronunciation	Some lapses in control, but can be generally understood throughout.

Examiner: What technology do you often use, computers or mobile phones[3]?

Candidate: As a student, I use both of them usually. But in daily life, I use cell phones[3] more.

Examiner: What electronic devices have you bought lately?

Candidate: A USB drive with a large capacity of IT. I bought it about one week ago. The space of my desktop is limited. So I bought the drive to share the storage with it.

Examiner: Is technology important in your life?

Candidate: Definitely[4], yes. For studies, desktop is important for us to search for material and do experiments. For hospital, a variety of technology help to improve the accuracy, efficiency[1] and safety of the diagnosis[1].

Examiner: Is there any technology you don't like?

Candidate: Up to now[4], it seems not. If we use technology properly, it can become a good assistant in our life.

Examiner's Comment	
Grammar	Attempts complex structures, but these mostly have errors in them – 'a variety of technology help …' should be 'a variety of technology **helps** …'. They don't cause comprehension problems, though.
	Simple ☑ Compound ☒ Complex ☑ Compound-complex ☒
Lexical Resource	A successful attempt at paraphrasing (***mobile phones→cell phones***), but there are many words used incorrectly – 'of IT' should be deleted from 'A USB drive with a large capacity of IT'.
	Less Common Language[1] ☑ Collocations/Idiomatic[2] ☒ Paraphrasing[3] ☑ Discourse Marker[4] ☑
Fluency	Some of the answers a not extended enough, and the speech is occasionally slow.
Pronunciation	Can be mostly understood, with a few mispronunciations.

Examiner: What technology do you often use, computers or mobile phones³?

Candidate: Well⁴, both. I use my smartphone³ almost hourly with messages, videos and the like, but I also use my laptop daily. Up until recently⁴, I've used my laptop for my classes, which has been interesting.

Examiner: What electronic devices have you bought lately?

Candidate: To be honest⁴, I haven't. The most recent purchase I've made that's even remotely electronic was a new pair of earphones for my phone. I can tell you what my next purchase will be, though, and that is a PS5. I've wanted one of those for nearly two years, and now that I have the money saved up², I will probably buy one next month.

Examiner: Is technology important³ in your life?

Candidate: Oh, without a doubt⁴. I think the IT of today is essential³ in everybody's life. It is really instrumental³ in everything we do, whether this is an alarm on my phone to get up, the technology in the electric bus for me to get to campus, or even the apps on my phone that allow me to pay for lunch. We can't get away with it.

Examiner: Is there any technology you don't like?

Candidate: Erm, that's an interesting question and one I've never thought about before. I suppose, no, not really. I know there are lots of people worried about or even afraid of AI, but for me, sci-fi robots that take over² the earth are still light years away². I'm really one of these people that enjoys all advancements¹ in technology and can't wait for the flying cars.

	Examiner's Comment
Grammar	Minor mistakes in the range of structures given – 'I use my smartphone … with messages' should be 'I use my smartphone … *for* messages'. Nothing that would cause communication problems. Simple ☑ Compound ☑ Complex ☑ Compound-complex ☑
Lexical Resource	A flexible range of vocabulary used with less common language, collocations and paraphrasing (*mobile phones→smartphone; important→essential/instrumental*) all successfully used. Less Common Language¹ ☑ Collocations/Idiomatic² ☑ Paraphrasing³ ☑ Discourse Marker⁴ ☑
Fluency	Some language-related pausing between/within sentences, but speaks fairly effortlessly and has a good range of discourse markers.
Pronunciation	L1 accent affects the understanding occasionally, but overall has good control over several features.

Examiner: What kinds of websites do you often visit?

Candidate: Website where hit[1] events are presented and where study materials are provided.

Examiner: What is your favourite website?

Candidate: Websites where study materials are posted through where I kill my time and know what is happening recently.

Examiner: Are there any changes to the websites you often visit?

Candidate: Yes. The format of it becomes varified. But it is a little annoying[1] that advertisements have been put on the site.

Examiner: What kinds of websites are popular[3] in your country?

Candidate: One is for a variety of news which I think has the largest quantity[3]. Another is for sport games, and we can see live games through them.

Examiner's Comment	
Grammar	Simple and complex structures are offered, but the wording of the complex structures is sometimes repeated – '*where* hit events ... *where* study materials ...', '*where* study materials ...'. This shows a limited range.
	Simple ☑　　Compound ☑　　Complex ☑　　Compound-complex ☑
Lexical Resource	Attempts at paraphrasing and less common language but, in this instance, the paraphrase (*popular→largest quantity*) isn't entirely correct. No collocations or idioms are used, and some words are incorrect – 'varified'.
	Less Common Language[1] ☑　　Collocations/Idiomatic[2] ☒　　Paraphrasing[3] ☑　　Discourse Marker[4] ☒
Fluency	The answers are a little short and spoken quite slowly. No discourse markers are given.
Pronunciation	Some words are difficult to understand 'varified'. It's difficult to know if this is supposed to be 'verified' or something else entirely. Some control of other features is given.

Look at this: *An examiner may get confused about what is said because the word 'varified' is inappropriate for that sentence in this answer, which should change to 'varied'. It will affect not only lexical resource, but also pronunciation scores.*

注意：因为在本答案的句子中使用了 varified 这个不恰当的单词（应改为 varied），考官会产生误解。这既会影响你的词汇多样性的分数，还会影响发音的分数。

Examiner: What kinds of websites[3] do you often visit?

Candidate: Being a student, I regularly visit educational websites because of my studies. These may include the university library website or maybe some pages[3] I use for my classes, like the New Channel or EDUZMS sites. I'm not really one that visits all these shopping websites. If I do need to buy something, I generally know where to find it quickly and don't really need to surf too much.

Examiner: What is your favourite[3] website?

Candidate: I think my favourite website is one of these video streaming sites, you know[4], like iQiyi or Tencent. I can generally find a TV series that I like, or movie that I love whenever I want to, so although I wouldn't say I visit it often, it's by far the one I enjoy the most[3].

Examiner: Are there any changes to the websites you often visit?

Candidate: Not that I've noticed. Maybe a course gets added to a site, or some new research papers get uploaded[1], but the general structure and format are always the same.

Examiner: What kinds of websites are popular in your country?

Candidate: Well[4], I think that depends on who you talk to. For bookworms[2] like me, I will use educational websites with maybe some entertainment ones bolted on[2]. For business people, I'm sure they would use completely different sites. In my opinion[4], websites are dying. These days it's all mobile apps which, in my mind, are different.

	Examiner's Comment
Grammar	A good mix of structures with very minor errors that are typically missing articles – 'a TV series … or movie' should be 'a TV series … or **a** movie'. Simple ☑ Compound ☑ Complex ☑ Compound-complex ☑
Lexical Resource	The beginnings of range with vocabulary usage and some use of idiomatic language and paraphrasing(***website→pages; favourite→enjoy the most***). Less Common Language[1] ☑ Collocations/Idiomatic[2] ☑ Paraphrasing[3] ☑ Discourse Marker[4] ☑
Fluency	Uses extended answers but is a little slow in the delivery sometimes. Some basic discourse markers are also provided.
Pronunciation	Some use of features, but not always sustained. Can be generally understood.

Look at this: *Some examiners may not think that the missing article 'a' (shown above) is needed in spoken English, whereas others may think it is. This is one example of where it depends on the examiner's discretion.*

注意: 有些考官可能觉得少了冠词a——见上表, 在英语口语中是可以的, 但其他考官认为不行。这种情况得看考官的自行决定。

Examiner: What apps have you recently used?

Candidate: Wechat, TikTok and QQ music.

Examiner: What kinds of apps are you usually interested in?

Candidate: For social conversation[1] and music. Also, some apps for language learning attracts me, too.

Examiner: What was the first app you used?

Candidate: QQ, I think. When I was young, this app was the most popular, and every classmates felt proud[1] of having an account.

Examiner: What kinds of apps would you like to use in the future?

Candidate: I'd like to use some apps which can instruct me to do sports and exercise. Also, apps with high ability of translating would be excellent.

Examiner's Comment	
Grammar	Most of the sentences are simple structures and sometimes contain mistakes – 'some apps … attracts me' should be 'some apps … ***attract*** me'. Attempts at complex structures are given but have minor errors – 'every classmates' should be 'every ***classmate***'.
	Simple ☑ Compound ☒ Complex ☑ Compound-complex ☑
Lexical Resource	Some less common language is used, but no idioms, collocations or paraphrasing are given.
	Less Common Language[1] ☑ Collocations/Idiomatic[2] ☒ Paraphrasing[3] ☒ Discourse Marker[4] ☒
Fluency	The answers are a little short and not what I would call extended. In addition, no discourse markers given. Speech is also a little slow sometimes with multiple pauses.
Pronunciation	Limited uses of features. It's challenging to measure due to the repetitious pausing. It's also a little monotonous.

Answer 2 (★★★☆) 🎧 111

Examiner: What apps have you recently used?

Candidate: Oh[4], loads. Just today, I've probably used about half a dozen. When I get up in the morning, I start with my Calendar App to figure out what I'm supposed to be doing that day. Then it's on to WeChat to see if I have any messages and maybe to check some of my friends' Moments. Lastly[4], onto Douyin for a little splurge[1] of mindless[1] fun.

Examiner: What kinds of apps are you usually interested in[3]?

Candidate: Like I mentioned just now[4], time management and communications Apps are going to be top of my list, and I'm including the Social Media stuff as communication. These days, the only other apps that I'm concerned about[3] is either language dictionaries or online learning apps.

Examiner: What was the first app you used?

Candidate: Cor, now you're asking. It was a few years ago, so I don't really remember the actual first. I would think maybe email or QQ messaging, something like that. When I was much younger, we didn't have smartphones, so the apps we had were very basic by today's standards.

Examiner: What kinds of apps would you like to use in the future?

Candidate: In the near future, probably more research and learning apps to help me with my studies. Beyond that, I don't know. Maybe something to do with my job, whatever that turns out[2] to be.

	Examiner's Comment		
Grammar	A good mix of simple and complex structures, with only minor errors that wouldn't cause communication difficulties.		
	Simple ☑ Compound ☑ Complex ☑ Compound-complex ☑		
Lexical Resource	A successful attempt at paraphrasing(***interested→concerned about***) and some good use of less common language and collocations.		
	Less Common Language[1] ☑ Collocations/Idiomatic[2] ☑ Paraphrasing[3] ☑ Discourse Marker[4] ☑		
Fluency	No noticeable effort while speaking and good extended answers for each question.		
Pronunciation	Features are mostly controlled with only a few lapses. Occasional interference by the L1 accent.		

■ Nature

Examiner: Would you like to work in a company related to environmental protection?

Candidate: Yes. I think this kind of job is closely related to our daily life. Also, I am willing to observe the surroundings.

Examiner: How can we protect the environment?

Candidate: First[4], we have to develop the awareness[1] of protecting environment. Second, we
具体的
should do concrete[1] actions like saving the water, classifying the litter[2] and so on. Last,
垃圾分类
we have to prevent others from damaging the environment.

Examiner: Do you think you have done enough to protect the environment?

Candidate: No. The greenhouse effect[2] is becoming more serious. And in recent years, other natural disasters occur[1], which prove that we haven't done enough.

Examiner: Is there education about environmental protection in school?

Candidate: Yes. According to my knowledge[4], in lower grade there would be specific courses about environmental protection. And for higher education, this is a hot topic all the time.

Examiner's Comment	
Grammar	Mostly, simple structures used, with limited use of complex ones. Errors are found in most sentences but wouldn't necessarily cause comprehension problems –'... which prove that ...' should be '... which **proves** that ...'.
	Simple ☑ Compound ☒ Complex ☑ Compound-complex ☒
Lexical Resource	Some good use of less common language and offers at least one collocation but doesn't attempt paraphrasing, and the vocab, in general, is limited in range.
	Less Common Language[1] ☑ Collocations/Idiomatic[2] ☑ Paraphrasing[3] ☒ Discourse Marker[4] ☑
Fluency	Generally keeps going, and the answers are a good length. Attempts at discourse markers but not always correct.
Pronunciation	Occasional control of features, but not sustained with occasional mispronunciations.

Examiner: Would you like to work[3] in a company related to environmental protection?

Candidate: I realise that companies that focus on[2] environmental protection can play a significant role in addressing the pressing environmental challenges we face, such as climate change, deforestation[1], air and water pollution, and loss of biodiversity[1] (生物多样性), but it's not something I could do for a job[3].

Examiner: How can we protect the environment?

Candidate: Oh[4], there are tons of[2] (许多) ways individuals and communities can help look after the environment. Things like recycling, conserving energy, you know[4], turning lights off when you leave a room, as well as choosing some green transport.

Examiner: Do you think you have done enough to protect the environment?

Candidate: Well[4], I'm not sure about enough, but I certainly do my part[2] (尽自己的本分). For most of the year, I use my bicycle to get to and from campus, turn any lights off that I'm not using. I also try and save water where I can by using my shower water for my plants etc.

Examiner: Is there education[3] about environmental protection[3] in school?

Candidate: Yes, we do learn about[3] looking after[3] our environment when we're quite young. I think perhaps one of the most useful things we learn is about the recycling. The different coloured bins at apartments are a fairly recent introduction but we've been encouraged to recycle for many years.

	Examiner's Comment			
Grammar	A good range of grammar structures is offered with only a few very minor errors.			
	Simple ☑	Compound ☑	Complex ☑	Compound-complex ☑
Lexical Resource	Demonstrates a good range of vocabulary with a variety of less common language, idioms and paraphrases (**work→job; education→learn about; protection→looking after**).			
	Less Common Language[1] ☑　　　　Collocations/Idiomatic[2] ☑ Paraphrasing[3] ☑　　　　　　　　　Discourse Marker[4] ☑			
Fluency	No noticeable effort for the most part and only some language-related hesitation. A range of basic discourse markers is also given.			
Pronunciation	Some minor mispronunciations of some of the longer, more complex words. Most features are controlled well with only minor lapses.			

Examiner: What kind of weather do you like most?

Candidate: I like the sunny day. In this day, I can go out to entertain. And I love the sun bath.

Examiner: What is the weather like in your hometown?

Candidate: Its four seasons have different weathers. Summer is very hot and winter is extremely cold. And it often rains.

Examiner: Do you like the weather in your hometown?

Candidate: I don't like. If it rains, I can't have a happy travel. And the mud will make my shoes dirty.

Examiner: Do you prefer dry or wet weather?

Candidate: I pre … prefer dry weather. In wet weather, everything seems to be cold. This make me feel uncomfortable.

Examiner's Comment	
Grammar	Only simple sentences are used, and some of them are incorrect. For example, 'This make me uncomfortable.' should be 'This **makes** me uncomfortable.'. No complex structures attempted.
	Simple ☑ Compound ☑ Complex ☑ Compound-complex ☒
Lexical Resource	Only basic words are used with some words repeated – weather – for example.
	Less Common Language[1] ☒ Collocations/Idiomatic[2] ☒ Paraphrasing[3] ☒ Discourse Marker[4] ☒
Fluency	The connective 'and' is repetitively used with no others given. Speech is slow and broken.
Pronunciation	Limited range is used, with no proper control. Mispronunciations cause some difficulty in understanding.

Examiner: What kind of weather do you like most?

Candidate: Oh, sunshine. Definitely. I'm what you'd call a fair-weather[1] person. Can't stand the cold, hate it, with a passion. Keep the snowmen, and the skiing. Just give me a beach, a

呼吸管
snorkel[1] and 35 degrees.

Examiner: What is the weather[3] like in your hometown?

Candidate: Well[4], you can tell it's got four distinct seasons. But, I'd say, overall, the climate[3] where I'm from is mostly quite dry. It does rain, of course[4], but not often and even then, not all that much, and we might get an inch or so of snow during the winter. Not cats or dogs[2], not even a mouse.

Examiner: Do you like the weather in your hometown?

Candidate: On the whole, no. The summers are too hot, and the winters are too cold, with a little bit of nice in between. Like I said earlier, I'm not a fan of the cold, so I'd really like warm weather all year round. Somewhere like Kunming, maybe.

Examiner: Do you prefer dry or wet[3] weather?

Candidate: Well, considering the fact that I don't like cold, I think that you can guess that I don't like wet either. Having said that[4], though, I do like the smell of grass after a

暴雨
downpour[1/3].

	Examiner's Comment
Grammar	A good range of grammar with a mix of simple and complex structures. Some of the structures are deliberately incorrect, but more native because of it – 'Can't stand the cold, hate it, with a passion.', no subject is explicitly given.
	Simple ☑ Compound ☑ Complex ☑ Compound-complex ☒
Lexical Resource	The beginnings of a good range of less common words, paraphrases (***weather→climate; wet→downpour***) and idiomatic language, with some unusual discourse markers too.
	Less Common Language[1] ☑ Collocations/Idiomatic[2] ☑ Paraphrasing[3] ☑ Discourse Marker[4] ☑
Fluency	The occasional pause before some of the more advanced language and a good range of connectives and discourse markers.
Pronunciation	A few lapses in features and the occasional mispronunciation of words, but is easy to understand throughout.

Examiner: Do you like to look at the sky?

Candidate: Yes, I do. I will look at the sky when I am free. It feels good.

Examiner: Can you see the moon and stars at night where you live?

Candidate: It depends[1] on the weather condition. If it is a good weather, I can see the moon and stars.

Examiner: Do you prefer the sky in the morning or the sky at night[3]?

Candidate: I prefer the sky in the evening[3]. Sometimes in the morning, the sun is too shiny and makes my eye not able to open. At night, the light is milder[1].

Examiner: Do you want to live on other planets?

Candidate: Absolutely[4] no. I think that is dangerous. The earth where I live is a good place.

Examiner's Comment	
Grammar	Mostly correct simple sentences, with attempts at complex structures. There are a few mistakes. 'If it is a good weather' should be 'If the weather is good'. 'the sun … makes my eye …' should change to 'the sun … makes my ***eyes*** …'.
	Simple ☑ Compound ☑ Complex ☑ Compound-complex ☒
Lexical Resource	One successful attempt at paraphrasing (***night→evening***). Limited flexibility with most language. The candidate seems to repeat the same words as the question too much.
	Less Common Language[1] ☑ Collocations/Idiomatic[2] ☒ Paraphrasing[3] ☑ Discourse Marker[4] ☑
Fluency	Generally keeps going, but the sentences are a little short, so can't give 'willing to speak at length' in 6.
Pronunciation	Some difficulty with features. Not really enough speech to properly measure.

Examiner: Do you like to look at the sky?

Candidate: Yes. When I am walking to or from university, I quite often look up and see what's happening above me. Recently there haven't been many planes, so if there's a noise from above, I'm curious[1] as to what it is.

Examiner: Can you see the moon and stars at night where you live?

Candidate: On occasion[2] ⌐有时, yes. The moon more than stars if I'm just looking up as I can't see too many because of the light. But it needs to be clear if I'm looking through the telescope[1] ⌐望远镜. If it's cloudy, I must use the radio one.

Examiner: Do you prefer the sky in the morning[3] or the sky at night?

Candidate: At night. Then I can collect data about the stars, and they look more pretty at night. Obviously, you can't see the stars in the daytime[3], but they're still there. And there's something about moonlight that I prefer to sunlight. Maybe it's more romantic[1].

Examiner: Do you want to live on other planets?

Candidate: That's not something I've thought about before. Erm … I would say no. Even if the environment would be OK for humans, I think I'd still prefer to stay here. This is home after all.

	Examiner's Comment		
Grammar	A good range of simple and complex structures with very few errors.		
	Simple ☑ Compound ☑ Complex ☑ Compound-complex ☑		
Lexical Resource	Quite a good range of vocabulary with some less common language mixed in. Some limited paraphrasing (***morning→daytime***) and idiomatic language.		
	Less Common Language[1] ☑ Collocations/Idiomatic[2] ☑ Paraphrasing[3] ☑ Discourse Marker[4] ☒		
Fluency	Shows 'willing to speak at length', but no obvious discourse markers and no effective use of connectives.		
Pronunciation	Mixed control and not sustained with regards to the features assessed, but can be generally understood throughout.		

Examiner: Do you like[3] to watch TV programs about wild animals?

Candidate: Yes. I love[3] them very much from childhood to now.

Examiner: Did you learn something about wild animals at school?

Candidate: Yes. I had biology class in the high school, in which we will learn some basic knowledge of wild animals. And in some reading class, we would learn some articles about wild animals.

Examiner: Where can you see wild animals?

Candidate: Zoo is a great place for common people. And if possible, to go the natural reserve is the best choice. To see them on the screen is a compromise[1]. 折中办法

Examiner: In which country do you think you can see many wild animals?

Candidate: China is a good choice to see wild animals. And in some African countries or Brazil, many wild animals exist because of their specific environment.

Examiner's Comment	
Grammar	Attempts complex structures, but these also contain small errors. Nothing that would cause comprehension problems. Simple ☑ Compound ☒ Complex ☑ Compound-complex ☒
Lexical Resource	A limited range of vocabulary used, with a successful attempt at paraphrasing (*like→love*) and less common language. No collocations or idioms are used. Less Common Language[1] ☑ Collocations/Idiomatic[2] ☒ Paraphrasing[3] ☑ Discourse Marker[4] ☒
Fluency	Often pauses and hesitates between and in the middle of sentences. No discourse markers are given and the sentences are a little short.
Pronunciation	It's quite challenging to measure pronunciation due to all the pausing. Some features are used, but there is a severe lack of control during the answers.

Examiner: Do you like to watch TV programs about wild animals?

Candidate: Personally[4], I don't have real preferences, but I can tell you that many people are interested in watching TV programs about wild animals. These programs can offer a glimpse into[2] (初步的认识) the lives and behaviours of animals in their natural habitats[2], and can also educate viewers about the importance of conservation and environmental protection.

Examiner: Did you learn[3] something about wild animals at school?

Candidate: Yes, we did. We'd occasionally watch documentaries[1] about wildlife in different countries around the world. It's not that we studied[3] them or anything, more like we were told they existed and given a bit of information about their habitat.

Examiner: Where can you see wild animals[3]?

Candidate: You can see wild animals in a variety of environments, depending on the species[3] you are interested in observing. A lot of people would simply go to a zoo or maybe a wildlife sanctuary[1] (鸟兽保护区), but you could also go to, like, a National Park or something.

Examiner: In which country[3] do you think you can see many wild animals?

Candidate: Oh wow[4], that's actually quite difficult to say because there are several places[3] around the world that are known for their abundant[1] wildlife populations and diverse ecosystems[1]. Kenya is known for its spectacular savannas[1] (稀树草原) and abundant wildlife, including lions, elephants, giraffes, and zebras and is somewhere I definitely want to go.

Examiner's Comment	
Grammar	A good range of simple and complex structures with very few errors. Simple ☑　　Compound ☑　　Complex ☑　　Compound-complex ☑
Lexical Resource	A good range of vocabulary is used with some flexibility. A variety of less common words and paraphrases (*learn→studied; animals→species; country→places*) are used, with some use of collocations. Less Common Language[1] ☑　　　Collocations/Idiomatic[2] ☑ Paraphrasing[3] ☑　　　　　　　Discourse Marker[4] ☑
Fluency	Some very minor pausing before some words, but mostly keeps going and offers the beginnings of a range of discourse markers. The answers are also of a good length to be considered extended.
Pronunciation	Can be understood most of the time, with occasional mispronunciations. Features are not always sustained, but a good range is used.

Examiner: Do you like planting trees? Why?

Candidate: Yes. I think seeing the growth of a tree is a wonderful thing. Every time I see it, it may change. Also, planting trees are good for the environment.

Examiner: What kind of trees do people usually plant in your country?

Candidate: I think the laurel trees, which release sweet odour[1] and a kind of trees with fan-like[2] leaves, are popular in China. Also, pines are common to see, too. China has a huge territory[1], so there are various kinds of trees.

Examiner: Have you ever planted a tree?

Candidate: Yes. When I was in elementary school, the teacher asked us to plant a tree on the Planting Day, so I bought a tree and plant it in the yard.

Examiner: What kinds of trees would you plant?

Candidate: One is the laurel tree, and the other is a kind of tree with bowl-like[2] white flowers. I like trees which can produce flowers.

Examiner's Comment	
Grammar	Some attempts at complex sentences, but these are incorrect in some way and of the same structure – '… so …'. There are also multiple errors in the simple sentences. For example, 'planting trees are good' should be 'planting trees *is* good'; '… bought a tree and plant it …' should be 'bought a tree and *planted* it in …'.
	Simple ☑ Compound ☑ Complex ☑ Compound-complex ☑
Lexical Resource	Vocabulary has a limited range, and some words are used repetitively, 'tree', for example. No paraphrasing is attempted, and very limited less common language given.
	Less Common Language[1] ☑ Collocations/Idiomatic[2] ☑ Paraphrasing[3] ☒ Discourse Marker[4] ☒
Fluency	Simple speech is often fluent, but complex structures slow the candidate down. No real range of connectives or discourse markers is given.
Pronunciation	Generally understood throughout, but the use of features is not sustained.

Examiner: Do you like planting trees? Why?

Candidate: To be honest with you[4], I've never planted one. I've seen it done on TV generally by heads of state when they're trying to make a point about the environment. Tell you what[4], when I'm a president, I'll let you know.

Examiner: What kind[3] of trees do people usually plant in your country?

Candidate: I couldn't tell you, and I'm really not a tree expert. I know that there are lots of trees dotted around[2] Beijing, and they line many of the roads here, but I haven't a clue[2] what type[3] they are, sorry.

遍布的 — dotted around
不知道 — haven't a clue

Examiner: Have you ever planted a tree?

Candidate: Like I said earlier, no. I don't think I'll ever plant one in the future, either. It's not the kind of thing I'd have the opportunity, or desire[1], to do.

Examiner: What kinds of trees would you plant?

Candidate: If I had to make a choose, then probably some kind of fruit tree because apple, pear, peach, and cherry trees not only add beauty to a landscape[1], but also provide edible fruit.

Examiner's Comment	
Grammar	Both simple and complex structures are given, and only a minor error in one of the sentences – 'make a choose' should be 'make a **choice**'. Simple ☑ Compound ☒ Complex ☑ Compound-complex ☑
Lexical Resource	A good range of vocabulary given, with successful attempts at less common language, collocations as well as paraphrasing (***kind→type***). Less Common Language[1] ☑ Collocations/Idiomatic[2] ☑ Paraphrasing[3] ☑ Discourse Marker[4] ☑
Fluency	No noticeable effort while speaking and gives a good range of discourse markers and connectives.
Pronunciation	Some good use of features, but not all the time. The occasional mispronunciation of words reduces clarity at times.

Look at this: *Your answers don't always have to be positive. If you haven't done, or don't like, something, that's perfectly acceptable as long as you can explain your position/thoughts to the examiner.*
注意：你不需要总是肯定作答。如果你没有做过或不喜欢某事，可以向考官解释你的立场或想法，这样是完全可以接受的。

Abstract Topics

Examiner: Do you enjoy your current stage of life?

Candidate: Yes. Busy while fulfilled[1]. Arduous[1] while hopeful.

Examiner: In which stage of your life were you the happiest?

Candidate: Before the College Entrance Examination, during which time the only thing that I had to do is to improve my score. But now, I have to encounter and deal with a lot of things beside the grades.

Examiner: Which stage of your life do you think is the most important?

Candidate: I think from 20 to 30 years old. In this stage, I will not only have further study but also step into the society. If I found a solid base during this ten years, the latter life will be promising.

Examiner: What is your plan for your next stage of life?

Candidate: The most important is to apply for a famous university to gain my Master's degree. Later, I might go on the academic way to apply for a Doctor's degree.

	Examiner's Comment
Grammar	Most complex structures contain errors, but these are fairly minor. For example, 'beside the grades' should be '***besides*** the grades'; 'during this ten years' should be 'during ***these*** ten years'.
	Simple ☑ Compound ☑ Complex ☑ Compound-complex ☒
Lexical Resource	A limited range is given, but there are no collocations, paraphrases or idioms offered. Some less common language, but it seems to have been memorised.
	Less Common Language[1] ☑ Collocations/Idiomatic[2] ☒ Paraphrasing[3] ☒ Discourse Marker[4] ☒
Fluency	Pauses occasionally and is quite slow throughout, but usually keeps going. There are no discourse markers spoken, and there are the beginnings of a range of connectives.
Pronunciation	A few mispronunciations, and a little monotonous, but can generally be understood.

Examiner: Do you enjoy your current stage of life?

Candidate: Oh, definitely[4]. I can't really think of a better time, and although I know I've got a lot more ahead of me, I think this might be the happiest time of my life. I've finished my childhood, and I'm now into adulthood and looking forward to[2] my career once I graduate.

Examiner: In which stage of your life were you the happiest?

Candidate: Like I just said[4], this one. According to my knowledge, there are only three stages of life: childhood, adulthood and old age[3]. I'm at the beginning of the second one, which I'm looking forward to.

Examiner: Which stage of your life do you think is the most important[3]?

Candidate: I suppose that would really depend on[2] who it is essential[3] to and for what. Childhood, for example, is your formative years[1] and probably the most important to you as a person. Adulthood is going to be important to the government, the company you work for, and whomever[1] you marry. Finally, when you're elderly[3], you're probably most important to your family because of your experience. So, it's actually a complicated question to answer.

——个性形成时期

Examiner: What is your plan for your next stage of life?

Candidate: Well[4], as I've only just entered it, I'd like to talk about my adulthood rather than my old age. My plan, certainly for the next three or four years, will be to finish my master's, and then I'm going to find a good job. After that, well, it will probably include marriage and children.

	Examiner's Comment
Grammar	A good mix of grammatical structures, and most sentences are error-free. Simple ☑ Compound ☑ Complex ☑ Compound-complex ☑
Lexical Resource	A good range of vocabulary given with a selection of less common language, paraphrasing (***old age→elderly; important→essential***) and collocations. Less Common Language[1] ☑ Collocations/Idiomatic[2] ☑ Paraphrasing[3] ☑ Discourse Marker[4] ☑
Fluency	Good extended answers and no noticeable effort when speaking. Also gives a range of discourse markers and connections.
Pronunciation	Can generally be understood with occasional lapses of feature control.

Examiner: What do you always do in a hurry? Why?

Candidate: Yes. I tend[1] to finish the task until the deadline, because I think the efficiency[1] in that period is the highest.

Examiner: What kind of things would you never do in a hurry?

Candidate: Cooking. I enjoy the process of cooking. I would rather reduce the number of dishes to ensure[1] their tasty flavour.

Examiner: Do you usually go out in a hurry?

Candidate: Yes, I prefer to tidy myself up and choose the suitable clothes before I go out. And this will cost me a lot of time, which makes me in a hurry to keep to the set time.

Examiner: Do you like to be in a hurry?

Candidate: No, actually[4]. Because doing things in a hurry requires to be highly focused and fully clear in mind. Although the efficiency can be high, accidents are always unexpected.

Examiner's Comment	
Grammar	A mix of simple and complex structures, with a variety of errors. Some mistakes would cause miscommunication. For example, 'finish the task until the deadline' should be 'finish the task **by** the deadline'; 'doing things in a hurry requires to be highly focused' should change to 'doing things in a hurry requires **me** to be highly focused'.
	Simple ☑ Compound ☒ Complex ☑ Compound-complex ☒
Lexical Resource	A limited range of vocabulary, but some good less common language. Some of the word choices are inappropriate, though.
	Less Common Language[1] ☑ Collocations/Idiomatic[2] ☒ Paraphrasing[3] ☒ Discourse Marker[4] ☑
Fluency	Occasionally speaks a little slowly, but generally able to keep going. Only one discourse marker.
Pronunciation	Some use of features, but not sustained, and slight mispronunciations are frequent.

Examiner: What do you always do in a hurry³? Why?

Candidate: I suppose most of the time I will always eat quick³. For me, food is a necessity rather than any particular pleasure. Sometimes I really enjoy my food and will take my time² (慢慢来), especially if I haven't had that particular type of meal for a long time, but not often.

Examiner: What kind of things would you never do in a hurry?

Candidate: That's a really good question. I suppose banking would be one of them. Not because I don't necessarily want to do it speedily³, but more because I can't. For some reason⁴, every time I go to the bank, it takes me more than an hour, which to be honest⁴, is really annoying¹.

Examiner: Do you usually go out³ in a hurry?

Candidate: No, not really. Or, at least, not often. I mainly plan things fairly³ well so that if I do need to pop out³ for any reason, whether this is to class or to go shopping or something, I don't have to be hurried and stressed before I get there. It is not that I want to go out at a snail's pace² (缓慢地), just that I don't want to imitate¹ the white rabbit.

Examiner: Do you like to be in a hurry?

Candidate: Absolutely not⁴. It's not a feeling I relish¹ (喜爱), and as I said earlier⁴, I've become relatively³ good at planning my time and will generally have a plan B even if plan A fails.

	Examiner's Comment			
Grammar	A good mix of simple and complex sentence structures with very few mistakes.			
	Simple ☑	Compound ☒	Complex ☑	Compound-complex ☑
Lexical Resource	A good range of vocabulary with some good, less common language as well as idioms and paraphrases (*hurry→quick/speedily; go out→pop out; fairly→relatively*).			
	Less Common Language¹ ☑ Paraphrasing³ ☑		Collocations/Idiomatic² ☑ Discourse Marker⁴ ☑	
Fluency	Extended answers throughout with a range of connectives and discourse markers.			
Pronunciation	Mixed control of features, which isn't sustained. Can be generally understood throughout, though.			

Examiner: Is it difficult for you to stay focused on something?

Candidate: Yes, especially sitting and doing something for long.

Examiner: What do you do to help you concentrate?

Candidate: I usually close all the social media and set a time limit. A cup of coffee helps, too.

Examiner: What may distract you when you are trying to stay focused?

Candidate: Messages from others, noise from the outside, and sometimes pain from my body due to long-time sitting.

Examiner: When do you need to be focused?

Candidate: When I am working on a long essay or a complicated task and when I am having a class. In these occasion[1], one moment of distraction[1] may means a miss of a inspiring[1] thought or key point.

Examiner's Comment	
Grammar	A limited range of complex structures that contain errors. In fact, most sentences have some kind of error. For example, 'In these occasion … may means a miss of a inspiring …' should be 'In these ***occasions*** … may ***mean*** a miss of ***an*** inspiring …'.
	Simple ☑ Compound ☑ Complex ☒ Compound-complex ☒
Lexical Resource	A limited range of vocabulary is used with some good attempts at less common language. No paraphrasing or idiomatic language is offered, though.
	Less Common Language[1] ☑ Collocations/Idiomatic[2] ☒ Paraphrasing[3] ☒ Discourse Marker[4] ☒
Fluency	Relatively slow speech all the way through, with a few noticeable pauses.
Pronunciation	A number of mispronunciations, which makes it difficult to understand sometimes. The number of pauses also makes it difficult to follow the required features.

Examiner: Is it difficult for you to stay focused[3] on something?

Candidate: As a general rule[4], no, but it really depends on how important something might be. If I'm writing a draft of a paper, and I have the TV on in the background, then yes, I do get distracted[1] sometimes. In something like an exam, though, or driving a car, I can give it my full attention[3].

Examiner: What do you do to help[3] you concentrate?

Candidate: I suppose it would depend on what I'm trying to do. Changing the environment sometimes helps, certainly if there are too many people around or it's too noisy. And making sure I'm sitting comfortably might assist[3] my focus.

Examiner: What may distract you when you are trying to stay focused?

Candidate: Like I mentioned earlier[4], I occasionally have the TV on in the background when I'm writing papers or doing my homework. When I start to get tired, I find myself watching TV more and more. I also think of other things that I can do in order to procrastinate[1] (拖延) finishing the paper.

Examiner: When do you need to be focused?

Candidate: In my opinion[4], most of the time. If I'm in class, I need to be focused on what is being said. If I am playing sports, I need to be absorbed[3] in that too. I think the only time I actually try and switch my brain off[2] (让大脑放松) is if I'm watching TV and can just flop on[2] (因疲惫而重重坐下) the couch.

	Examiner's Comment
Grammar	Frequent error-free sentences in the sentence structures, which are mostly complex in nature.
	Simple ☑ Compound ☒ Complex ☑ Compound-complex ☑
Lexical Resource	Uses a good range of vocabulary together with a number of collocations, idioms and paraphrases (***help→assist; focused→full attention/absorbed***).
	Less Common Language[1] ☑ Collocations/Idiomatic[2] ☑ Paraphrasing[3] ☑ Discourse Marker[4] ☑
Fluency	No noticeable effort while speaking with a range of discourse markers given.
Pronunciation	Is easy to understand throughout, with only minor mispronunciations and lapses in features.

Examiner: Do you have a talent or something you are good at?

Candidate: Yes. I think I have a talent for cooking. I often cook in the middle school.

Examiner: Was it mastered recently or when you were young?

Candidate: When I was in the middle school, I cooked for a whole summer vocation at home. I was very good at slicing food and seasoning[1] at that time. But later, I seldom cook because I became lazier.

Examiner: Do you think your talent can be useful for your future work? Why?

Candidate: Yes. Eating is one essential[1] thing for every human in the world. What's more[4], different countries share different cultures of cooking. Through talking about cooking, better understanding can be achieved.

Examiner: Do you think anyone in your family has the same talent?

Candidate: Yes. My grandfather used to be a chief in a restaurant and in the local school. I am excited to be his assistant when he is preparing the meal.

Examiner's Comment	
Grammar	Attempts at complex structures, but these usually contain mistakes. They don't cause many difficulties in comprehension, though.
	Simple ☑ Compound ☒ Complex ☑ Compound-complex ☒
Lexical Resource	A limited range of vocabulary is given, with some less common words offered. There are several inappropriacies and inaccuracies – 'summer vocation' should be 'summer vacation'.
	Less Common Language[1] ☑ Collocations/Idiomatic[2] ☒ Paraphrasing[3] ☒ Discourse Marker[4] ☑
Fluency	Normally keeps going but is quite often slow and occasionally pauses. Some good use of connectives and discourse markers.
Pronunciation	Some use of features, but monotonous at times with occasional mispronunciation.

Answer 2（★★★★） 🎧 129

Examiner: Do you have a talent or something you are good at?

Candidate: Well[4], I like to think of myself as quite good with numbers, as I can calculate[1] things fairly quickly in my head without the need for a calculator. I'm not really talking mathematical formulas here, more like percentages, fractions or square roots of numbers, that kind of thing.

Examiner: Was it mastered recently or when you were young?

Candidate: Oh[4], when I was young[3]. As a kid[3] in middle school, I was often bored by my teachers, so I would do things like figuring out[2] the square root of two during class. As you may know, that is an unending[1] 无尽的 number. I think I got to about 8 or 9 decimal places[1] 小数 before I calculated something else.

Examiner: Do you think your talent can be useful for your future work? Why?

Candidate: I would think so, yes. Everyone needs to be able to do some level of numeracy in their head, but unfortunately, especially these days, the first thing anyone does when they need to add something up[2] is reach for a calculator. Personally[4], I think we're losing the ability to use our brains over technology.

Examiner: Do you think anyone in your family has the same talent?

Candidate: I'm reasonably sure they don't. My mother and father hate[3] anything mathematical, and although my big sister is great at mathematics and formula, she still reaches for a calculator when she's dividing two numbers. I think it's that I will see it as a mental challenge[2] and something to relieve[1] boredom, whereas they just think it's difficult and don't like[3] it.

	Examiner's Comment
Grammar	A good range of complex structures are given, and they are mostly error-free. Simple ☑ Compound ☑ Complex ☑ Compound-complex ☑
Lexical Resource	A good range is given with good examples of less common language as well as collocations and paraphrasing (***young→kid; hate→don't like***). Less Common Language[1] ☑ Collocations/Idiomatic[2] ☑ Paraphrasing[3] ☑ Discourse Marker[4] ☑
Fluency	Generally keeps going, with only occasional hesitation. Some good use of basic Discourse Markers and connectives.
Pronunciation	Can generally be understood, with occasional lapses in control and sustainability.

Now that you have read through all the different Part 1 topics, you will hopefully have an idea on what different types of language can be used to answer a multitude of questions. I have tried to use a variety of less common language as well as different collocations and idioms. Don't forget that during the IELTS exam you'll be asked one of the frequently asked topics, plus two others, so don't worry if you don't always use language required for a band 6 or 7 for EVERY answer.

通读完所有 Part 1 的话题后，希望你能了解哪些不同类型的语言可以用于回答各种各样的问题。本书中用了各种非常见的语言以及不同的搭配和习语。别忘了在雅思考试中，你会被问到一个核心话题和另外两个话题，所以，如果不是**每个**问题都用的是 6—7 分水平的语言，也不用担心。

One other last piece of advice, KEEP GOING. If you're unfamiliar with the topic, say so. The examiner won't laugh at you because you haven't heard of a particular sport, or type of tree. For example:

最后一条建议：坚持！如果你对所问的话题不熟就说出来。考官不会因为你没有听说过某项运动或某种树而嘲笑你。例如：

I'm sorry, but I don't really know anything about this topic, so I'm finding it incredibly challenging to answer these questions intelligently. It might be that I don't entirely understand the subject. Can we try the next question?（我很抱歉，但是对于这个话题我真的是一无所知，所以我感觉要答好这些问题很难。可能是因为我完全不懂这个话题。我们能试试下一个问题吗？）

The example answer above is grammatically correct, has a complex structure and uses less common language. This is all the examiner is listening for. And NO, you can't use this for every answer in a topic. One previous sentence that I heard during my days helping other students was:

上述答案范例语法正确、句型复杂，还使用了非常见的语言。考官想听的就是这种答案。当然，你不能每个话题都用这种答案。我之前教学生时听到这样一句话：

I can't think of an answer to this question. I'm sure if I had time to look it up on the Internet, I could give you a good answer.（对于这个问题，我想不到答案。我确定，如果我有时间在网上查一下的话，我就能给你一个很棒的答案。）

This, in itself, is a reasonable statement with correct grammar, but when the question is 'What's your name?' or 'What's your favourite colour?', it stands out as a memorised sentence and will not help you increase your score.

这个答案本身很合理，语法也是对的，但是如果问题是"你的名字叫什么？"或者"你最喜欢的颜色是什么？"，这显然是个记下来的句子，不会帮你加分。

Section III

Parts 2&3 Preparation and Topics

如何准备 Parts 2&3

In this section, I will cover the exam questions in Parts 2 and 3. Similarly to what I've covered with the Part 1 examples, please use what I give here to learn different ways of saying things and hopefully some new vocab and techniques.

在本部分，我会谈到 Part 2 和 Part 3 的考题。与我所提供的 Part 1 答案范例一样，请使用我给的范例去学习不同的表达方式、新的词汇以及技巧。

Again there are two example answers per topic, but this time I have simply answered them using different language and ideas. They all are around the ★ ★ ★ ★ mark. Also, I'll focus on the language and list some good expressions in the Lexical Resource table after each answer.

本部分的每个话题同样都提供两种答案，但是我仅仅使用了不同的语言和思路。它们的分数都是 ★ ★ ★ ★。此外，我会更关注语言，并在每个答案后的"词汇多样性"表格中列举了一些好的表达。

▶ Part 2 Exam Information

In Part 2 of the exam, the topics are considered 'unfamiliar'. You'll notice that this is occasionally mentioned in the criteria, so when it is, it is in direct reference to Parts 2 and 3. Perhaps one of the main elements of the criteria that relates to Parts 2 and 3 (although it does refer to Part 1 as well) is 'speaks at length' under the Fluency Section. As part of the instructions, the examiner tells you that you have to speak for '1 to 2 minutes' and that they will stop you at two minutes '... when the time is up'. I would strongly advise that you speak until the examiner says, 'stop'. After all, if you only spoke for 1 minute, when you have two, would YOU consider that 'speaking at length'?

在口语考试的 Part 2 中，话题是"不熟悉的"。你会留意到，这一点只在评分标准中偶尔提到，因此，当提及这一点，主要是指 Parts 2&3。或许，与 Parts 2&3 相关的一个主要因素就是流利性这个评分标准中提到的"畅谈"。在考试指令中，考官会告诉你需要发言"一至两分钟"，"时间到后"他们会在两分钟时让你停下来。我强烈建议你一直说到考官说"停"为止。毕竟，你明明有两分钟的时间，却只说了一分钟，你会认为这是"畅谈"吗？

You'll notice from the following topics that there are always four elements that you are asked to cover about the subject, and the last of these is nearly always asking 'why' you feel a certain way or how' you feel about it. When preparing any topic, I would suggest this should be where you start, as it will push you to think about the subject from different angles. For example, if a topic asks you to describe a piece of electronic equipment that you use, it's easy to say what it is, but it's more challenging to say why you enjoy using it.

你会从接下来的话题中注意到，你总会被问及四个与某个主题相关的问题，而最后一个几乎总是会问"为什么"你这样想，或你"怎么"看？准备任何话题时，我建议你从最后一个问题开始，因为这样能迫使你从不同的角度考虑该主题。例如，如果该主题让你描述一个你用的电子设备，说出这个设备是什么很简单，但是要解释你为什么喜欢用它就难多了。

At the beginning of Part 2, once you have been given the topic that you need to talk about, you have one minute to make 'notes'. MAKE NOTES! My advice is to quickly divide the paper/whiteboard into four sections, as exampled below. I have found this method to be faster and better than making a simple list, mainly because you can write more clearly by using the entire space on the paper/whiteboard.

在 Part 2 开头，考官给了你要讨论的主题后，你会有一分钟的时间做"笔记"。一定要"做笔记"！我建议迅速地把纸 / 白板分为四个部分（如下图）。我发现这种方法比列清单更好、更快，因为这样用纸 / 白板，你的笔记更清晰。

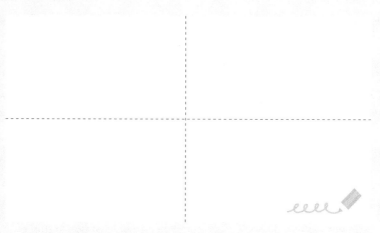

▶ Part 3 Exam Information

In Part 3, the examiners listen for some particular language because their questions cover the following areas. Here is a labelled list of the most common types and possible beginnings of answers:

在 Part 3，考官想听到一些不寻常的表达，因为他们的问题包括以下几种类型。最常见的问题类型和可以使用的答案开头见下表：

Types	Questions	Answers
Opinion	Do you think that ...? Is ... popular ...?	I think ..., In my opinion ..., I believe ...
Evaluate	Is ... good for ...? Can ... influence ...?	I agree ..., I don't think that's right ...
Compare & Contrast	These days, is ... the same as the past? What are the differences between ...?	however, as well as ...
Hypothesise	Will ... change in the future? If you ... would ... happen?	maybe, would ...
Speculate	What's the best way to ...? Can we ...?	perhaps this will/probably/possibly/may happen ...
List	What kinds/types of ...? How many ...?	there are various/multiple ...

When answering Part 3 questions, you should first identify the type of question being asked from the list above and then give the appropriate answer structure. Typically, it means the first few words of the sentence, as the content will change depending on the topic. For example:

回答 Part 3 的问题时，你首先要确定问题属于上面提到的哪一类，再使用恰当的答题结构。问题类型往往体现在句子开头的几个单词中，因为后续内容取决于所问话题。例如：

> *In my opinion, mobile phones are great.*
> *In my opinion, online learning is excellent.*
> *In my opinion, homework is awful.*

Here, you can see that the beginning of each sentence is the same and would be perfectly acceptable for the start of an answer to an Opinion question. It's just the remaining content that would differ.

从上述例子中你会发现，每个句子的开头都一样，很适合用在观点类问题答案的开始。只是后面的答案内容不一样而已。

For the List questions, make sure that you're clear about whether the examiner is asking about one, or multiple things. For example, 'What kind of' is singular, whereas 'What types of' is plural. If it's a plural that the examiner has asked about, make sure you give at least two examples.

对于列举类的问题，要清楚考官问的是一样还是几样东西。例如 What kind of 是单数，而 What types of 是复数。如果考官用的是复数，那你至少需要给两个例子。

Some of the questions can be interchanged. 'What are the differences between …?' in the above table could be considered as a List, certainly if you mentioned multiple differences. The important thing to take away here is that there are specific types of questions that will be asked and can be answered in different ways.

一些问题的类型可以互换。如果你提到多种差异的话，上表中的"两者有哪些区别？"这个问题当然也可以视为列举。重要的是，问题有特定类型，也有不同的回答方式。

Something else to remember is that many Part 3 questions are not just of one specific type. So, you might be able to express an opinion while comparing something. There are multiple ways to answer most of these questions, so when you are studying this book and learning from the answers, please play with the styles and types of answers. Mix them up and see how you can answer one question differently. Don't forget that the ability to use language in different ways is a large part of the test.

还要记住，Part 3 的很多问题很难归为一种类型。所以，有可能你在对比时还要表达个人看法。回答这些问题的方法很多，所以在使用这本书时，学习本书中的答案，请注意答案的风格和答题类型。将它们糅合起来，试试如何用不同的方式回答同一个问题。别忘了，用不同方式使用语言的能力占测试的大部分。

This section is an opportunity to show off your grammar by using a 'range of complex structures' (Level 7 in Grammar, Range and Accuracy). It also allows you to use different phrases to express these different structures, which should help your score in 'lexical resource' improve simultaneously by showing 'range' there too.

在本部分，你有机会通过使用"一系列复杂的结构"来展示你的语法（7分水平的语法、结构和准确性）。此外，你还能运用不同的短语来表达这些句型结构，这样的话，你在提高"词汇多样性"得分的同时，还能展示"结构的多样性"。

Little Reminder: *Each answer for Part 3 should be around 30 seconds long – about 3 or 4 sentences. This would be recognised as an 'extended answer'.*

小提醒：Part 3 每个答案的长度应该是 30 秒左右，即三至四句话。这样就可以视作"拓展答案"。

Disclaimer: *The answers I've written are provided as examples of the different scores based on the information given in the Public IELTS Speaking criteria. They are not a guarantee that anyone would achieve those scores in a real IELTS exam and should be taken as guidelines only. It should also be understood that the marks given by examiners are for the test as a whole, not the individual parts. I give marks for individual sections based on the prediction that other answers would be of similar quality.*

免责声明：本书中答案范例所给的分数依据的是公众版雅思口语评分标准。不能保证任何持有这些答案的考生在真实的雅思考试中能拿到一样的分数，这些答案仅作参考。同时需要清楚的是，考官所给的分数是基于整场口语考试，而不是每个部分单独打分。而我在每个部分单独给分是假定考生在每个部分的表现是相似的。

■ Advice for People and Animals topics

With topics about people, there are some occasions where you can use the same kind of idea and sentence structure across multiple topics. When you're talking about a famous person, for example, they might be an athlete, singer, or actor as well, but don't get drawn into the idea that you can always do this, or that what you say should be repeated for different Part 3 questions.

对于人物类的话题，有时候你可以在不同的话题中使用同样的思路和句型。例如谈论名人这个话题时，名人也可能是运动员、歌手或演员。但不是所有情况都可以这样，也不要以为应该在不同的Part 3中重复使用（一样的思路和句型）。

▶ Details you could use 使用细节信息

Think about exactly who you are trying to describe and why you have chosen that particular person. So, if they're a singer, talk about their songs; if they're an actor, talk a little about their films, their co-stars etc. Describe them, in detail: character, personality, physical features and the like.

仔细考虑你想描述谁，为什么你要选这个人。如果你选的是位歌手，那就谈谈他唱的歌；如果是位演员，可以谈论他参演的电影、联合主演等。详细描述他们的性格、个性、身体特征等。

For animals, think about what they look like, are they common in your country? Why you thought of a cat, rather than a dog, for example.

对于动物类话题，可以考虑它们长什么样，它们在本国常见吗？例如，为什么你会考虑猫而不是狗。

▶ Thinking around the topic 围绕话题思考

Imagine a stranger is asking you about these people because they have no idea about them in your country. If you're talking about musicians, it's pretty evident that people would like to know more about different types of music or musician; how, when, where you would listen to music; how and when people learn a musical instrument; what instrument would be popular; as well as the past and future of music.

想象一下有位陌生人问你有关这些人的情况，因为他们不了解你们国家的这些人。如果你们正在谈论音乐家，很显然人们应该会想更多地了解不同类型的音乐或音乐家，你想何时、在哪里、怎样听音乐，人们何时、如何学习一门乐器，什么乐器流行，以及过去和将来的音乐。

Regarding animals, you can think of where or when you might see or look after an animal. Also, think though of the opposite: What animals CAN'T you see in your country, why not? Would you like to see or have that animal as a pet? Has the knowledge of animals changed over the last few years? – think about documentaries on TV, the price of travelling to different countries, the new animals in zoos etc.

关于动物，你可以考虑你何时或在哪儿想参观或照顾动物。另外，也可以反向思考——在你们国家看不到什么动物？为什么？你想去看看那种动物或养一只当宠物吗？与动物有关的知识在近几年变化了吗？想想电视上的纪录片，去不同国家旅游的费用，动物园里新出现的动物等。

■ Advice for Things topics

> ● **General things to think about** 可以考虑的共性问题

With topics about things or objects the range could vary hugely. I believe that there would be a few general things to think about:

物品类话题千差万别，我认为可以考虑一些共性问题：

- *Type of thing/object*（事物的类型）
- *Time of thing/object*（与事物有关的时间）
- *Importance of thing/object*（事物的重要性）

Simply put, these would cover what kind of thing it is, when it was/will be used and how you feel about the thing/object. For example, a book or a photograph can be described in the same way:

简而言之，问题会包含它是什么，什么时候用，以及你对它的感情。例如，一本书或一张照片可以用同样的方式描述：

Book

Type of thing/object	paper book/E-book, genre (Sci-Fi, Fantasy, etc.), author, popular? gift?
Time of thing/object	when read? when written? when given?
Importance of thing/object	sentimental value, placed where? (pride of place, or hidden in a drawer?), gift from dead grandmother?

Photo

Type of thing/object	holiday, girlfriend, family, digital or printed?
Time of thing/object	when taken? holiday? important trip? first time to that place?
Importance of thing/object	sentimental value? placed where? (pride of place, or hidden in a drawer?), taken with dead grandparents?

> ● **Details you could use** 可以使用的细节信息

In English, a common phrase that could describe what you need to think about is: 'The devil is in the details'. What this means is, don't just say 'Oh, it's a book' or 'It's a photo'. Who, What, When, Where, Why, and How are the questions you should be asking yourself. These work not only with things/objects, but any topics that arise in Part 2 or Part 3.

英语中有一个可以用来描述你需要思考的内容的常用表达："魔鬼藏在细节里"。这句话的意思是不要只是说"哦，是一本书"或"是一张照片"。Who、What、When、Where、Why 和 How 才是你应该问自己的问题。这个方法不仅适用于回答事物类话题，也适用于 Part 2 或 Part 3 中的任何话题。

■ Advice for Activities and Events topics

▶ General things to think about 可以考虑的共性问题

If you check the wording of the topics, many of them begin with 'Describe an occasion ...' or 'Describe a time ...'. With topics about activities or events, I believe that there would be a few general things to think about:

如果你留意下活动与事件类话题的用词，会发现许多题目都是以"描述一个场合"或"描述一个时间"开头的。我认为事件类话题有一些共性问题可以考虑：

- *Type of activity/event* (活动 / 事件的类型)
- *Time of activity/event* (活动 / 事件的时间)
- *Who you do this activity/event with* (你和谁一起参与的这个活动 / 这件事)

Simply put, these would cover what kind of thing it is, when it was/will be used/done and who you were with during this activity or event. Another thing to think about is why you do this thing.

简而言之，问题会包含什么事、什么时候做的 / 将要做的 / 已经做完的，以及你和谁一起做的这件事。另外要思考的是你为什么要做这件事。

▶ Details you could use 可以使用的细节信息

With these topics you can focus on details like:

这类话题你可以关注以下细节：

- *Is it a regular activity/event, or a one off?* (活动是定期举办还是一次性的？)
- *Time of day/year that this happens ... why?* (举办的日期以及为什么在这一天？)
- *Who do you do it with, family, friend, classmate, girlfriend? How do you know them? What's their name?* (你当时和谁在一起？家人、朋友、同学、恋人？你怎么认识他们的？他们叫什么？)

This will allow you to add information that can fill up the time for the part 2 or the part 3.

你可以照此添加信息，填补 part 2 或 part 3 的时间。

Use activities or events that you know a lot about. Sometimes they need you to talk about festivals or celebrations, for which you can use family get-togethers as a template. Describe your family, and where does this happen? Don't just say 'at home' – Where's home? Which province? Which city? Where is the city? Is it a big city?

描述你非常熟悉的活动或事件。有时考官让你谈论节日或庆典，你可以用家庭聚会作为模板。描述一下你的家庭以及庆典发生在哪里？不要只说 at home——家在哪里？哪个省？哪个城市？城市在哪里？是大城市吗？

My advice would be to NOT say:

我不建议说：

> *My family comes over for dinner, and we eat together.*

What you could say is:

你可以说：

> *All my family comes over dinner. Normally, both my uncles come over with my cousins. They're on my mother's side – she's the youngest of the three. Both sets of grandparents also join us as they're still young enough to be able to travel. Generally, they all come together as they live close to each other. As we live far from them, about 800 km, they take a flight from Beijing to Weihai, which is in Shandong province. We're pretty near the airport, so it's not an issue for us to go and meet them ...*

One takes about 3 seconds to say, the other takes 30 or more. You're still saying the same thing, just adding a little more information.

第一个回答只够说3秒，第二个可以说30多秒。你说的还是同样的事，只是补充了一点信息。

■ Advice for Places topics

With topics about places, the most obvious detail that you need to talk about is where this place is, so this is something that you can focus on and give specific details. You'll notice from all the questions in this book about places that 'Where …?' is in all of them, and the next most popular question is 'What did you do there?', quickly followed by 'How do you feel about this place?'.

关于地点的话题，你首先需要说的细节就是这个地点在哪里，你可以给出具体细节。你会发现本书所有关于地点的第一个问题都是"……在哪?"，其次是"你在那里做了什么?"，最后是"你觉得这个地方怎么样?"。

Where	city name, north/south, near the x, not far from y, 5 minutes a walk from z
What you did	relaxed myself, had a look around/meal/coffee, used their Wi-Fi/Internet because …
How you felt	amazed/relaxed/awe-struck/peaceful because …

▶ Thinking around the topic 围绕话题思考

As discussed above, some of these questions will be focussed on the place itself, some on what you do there, and some on your feelings about the place. Even if the question is focused more on your feelings, you can still include details on the other two. You could also include information about how you found out about this place: from a friend, on the Internet, or walked past it by chance.

如上所述，有些问题关注这个地点本身，有些关注你在那里做什么，有些关注你对这个地点的感觉。即使问题主要问你的感受，你仍然可以谈论其他两个方面的细节。你也可以说你是如何发现这个地点的，是从朋友那得知或网上看到还是偶然路过。

The age of the place would also be an interesting detail that you could include. You would not necessarily need the exact year. You could say whether it's new or old, or maybe generalise about the age.

这个地点存在的时间也是一个你可以谈论的有趣细节。你不需要确切的年份，你可以说这个地点是新还是旧，或者笼统说下年份。

Chapter 2 People and Animals

人物与动物篇

A favourite singer

> **Describe your favourite singer or actor.**
>
> **You should say:**
>
> > **who he/she is**
> >
> > **what his/her personality is**
> >
> > **what kind of style his/her music/acting belongs to**
>
> **and explain why he/she is your favourite singer/actor.**

The singer I want to talk about is Freddie Mercury. He was a British singer, songwriter and record producer, best known as the lead vocalist of the rock band Queen. He was born Farrokh Bulsara back in September of 1946 in Stone Town, Zanzibar and was known for his flamboyant stage presence and powerful vocals, and is considered one of the greatest singers in the history of rock music.

His personality was dynamic, energetic and charismatic. He had a great sense of humour and was known for his wit and sarcasm, both on and off stage. Despite his larger-than-life persona, he was also known for his humility and kindness towards his fans and those around him.

His music can be classified as rock, hard rock and heavy metal, with elements of opera, classical music and progressive rock. His voice was powerful, soulful and versatile, and he had a remarkable range that allowed him to sing in different styles, from soft ballads to hard rock anthems. He was also known for his flamboyant stage performances and dynamic showmanship, which made him one of the greatest performers in the history of rock music.

He is the singer I like the most because of his unique vocal abilities and dynamic stage presence. His powerful and soulful voice, combined with his larger-than-life personality, made him one of the most captivating performers in the history of rock music. His music continues to inspire and influence new generations of artists, and his legacy will always be remembered as one of the greatest voices in the history of rock and roll.

Examiner:	Do you think the most popular singer is the best one? (Opinion)
Candidate:	Popularity does not necessarily equate to quality or talent. While a singer's popularity can be an indication of their success in the music industry, it is not a reliable measure of their overall skill or musical ability. I think, the best singer is subjective and can depend on individual preferences and opinions.
Examiner:	What kind of music is popular in your country? (Opinion)
Candidate:	Well, these days, Pop music in China encompasses a wide range of genres, including Mandopop, C-pop, rock, hip-hop, electronic dance music, and traditional Chinese music. Mandopop is perhaps the most popular genre, which is sung in Mandarin Chinese and is influenced by both Western and Chinese music styles. Some of the most popular Chinese singers include Jay Chou, Li Ronghao, and G.E.M. In recent years, hip-hop and EDM are becoming more popular.
Examiner:	What kind of music do people like at different ages? (Compare & Contrast)
Candidate:	I don't think that's a particularly easy question to answer, because each person will be different. As a general rule, I think younger people prefer music that's quite loud, and that has a heavy beat, whereas as you get older the music will become tamer and softer.
Examiner:	Do people learn to sing nowadays? (Evaluate)
Candidate:	Yes, a lot of people still study singing nowadays. Singing is a popular activity, and there are many ways to learn how to sing, including taking singing lessons, joining a choir or vocal group, participating in music programs or workshops, and watching instructional videos online. But, you know, I do think it's a diminishing activity.

Mandopop — 华语流行音乐

EDM — 电子舞曲

heavy beat — 强拍

Lexical Resource	
Less Common Language	flamboyant, charismatic, hard rock, versatile, showmanship, Mandopop
Collocations/Idiomatic Language	larger-than-life, heavy beat
Paraphrasing	favourite→like the most, learn→study
Discourse Marker	well, you know

> **Describe your favourite singer or actor.**
>
> **You should say:**
>
> > who he/she is
> >
> > what his/her personality is
> >
> > what kind of style his/her music/acting belongs to
>
> **and explain why he/she is your favourite singer/actor.**

I think my all-time favourite actor is Jackie Chan. He's been making films since way before my time, around the 1960s, I think. From memory, I think he's done over 100 movies over a span of 60 years. His character, from what I've seen, is calm and controlled. I've never actually met the man, but from what I've seen of him on TV during interviews and the like, he seems like a very personable gentleman.

Most of his movies, I would say, belong to the martial arts genre, and certainly his older movies are all like that. He trained both as a gymnast and a martial artist when he was a kid and has grown up doing both. It wasn't until the *Cannonball Run* film that I think he started getting a taste for comedy. A lot of his movies through the '80s, '90s and into the Naughties, like the *Rush Hour* films, I would say, are more comedy than martial arts. Having said that, though, there's still a lot of fighting in them.

I think he's the one I like the best because his head doesn't seem to be in the clouds, you know, even though he's a worldwide A-List actor, his feet are still firmly on the ground. He's also sponsored lots of things for poor children as well as setting up a charity to help those less fortunate. So, in my book, he's an all-around good guy both on and off the screen, and I hope to see some more of his movies soon.

Examiner: Do you think the most popular singer/actor is the best one? (Opinion)

Candidate: Not always. Some people shoot to fame very quickly and are raved about for a time and then kinda fade away into history. People like Jackie Chan might not be the most popular right now, but he's been up there with the best of them for 50 years. He hasn't faded away. Not yet, anyway.

Examiner: What kind of music is popular in your country? (Opinion)

Candidate: Well, I'd have to say Pop music. It's kind of in the name, isn't it? More specifically K-Pop has hit the music scene in a big way over the last few years, you know, girl and boy bands from South Korea. MandoPop is another one that's up and coming among the younger crowd. That's the Chinese version of K-Pop. Similar groups, but more designed for the Chinese market.

Examiner: What kind of music do people like at different ages? (Compare & Contrast)

Candidate: I think they continue to like the music they enjoyed when they were teenagers or even maybe young adults. My parents still listen to music from the '80s and '90s, and my grandparents still listen to some stuff from the '60s, as well as some classical tunes. None of the generations appreciates music from either of the others, in my experience. I can't really stand my grandparents' listening habits, and they don't enjoy my parents' tastes either.

Examiner: Do people learn to sing nowadays? (Evaluate)

Candidate: I'd say so, yes. I sang a little bit during my junior school years but gave it up when my voice broke. I know there's a singing club at my university that meets on a Wednesday evening because I hear them sometimes from the study room I go to. It sounds wonderful. So, maybe not as many people train their voices nowadays, but it does still happen.

Lexical Resource	
Less Common Language	controlled, genre, gymnast, appreciates
Collocations/Idiomatic Language	martial arts, the Naughties, in the clouds, A-List, in my book, shoot to fame, raved about, fade away into history
Paraphrasing	favourite→like the best, films→movies, music→tunes, learn→train
Discourse Marker	I would say, not always, well, you know

A foreign celebrity

> **Describe a foreign celebrity you want to meet in person.**
>
> **You should say:**
>
>   **who this person is**
>
>   **how you knew about this person**
>
>   **what this person does**
>
> **and explain why you want to meet this person.**

One foreign celebrity that many people admire, including myself, is Leonardo DiCaprio.

He's an American actor, film producer, and environmental activist. He was born on November 11, 1974, in Hollywood, California, and is widely regarded as one of the greatest actors of his generation. He has appeared in many critically acclaimed films, such as *Titanic*, *The Wolf of Wall Street*, *Inception*, and *The Revenant*, and has received numerous awards and nominations for his work.

I learned about him through his films, which are widely popular and widely recognized. He's known for his versatility as an actor, his ability to bring depth and emotion to his characters, and his commitment to environmental causes.

I would want to meet him because of his talent as an actor and his dedication to environmental issues. He is a role model for millions of people around the world, and his work has inspired many to take action to protect our planet. I believe that meeting him in person would be a once-in-a-lifetime experience, and I would be grateful for the opportunity to learn from his experiences and perspectives. Additionally, I am a fan of his acting, and I would be excited to see his ability and charisma in person.

Examiner: How can people become famous? (Speculate)

Candidate: Becoming famous is a complex and multifaceted process that often involves a combination of talent, hard work, timing, and luck. For example, people who have exceptional talent or skills in fields such as music, sports, acting, or comedy can gain fame by honing their craft and building a following.

Examiner: What influences can famous people have on society? (Evaluate)

Candidate: Famous people can have a significant influence on society due to their large following and visibility. Celebrities can influence societal norms and values through their work and personal lives. For example, they can bring attention to critical social issues or advocate for specific causes, which can impact public opinion and lead to social change.

Examiner: What are the advantages and disadvantages of becoming a celebrity? (Compare & Contrast)

Candidate: Well, the most obvious advantage of becoming a celebrity is the potential to earn a lot of money and become well-known, which can lead to various opportunities such as brand endorsements, appearances, and merchandise deals. However, one of the biggest downsides of being a celebrity is the lack of privacy. Celebrities are often followed by paparazzi, and their personal lives can be subject to public scrutiny.

Examiner: Why can some celebrities stay famous for a long time while some cannot? (Hypothesise)

Candidate: Celebrities who are able to stay relevant and adapt to changes in the industry are more likely to maintain their fame over time. This may involve staying up-to-date with current trends and styles, exploring new opportunities, and adapting to changing audience preferences. I think someone like Jackie Chan would be a good example.

Lexical Resource	
Less Common Language	activist, acclaimed, following, paparazzi, scrutiny
Collocations/Idiomatic Language	once-in-a-lifetime, honing their craft, lack of, up-to-date
Paraphrasing	talent→ability, famous people→celebrities
Discourse Marker	well, however

> **Describe a foreign celebrity you want to meet in person.**
>
> **You should say:**
>
>   **who this person is**
>
>   **how you knew about this person**
>
>   **what this person does**
>
> **and explain why you want to meet this person.**

Well, the first person that comes to mind is the new King of England, Charles. He was coronated last [加冕] week, so although many people have been calling King Charles for a while now, it's only just become official.

As for how I know about him, I don't think there's a person on the planet that doesn't know of him. His mother was hugely famous around the world, and he, until recently, when she died, was forever in her shadow. But now, he can step into the light, if you will [请允许我这么说], and with Camilla, who's now the queen consort, can really begin to shine.

Beyond the obvious of being the King of England and head of the Church of England, I don't honestly know. I know part of the role is meeting with the UK Prime Minister each week and that he can meet foreign dignitaries [显要人物] as the new Head of State, but beyond that and what the Crown has shown on TV, I can't say for sure. I know that previously he ran things like The Prince's Trust, but I assume his son William, the new Prince of Wales, will take over that role.

I'd just like to be able to shake him by the hand and ask him how he found the patience to have been the longest-living heir [王位继承人] to a throne. To tell you the truth, I also want to find out how much of The Crown is actually true. Get the inside scoop [获取内幕消息], as it were. Also, though, more seriously, just to try to understand more about the man. After all, it must be a horrible position to be in, knowing that the only way you can be promoted is if your mother dies.

Examiner: How can people become famous? ⟨Speculate⟩

Candidate: These days? Have a Douyin account! There are now 无数的 countless people uploading all sorts of content to the platform that seems to have tens of thousands of followers. I really don't know how they do it, but they have 一举成名 shot to fame in a matter of days, sometimes. I've uploaded some of my photos, and only my friends ever like them.

Examiner: What influences can famous people have on society? ⟨Evaluate⟩

Candidate: Oh, a varied and huge amount. It might be that they advertise some products that people then buy in order to be like them, or maybe there's a cause or charity that they believe in, so they ask people to give money to 慈善事业 worthy causes. I think well-known celebrities that use their influence in an 值得尊敬的 honourable way and help better the world we live in are undoubtedly worth listening to.

Examiner: What are the advantages and disadvantages of becoming a celebrity? ⟨Compare & Contrast⟩

Candidate: For me, I think that beyond the obvious advantages of wealth and fame, as I said just now, you can help make the world a better place by 为……而斗争 fighting for 公益事业 good causes that you believe in and persuading others to do the same. I suppose one of the big disadvantages is that you can never really have that much of a private life. Everybody who sees you will want to say hi and get your autograph or something.

Examiner: Why can some celebrities stay famous for a long time while some cannot? ⟨Hypothesise⟩

Candidate: In my opinion, I think one of the reasons is whether they are a 'reality' celebrity and are famous for doing one specific thing, or whether they're a trained singer or actor that has made their life's work being famous. For the former, they 回到现实中 come back down to earth with a bump very quickly after being a 昙花一现 one-hit-wonder, whereas the latter may do films or music over an extended period of time. Decades normally.

Lexical Resource	
Less Common Language	coronated, dignitaries, countless, honourable
Collocations/Idiomatic Language	get the inside scoop, shot to fame, worthy causes, good causes, come back down to earth with a bump, one-hit-wonder
Paraphrasing	famous people→well-known celebrities
Discourse Marker	if you will, to tell you the truth, as I said just now, in my opinion

A famous athlete

> **Describe a famous athlete you know.**
> **You should say:**
> > **who he/she is**
> > **how you knew him/her**
> > **what he/she has achieved**
> **and explain why he/she is famous.**

One famous athlete that I know, as a football fan, is Lionel Messi.

Lionel Messi is an Argentine professional soccer player, who currently plays as a forward for Paris Saint-Germain and the Argentina national team. He was born on June 24, 1987 in Rosario, Argentina and is widely considered one of the greatest soccer players of all time.

I became familiar with him through his career in soccer and his numerous achievements on and off the field. He has won numerous awards and accolades for his outstanding performance, including 7 Ballon d'Or awards, which are given to the best player in the world. Additionally, he holds several records, such as the most goals scored in a calendar year, and the most goals scored in a European club season.

Messi is famous for his incredible talent on the soccer field. He is known for his incredible speed, dribbling skills, and scoring ability. He has won many championships and titles with both Barcelona and Argentina, and has become a global icon for the sport. In addition to his on-field success, He's also widely recognized for his charitable work, and his efforts to give back to his community.

In conclusion, he's a famous athlete due to his exceptional talent, numerous achievements, and contributions to the sport of soccer. He is widely regarded as one of the greatest soccer players of all time, and continues to inspire fans around the world with his skills and dedication to the game.

Examiner: What kinds of exercises do Chinese people like? (List)

Candidate: There are many types of exercises that are popular in China, and different people may have different preferences depending on their age, interests, and health goals. Many young people enjoy running or playing badminton, whereas a lot of the elderly like things like Tai Chi or square dancing. I suppose it really depends on what you want to do.

Examiner: What characteristics do you think an athlete should have? (List)

Candidate: I think the most important personality trait for a top athlete is discipline. Athletes 自制力 need to be highly disciplined to achieve their goals. They must adhere to strict training 坚持 schedules and routines, maintain a healthy diet, and make sacrifices in their personal lives to ensure that they are in peak physical condition.

Examiner: Why are there so few top athletes? (Speculate)

Candidate: I think it comes down to the fact that being at the top is just that, the top. Not everyone 归结为 can be there. In many sports, the competition for the top spots is incredibly intense. Even among athletes with a high level of natural ability and talent, only a few will be able to rise to the top.

Examiner: What's the best way to become a top athlete? (Opinion)

Candidate: In my opinion, becoming a top athlete requires a combination of talent, hard work, 结合 dedication, and the right training and resources. You will need to set goals, develop a training plan and, perhaps more importantly, stay focused and disciplined so that you can complete everything else.

Lexical Resource	
Less Common Language	accolades, dribbling, championships, discipline, sacrifices
Collocations/Idiomatic Language	adhere to, physical condition, comes down to, a combination of, set goals
Paraphrasing	characteristics→personality trait
Discourse Marker	in conclusion, in my opinion

Describe a famous athlete you know.

You should say:

who he/she is

how you knew him/her

what he/she has achieved

and explain why he/she is famous.

One famous Chinese athlete that I know is Yao Ming. I first became aware of Yao Ming as a basketball fan, and I've followed his career since he was drafted to the NBA in 2002.

These days he's a retired professional basketball player who played for the Houston Rockets in the NBA. He is one of the most famous Chinese athletes of all time, and he is credited with helping to popularize basketball in my country. During his career, Yao Ming achieved a number of notable 重要的 accomplishments, including eight All-Star selections and five All-NBA selections.

One of the reasons why Yao Ming is so famous is his impact on the sport of basketball both in China and globally. As one of the first Chinese basketball players to achieve success in the NBA, he became a symbol of national pride for China and helped to inspire a generation of young Chinese basketball players. Additionally, his unique combination of size and skill on the court made him a fan favourite 主力 and a dominant force in the NBA for many years.

Beyond his athletic accomplishments, he has also become known for his philanthropy and activism. 慈善行为 He has been involved in a number of charitable organizations and initiatives, and he has worked 野生动物保护 to promote wildlife conservation and animal welfare. Overall, he's a beloved figure in China and a respected athlete and humanitarian worldwide.

Examiner: What kinds of exercises do Chinese people like? [List]

Candidate: A lot of people grow up playing badminton or table tennis, so these are certainly very popular. Nowadays, a lot more people are going to the gym to get exercise or maybe simply going for a run. Personally, I prefer cycling.

Examiner: What characteristics do you think an athlete should have? [List]

Candidate: I think if you're going to be, or at least attempt to be, a top athlete, the first thing you're going to need is dedication, with some perseverance following quickly behind. Without these, I can't see anything else mattering.

Examiner: Why are there so few top athletes? [Speculate]

Candidate: I think that's just the nature of competition. Not everybody can be first or at the top. Otherwise, it would kind of defeat the object of excellence. The China National Olympic team is a few hundred people strong and dwarfs many other countries, but obviously, out of a population of 1.4 billion, this number is minute.

Examiner: What's the best way to become a top athlete? [Opinion]

Candidate: Well, I think the first thing you have to have is some kind of innate talent in a sport. Then, it just comes down to lots of hard work and practice. You'd probably also need a fairly large dollop of luck in the mix as well.

Lexical Resource	
Less Common Language	notable, philanthropy, dedication, perseverance, dwarfs, minute
Collocations/Idiomatic Language	dominant force, wildlife conservation, a large dollop of luck
Paraphrasing	conservation→welfare
Discourse Marker	well, nowadays, obviously

■ A person on social media

> **Describe a person who you follow on social media.**
>
> **You should say:**
>
> > **who he/she is**
> >
> > **how you knew him/her**
> >
> > **what he/she posts on social media**
>
> **and explain why you follow him/her on social media.**

One person that many people follow on social media is Ellen DeGeneres.

Ellen DeGeneres is an American comedian, television host, actress, writer, and producer. She was born 60-odd years ago in Louisiana, and is best known for her daytime talk show, 'The Ellen DeGeneres Show.'

I became familiar with her through her daytime talk show, which has been on the air for many years and has won numerous awards. On social media, she posts a variety of content, including jokes, photos and videos from her show, as well as messages of positivity and encouragement.

People follow her on social media because of her entertaining and uplifting content. She is known for her sense of humour and her kindness, and her posts often reflect these qualities. Additionally, she is a strong advocate for many important causes, and uses her platform to raise awareness and make a positive impact in the world.

In summary then, Ellen DeGeneres is a person that many people follow on social media because of her entertaining and uplifting content, as well as her advocacy for important causes. Whether she is making people laugh with her jokes, or inspiring them with her messages of positivity, she continues to engage and inspire her millions of followers around the world.

Examiner: What can people do on social media? (List)

Candidate: People can do a variety of things on social media, like allowing people to connect with others around the world, including friends, family, and people with similar interests or backgrounds. Also, it can be a source of news and information on a variety of topics, from current events and politics to entertainment and lifestyle.

Examiner: Do you think older people and younger people will use the same kind of social media software? (Opinion)

Candidate: No, I don't think they do. Younger people tend to gravitate towards social media apps that offer more visual content, such as Instagram, Snapchat, and TikTok, while older people may be more likely to use social media apps that focus on text-based content, such as Facebook and Weibo.

Examiner: Do older people spend much time on social media? (Speculate)

Candidate: It kind of depends on what you mean by older people because most people are older than I am but, for people of my parents' age, I think they spend more time on it than my grandparents. Having said that, I don't spend nearly as much time as my generation does, and I think they use it more for work than pleasure.

Examiner: Are non-social media like television and newspapers still useful? (Compare & Contrast)

Candidate: Yes, they are. TV is set up as a one-way entertainment mechanism. You sit there and watch a TV series, and you don't have to interact with anybody else. The same kind of thing will happen with the newspaper. Well, I do think the news is firmly moving online, and the newspaper itself is basically dead.

Lexical Resource	
Less Common Language	uplifting, advocate, variety
Collocations/Idiomatic Language	on the air, raise awareness, gravitate towards, having said that
Paraphrasing	positivity→encouragement, older people→parents' age
Discourse Marker	additionally, in summary then, well

> **Describe a person who you follow on social media.**
>
> **You should say:**
>
> > who he/she is
> >
> > how you knew him/her
> >
> > what he/she posts on social media
>
> **and explain why you follow him/her on social media.**

This is actually quite a difficult question for me to answer effectively, for the main reason being that I don't actually follow anyone on social media. I find the whole idea of putting your life story online for 很多人 everyone and his dog to look at and potentially criticise not only stupid but downright 可笑的 ludicrous.

I realise I am one of the few that feel this way as there are quite literally billions of people that feel the need to post things everyday. I must admit that there are occasions where I think, 'Ooh, that might be interesting', but I've never actually got to the point of finding them online and then following them.

I'm an 热衷的 avid gamer and, hopefully, will get the new PS5 soon. And, like I said, I am aware of people that play games and make videos of themselves, but my thinking is that 到底 why on earth would I want to see someone else play the game when I can play it myself. I don't want the solution to problems, I don't want to know where the best sword or piece of equipment is, but I want to find it for myself.

So I realise I'm not answering the question as it is 说明 laid out, but I want you to realise that not everybody is a social media fan and that it's not necessarily a bad thing or that I'm deficient in any way. It's just that not all of our generation are necessarily the same.

Examiner: What can people do on social media? `List`

Candidate: As far as I know, quite a lot, but it's all based around with relative strangers. These days however, I know you can get a lot of different types of news from some of the business social accounts, which could be useful.

Examiner: Do you think older people and younger people will use the same kind of social media software? `Opinion`

Candidate: I don't think age makes a large difference in how a person uses social media. If you look at some of the figures, there are billions of people using Facebook and Weibo and WeChat. They are not all going to be youngsters.

Examiner: Do older people spend much time on social media? `Speculate`

Candidate: I think that would come down to what the older people do for a living, or if they even still work, in the case of my grandparents. What I mean is, people like my parents use it to connect to colleagues and customers, whereas my grandparents really only use it to keep in touch with me, so the usage is much smaller.

Examiner: Are non-social media like television and newspapers still useful? `Compare & Contrast`

Candidate: TV, yes, newspapers, not so much. I would rather watch a TV programme on an actual TV rather than my mobile phone. Although I do check the news daily, I'll do this with my smartphone all through my laptop. It wouldn't even occur to me to go out and buy a newspaper. I'm not sure you even can anymore.

Lexical Resource	
Less Common Language	ludicrous, avid, occur
Collocations/Idiomatic Language	everyone and his dog, on earth, laid out, come down to
Paraphrasing	stupid→ludicrous, mobile phone→smartphone
Discourse Marker	like I said, what I mean is, so

■ A businessman you admire

> **Describe a businessman you admire.**
>
> **You should say:**
>
> who this person is
>
> how you knew this person
>
> what kinds of business this person does
>
> **and explain why you admire this person.**

One businessman that I admire is Elon Musk. Elon Musk is a South African born entrepreneur, investor, and engineer. He was born on June 28, 1971 in Pretoria, South Africa, and is best known for his innovative and visionary work in the tech industry. He is the CEO of Tesla Inc., a leading producer 有远见的 of electric vehicles and renewable energy products, as well as the founder of SpaceX, a private space exploration company.

I became familiar with him through his work in the tech industry and his numerous business ventures. 开创性的 He is known for his innovative and groundbreaking ideas, and his determination to make the world a better place through his work.

I admire him for his ability to think and push the boundaries of what is possible. He has taken on many seemingly impossible challenges, you know, like developing electric vehicles and reusable rockets, and has made tremendous progress in these fields. He is also a strong advocate for sustainable energy and reducing our dependence on fossil fuels, and his work at Tesla is helping to drive the transition to a cleaner energy future.

So to summarize, Elon Musk is a businessman that I admire because of his innovative and visionary ideas, his determination to make the world a better place, and his commitment to sustainable energy. He is an inspiration to many people worldwide, and his work continues to positively impact our planet and our future.

Examiner: What do you think is the retirement age for men and women? (*Speculate*)

Candidate: The retirement age for men and women varies from country to country and is determined by various factors such as life expectancy 寿命, labour market conditions, and social and economic policies. I believe, here in China, it's about 60 for men and 55 for women, but I'm not sure.

Examiner: What kinds of qualities do people need to run their own business? (*List*)

Candidate: Running a successful business requires a combination of different qualities and skills. For a start, you need to be adaptable and have the ability to overcome any potential problems or changes in a market. On top of that 除此之外, I think they're going to be quite confident as well as a little bit of a risk taker.

Examiner: What do you think are the key factors that contribute to the success of a business? (*Speculate*)

Candidate: There are many factors that can contribute to the success of a business, but a couple of the most important ones, I think, are having clear and well-defined 明确的 goals and high-quality products or services. If you don't know where you're going with the business and don't have a good product behind you, I don't think you'll get very far.

Examiner: If you had the opportunity to have your own business, what business would it be? (*Hypothesise*)

Candidate: Well, one area that is growing in popularity and demand is sustainable and eco-friendly products or services. If I were to start a business, I might consider creating an online store that specializes in environmentally friendly and sustainable products, such as reusable bags, bottles, and containers, organic clothing, and biodegradable 可生物讲解的 cleaning products. That way I'm helping the environment and making money.

Lexical Resource	
Less Common Language	visionary, groundbreaking, determination, sustainable, biodegradable
Collocations/Idiomatic Language	renewable energy, life expectancy, well-defined
Paraphrasing	businessman→entrepreneur, key→important
Discourse Marker	you know, to summarize, on top of that, well

---

Describe a businessman you admire.

You should say:

who this person is

how you knew this person

what kinds of business this person does

and explain why you admire this person.

The businessman I would like to describe for you today is Bill Gates, you know, the Microsoft guy. I've had a lot of respect for him for a number of years, not only in his business empire but also in his charity and foundation work.

I first heard of him, like anybody else, through the news. It was a few years ago now, and I think he had just stopped being the chairman of Microsoft. I know he's from the same era as people like Steve Jobs and Steve Wozniak, and these guys were all the pioneers of what we know as computing and Operating Systems (OS) today.

I think he originally started Microsoft back in the 1970s with DOS. Personally, I'd never heard of it, but I remember asking my father about it. For me, it's all about Windows, and I've been using that since version 7. I also use the new Microsoft 365 suite and find it much better than anything else on the market. More recently, he has been focusing on his philanthropic ideas, although having said that, I think the Bill and Melinda Foundation is now going to split into two as he has recently gotten divorced.

Mr Gates had a vision of having every PC in the world with Windows on it, and although there are other OSs you can use, like Ubuntu or something, he's basically achieved what he set out to do. He had a singular determination to succeed, and that's precisely what he did. I think that's worth admiration and respect.

Examiner: What do you think is the retirement age for men and women? (Speculate)

Candidate: I'm honestly not sure. I think for males, it will be north of 65, but for females probably be around 55. It's not something I know a lot about, and both my grandparents are still working, but they have their own business, so it might be a bit different.

Examiner: What kinds of qualities do people need to run their own business? (List)

Candidate: I think perhaps one of the most important characteristics of a business owner is dedication. If they are not absolutely 100% sure that they want to do the business, it will almost definitely fail. I think you also need a charismatic personality, you know, in order to sell your product or perhaps get people to invest in your company.

Examiner: What do you think are the key factors that contribute to the success of a business? (Speculate)

Candidate: I think some of the important elements that will make a business successful are one, that the product is new or at least innovative, and two, that there is a clear market for that product. Without these two things, I don't think a business could be successful in the slightest.

Examiner: If you had the opportunity to have your own business, what business would it be? (Hypothesise)

Candidate: If I were to start my own company, I think it would have to be something in IT. I'm studying computer science and, in particular, AI, so I would love to do something in that field. I'm just not sure exactly what. It's not something I've actually ever thought about before.

Lexical Resource	
Less Common Language	suite, philanthropic, charismatic
Collocations/Idiomatic Language	split into, set out, north of, in the slightest
Paraphrasing	men/women→male/female, key factors→important elements
Discourse Marker	you know, personally, one, two

A family member you want to work with

> **Describe a family member who you want to work with in the future.**
>
> **You should say:**
>
>   **who he/she is**
>
>   **whether you worked together before**
>
>   **what kind of work you would like to do with him/her**
>
> **and explain how you feel about this family member.**

My big sister is a talented graphic designer, and I would like to work with her in the future, so, that's whom I'll talk about today.

She is someone who has a passion for creativity and design, and has honed her skills over the years through her work and education. I have known this person for my entire life, and have always been impressed by her talent and dedication to her craft.

We haven't worked together before, but I have often talked about the possibility of collaborating on a project in the future. I would like to work with this family member on a variety of design projects, ranging from logos and branding materials to web design and advertising campaigns.

I feel very positive about her and am eager to work with her in the future. I can appreciate her talent, her creativity, and her passion for design, and I believe that our skills and expertise will complement each other well, especially my CAD and Visio skills. I am confident that we will be able to produce high-quality work together, and am excited to explore the possibilities of a future collaboration.

I need to finish my master's first, but that should only take a year, and we could probably start collaborating before then, but I think it would probably be best if we waited. Just so that I can get some more information from my courses and potentially use that in the business.

Examiner: What kinds of family businesses are common in China? (List)

Candidate: A lot of family businesses are pretty small. Typically, they might be a small shop or restaurant. Many of the little supermarkets and grocery stores around my campus are all run by families.

Examiner: Is it good to work with family members? (Opinion)

Candidate: I think it can be an excellent option. You know, it's difficult to always trust business partners, but I think if they are a family member, that problem goes away. As far as I know, my sister, who I mentioned earlier, would never screw me.
欺骗

Examiner: Why do people want to do family business? (Speculate)

Candidate: I think it's probably because of the trust issue I just mentioned but also because you can keep the money and the profit within the family. So, if it is initially run by a mother and father, the son or daughter can take it over with a minimum of fuss. I think also, it
轻轻松松地
could just be a lot of fun. After all, you're spending time with the people you love.

Examiner: What benefits are there when working for big companies? (List)

Candidate: First off, you would hope that a large company isn't going to go bust, so it's unlikely
破产
that you would ever get made redundant. A second point I think would be for a large
被解雇
company you can meet lots of different people, whereas in a smaller one or even in the family business that we've been talking about, it would only be a few.

Lexical Resource	
Less Common Language	honed, CAD, passion
Collocations/Idiomatic Language	complement each other, screw, with a minimum of fuss, go bust, made redundant
Paraphrasing	collaborating→work together
Discourse Marker	typically, you know, first off

> **Describe a family member who you want to work with in the future.**
>
> **You should say:**
>
>   **who he/she is**
>
>   **whether you worked together before**
>
>   **what kind of work you would like to do with him/her**
>
> **and explain how you feel about this family member.**

Well, the family member I want to talk about today is my brother-in-law. He's in the education business and helps Chinese students, like me, go to the UK, the USA and Canada. I think he also sends students to other countries around the world but these are the main three.

We haven't actually worked together in the past, but he has helped me apply for my master's in the UK, which is the reason I'm doing this IELTS test. Having seen first-hand the processes needed, together with the preparation and technology involved, I think it's something that I could certainly help with.

For me, I enjoy talking to people, so I'm thinking of becoming one of his salesmen in order to drum up business. I'd like to be the sales manager, but I think nepotism only goes so far, and I would need to gain some experience first. I think I'd make a good salesman because I already intimately know the service as I have used it myself.

Even though he's not my actual blood, I have always gotten on very well with him, and we seem to be on the same page with a lot of our thoughts and ideas. Not only that I think having the very small family that I have, he would be the best option, if not the only. I couldn't imagine working for my mother or father, and although I love my sister, his wife, very much, we would drive each other up the wall if we saw each other day in day out.

Examiner: What kinds of family businesses are common in China? `List`

Candidate: I think it varies quite a lot. You have quite a lot of people open up little food places that sell Jiaozi or maybe Malatang. And then you have quite a lot that manufacture clothing and the like that have small factories in the countryside. I couldn't honestly tell you with any certainty which is more common.

Examiner: Is it good to work with family members? `Opinion`

Candidate: Personally, I don't think it's a particularly bright idea. I see enough of my family on a daily basis anyway, and although I love them to bits, I really can't imagine seeing them quite literally 24/7.

Examiner: Why do people want to do family business? `Speculate`

Candidate: This isn't something I've thought about an awful lot. But I suppose, at least for some people, it could be quite a lot of fun. It's also something that could be handed down to future generations as a way of creating a legacy.

Examiner: What benefits are there when working for big companies? `List`

Candidate: I think there are quite a few advantages of working for large corporations, not least of which would be job security. A company generally becomes large because it's successful, which means that unless you are fired, you're never going to get made redundant. Beyond that, I think it allows you to learn how things are done on a large scale, whether that be production or some kind of service.

Lexical Resource	
Less Common Language	first-hand, nepotism, legacy, redundant
Collocations/Idiomatic Language	drum up, on the same page, drive each other up the wall, day in day out, to bits, handed down, not least
Paraphrasing	before→in the past, benefits→advantages, big companies→large corporations
Discourse Marker	well, personally, beyond that

Someone older that you admire

> **Describe someone who is older than you that you admire.**
>
> **You should say:**
>
>   who this person is
>
>   how you knew this person
>
>   what kinds of things you like to do together
>
> **and explain how you feel about this person.**

Well, there's an older person I admire, who I met through a volunteer organization that we both belong to called the World Wildlife Fund. You may have heard of it. It's an organisation that looks after wild animals and hopes to prevent their extinction.

He is someone who has dedicated his life to helping others and making a positive impact on the world. He is kind, compassionate, and always willing to lend a helping hand. He is also knowledgeable and experienced, and I've learned a great deal from him about the world and about life in general.

I enjoy spending time with him, and I look forward to our volunteer work together. We both like to work on projects that benefit the native animals, and I'm inspired by his dedication and commitment to making a difference. I just wonder sometimes why there can't be more people like him around the world. I'm sure if that were the case, we'd come full circle and not actually need them.

I feel a great deal of respect and admiration for him, and I am grateful for the positive impact that he's had on my life. I appreciate his wisdom, kindness, and his unwavering commitment to helping others, and I truly believe that he is a true role model for people of all ages.

I hope that when I'm older, I will be able to have the same kind of impact and influence on someone younger so that I can pay everything forward to a generation.

Examiner: Why do people sometimes admire others? (Speculate)

Candidate: People may admire others for their accomplishments and achievements, such as reaching a personal goal, winning an award, or making a significant contribution to their field of work. Or it could be because of their successes, like Steve Jobs, or their position, like a president.

Examiner: Should famous people have a responsibility to the public? (Opinion)

Candidate: Personally, I believe that famous people, whether they are celebrities, politicians, or public figures, often have a significant influence on the public. As such,〔因此〕 they may have a responsibility to the public to act in a certain way or use their influence for the greater good.

Examiner: Is it good that young children admire others? (Evaluate)

Candidate: It's natural for young children to admire others, whether they're family members, friends, or famous people. Admiration can be a positive thing for children, as it can help them develop a sense of identity, build self-esteem, and develop aspirations〔志向〕 for their future.

Examiner: What can young and old people learn from each other? (Speculate)

Candidate: Both young and old people can probably learn from each other when it comes to empathy〔同情〕 and understanding. Young people can learn from older people's life experiences and perspectives, while older people can learn from younger people's openness and willingness to challenge stereotypes and biases.

Lexical Resource	
Less Common Language	unwavering, aspirations, empathy
Collocations/Idiomatic Language	dedicated his life to, lend a helping hand, come full circle, pay everything forward
Paraphrasing	impact→influence
Discourse Marker	well, personally, as such

Describe someone who is older than you that you admire.

You should say:

who this person is

how you knew this person

what kinds of things you like to do together

and explain how you feel about this person.

I know the normal answer for this kind of question would be someone who is famous, but actually the person I most admire is my mother.

The thing I most admire about what she does and has done is that however much work she has to do, she never complains. When she had me, and then my little sister, she kept working as a part-time nurse but also looked after us. At the time, I remember thinking this is just what mums did and didn't really take any notice of it. Now, however, I'm beginning to realise that in a lot of ways it's more difficult raising children than working in an office or a hospital in her case, and she did both! Not only has she got to be available every hour of every day for us children, she also managed to find time to cook and clean and occasionally meet with her friends.

As for how long I've admired her, to be honest, it is only a recent thing. Now that I am studying at university away from home and getting a little older, I am beginning to see exactly how much she did. Whereas I occasionally helped with the cooking and cleaning at home, now, I have to do it all myself, and when you start adding the hours I have to study for my course, I don't have time for anything else.

I think the other reason I truly admire her more than other people is because I know her. I'm not really one of these people that goes weak at the knees when I see an actor or actress, and I realise that what I see on TV isn't the real person. So, understanding what she has done, does, and will do for me and my family, this is why I admire her the most.

Examiner: Why do people sometimes admire others? (Speculate)

Candidate: I think it's probably because the other people can do something that you can't, especially if it's something difficult, and they do it at a very high level. For example, athletes. It's well known that a lot of Olympic and world-class athletes have a job too. This means they work all day and train all night in order to become particularly skillful or good at something. Most other people would admire this dedication, not necessarily because they couldn't do it themselves; they are just too lazy.

Examiner: Should famous people have a responsibility to the public? (Opinion)

Candidate: Yes, I think they should. A lot of children and even some adults will do things or even buy things, if a famous person says so. Popstars, for example, have a huge influence over the young, and if they behave badly, then the children will think that's okay, which it's not, by the way!

Examiner: Is it good that young children admire others? (Evaluate)

Candidate: To a degree, I suppose. A lot of children need a role model in their life and these days with parents having to work more and more, they look to famous people on TV and in movies. But I think that children need to learn that too much admiration for others isn't necessarily a good thing, you know, they should also try and admire themselves for what they have done.

Examiner: What can young and old people learn from each other? (Speculate)

Candidate: Young and old people can learn a lot from each other, as they bring different experiences, perspectives, and knowledge to the table. Older people have a wealth of life experience, which can provide valuable insights and lessons for younger people, whereas younger people are often more familiar with trends, and can bring fresh ideas and viewpoints not to mention help with new technologies.

Lexical Resource	
Less Common Language	occasionally, dedication, perspectives, insights
Collocations/Idiomatic Language	managed to, goes weak at the knees, world-class, a wealth of, fresh ideas
Paraphrasing	skillful→good, perspectives→viewpoints
Discourse Marker	at the time, to be honest, for example, to a degree

■ An interesting animal

Part 2　　Answer 1（★★★★）　　　　　　　　　　　　　　🎧 158

Describe an interesting animal.

You should say:

　　what it looks like

　　when you saw/knew it for the first time

　　where it lives

and explain why it is interesting.

Today I'm going to describe an animal that I find particularly fascinating, albeit (尽管) a little unusual, and that is the octopus.

An octopus has a distinctive appearance, with a soft and flexible body, eight long arms that are covered in suction cups, and two large eyes that can move independently from each other. They come in a variety of colours and patterns, and are capable of changing their appearance to blend in (协调) with their surroundings, making them skilled at hiding from predators.

I first learned about octopuses when I was a child and was absolutely enthralled (迷住) by their unusual appearance and behaviours. They can be found in oceans all over the world, and are most commonly found in tropical and temperate waters. I saw my first live one at the Sydney Aquarium a few years ago and loved it. When I then went scuba diving (戴水肺潜水) at the Great Barrier Reef, I managed to play with one in its natural habitat.

What makes the octopus particularly interesting is its incredible intelligence and problem-solving abilities. Octopuses have been observed opening jars to get to food, using tools, and escaping from tight spaces, which is remarkable for an animal with no bones and a relatively simple nervous system. They are also able to learn from experience, remember past events, and communicate with other octopuses. I think they're a particularly misunderstood and underrepresented (未受到足够关注) creature that people should learn more about. Hopefully, then, other people will also love them as I do, or at least understand them better.

Examiner: How do you like taking care of animals? (Evaluate)

Candidate: I've never taken care of any animals as I never had a pet, but I can tell you that taking care of animals can be a rewarding and fulfilling experience for many people. It can bring a sense of companionship, joy, and purpose to their lives. It's just something I've missed out on to date.

Examiner: Do you think it is safe for animals to live in the cities? (Evaluate)

Candidate: Well, I suppose it would really depend on the animal. If it's something like a dog or a cat that is very used to city life, I don't see a problem. However, if it's something more like a wild animal like a monkey, I'm not sure it could cope with it. I think it would have difficulty with noise, cars and the like.

Examiner: What problems will keeping pets bring? (List)

Candidate: I think the biggest challenge when it comes to looking after a pet is time. I don't think it's particularly fair to get yourself a dog and then go out to work 12 hours a day, leave them locked up in a room where they can't interact with anyone or anything. There're probably other issues, but I can't think of any right now.

Examiner: How are pets now different from those in the past? (Compare & Contrast)

Candidate: I think they've become a little bit more exotic. Previously people just owned a dog or a cat or maybe a fish. These days people own spiders, snakes, iguanas and all sorts. I'm not sure it's a positive development.

Lexical Resource	
Less Common Language	distinctive, enthralled, tropical, temperate, underrepresented, exotic
Collocations/Idiomatic Language	blend in with, scuba diving, a sense of companionship, missed out on
Paraphrasing	interesting→fascinating/enthralled, now→these days, in the past→previously
Discourse Marker	albeit, well, however

> **Describe an interesting animal.**
> **You should say:**
>> **what it looks like**
>> **when you saw/knew it for the first time**
>> **where it lives**
> **and explain why it is interesting.**

Well, when it comes to talking about an interesting animal, I would have to say the platypus because
although it's not my favourite animal, it is certainly one of the ones that makes me the most
fascinated.

From memory, it's less than a foot long and has a beak like a duck, a tail like a beaver, and fur like a
cat. Perhaps now you understand why I find it so fascinating.

I first saw it on a trip to Sydney in Australia a few years ago. I was looking around the city and decided
to go to the aquarium to have a look around. I don't know if you've ever been, but it's a marvellous
place with all sorts of sea life there. I came around to the platypus exhibit and, to be honest, was
very surprised. I couldn't believe how small the platypi were. I'd seen them on TV during wildlife
documentaries where I had the impression they were about the same size as a cat, but they're not;
they're tiny. I was gobsmacked.

As part of the marsupial family of animals, they are native to Australia, and I don't know if that fact in
itself has anything to do with its size. I don't think so, but you never know. Since that trip, I've never
seen another animal that even remotely compares to it because, as I said, it seems to me like a real
mix of different animals.

I'm hoping to go back to Australia soon and see them again, and maybe next time, I'll be able to see
them in their natural habitat rather than a tank in an aquarium.

Examiner:　How do you like taking care of animals? (Evaluate)

Candidate:　I like the idea of it; I'm just not particularly good at it. I've had a few animals over the years, and unfortunately, they all died. The terrapin I had lasted about a month. I've had countless fish die on me; even the rabbit only lasted a year. So I think I've learned my lesson now and will leave it to other people.

Examiner:　Do you think it is safe for animals to live in the cities? (Evaluate)

Candidate:　On the whole, no. In urban areas, there are just too many dangers the animals wouldn't necessarily understand that can kill them. Cars, for a start. Actually, that's what happened to my little dog. We had her for a few years and then moved from the outskirts of Beijing into the city centre. For her, she didn't really understand what all these big metal boxes were and eventually was hit by one. So, no, not a good idea.

Examiner:　What problems will keeping pets bring? (List)

Candidate:　I think there are lots of problems in looking after pets. A big one is money as you need to feed them and potentially give them a separate living area, like a fish tank or something that then needs to be maintained and beyond that medical bills. It's important that you keep up with any jabs or injections that are needed, typically for cats and dogs, as well, as if they simply get sick and need to take them to the vet.

Examiner:　How are pets now different from those in the past? (Compare & Contrast)

Candidate:　I don't think they are, really. In my experience, my friends and I all had pet fish or cats, dogs, rabbits, even a turtle or two and most of them still do. It might not be the exact same fish or rabbit, but the actual animal is the same.

Lexical Resource	
Less Common Language	aquarium, marsupial, jabs, injections, vet
Collocations/Idiomatic Language	looking around, gobsmacked
Paraphrasing	describe→talk about, interesting→fascinated, safe→danger
Discourse Marker	well, to be honest, on the whole, actually

Chapter 3 Things
物品类

■ A gift you'd like to buy

> **Describe a gift you would like to buy for your friend.**
>
> **You should say:**
>
> > **what gift you'd like to buy**
> >
> > **who you'd like to give it to**
> >
> > **why you'd like to buy a gift for him/her**
>
> **and explain why you'd choose that gift.**

I want to buy a present for my close friend, who loves photography and enjoys travelling. I've known her for years, and I wanted to get her something special for her 18th birthday. The 18th birthday is an important one here in China as it marks the day that you move from being a child into becoming an adult. I'm not sure if it's the same in other countries, but I have a feeling it might be.

I want to buy her a high-quality camera lens, specifically a wide-angle lens, that will allow my friend to capture stunning landscapes and wide vistas. I know that she has been using their current lens for a while, and I think she would appreciate an upgrade to her photography equipment.

I choose this gift because I want to show her how much I care about her interests and passions. I know that she is very passionate about photography and enjoys capturing her travels, and I believe that a high-quality lens will help her take her photography to the next level.

Additionally, I think that this gift will be practical and useful for her, as she will be able to use it for years to come. I am confident that it will bring her a lot of joy and satisfaction, and I am excited to see the beautiful photos that she will be able to capture with this lens.

It's not often that I can know exactly what to buy someone, and this lens is a little expensive, but in this case, I'm fairly sure I've nailed it, and I can't wait to see the look on her face.

Examiner: When do people normally send gifts to others? ⌐Speculate⌐

Candidate: I suppose the most obvious answer to this would be birthdays, like my friend's 18th. Besides that, I can think of a few, like wedding anniversaries, Chinese New Year, Christmas and the like.

Examiner: Do people give gifts or red packets at traditional festivals? ⌐Speculate⌐

Candidate: Yes, they do, but not all of them. The red pocket is traditionally given during Chinese New Year rather than any other holiday. It is known, though, that on very special occasions, exceptions can be made.

Examiner: Is it hard to choose a gift? ⌐Opinion⌐

Candidate: In my opinion, yes. At least for me. But I suppose it would also depend on the person that you're buying for. The lens for my friend is just such an obvious gift for her that it's fairly simple. Whenever I'm buying gifts for my parents, on the other hand, I find it incredibly difficult. Even though I know them very well, it's difficult to think of things to get them because they already have everything.

Examiner: Will people feel happy when receiving an expensive gift? ⌐Speculate⌐

Candidate: It's possible. I've never really thought about how expensive the gift is because that's not particularly important to me. I've always considered it more from the point of who's giving it to me, and have they actually thought about the gift. A 体贴的 considerate gift is of much more value to me than an expensive one.

Lexical Resource	
Less Common Language	capture, stunning, vistas, exceptions, considerate
Collocations/Idiomatic Language	wide-angle, nailed it
Paraphrasing	gift→present, red packets→red pocket, hard→difficult
Discourse Marker	additionally, though, in my opinion, on the other hand

Describe a gift you would like to buy for your friend.

You should say:

    what gift you'd like to buy

    who you'd like to give it to

    why you'd like to buy a gift for him/her

and explain why you'd choose that gift.

The present that I'd like to buy my best friend is a PS5. I'm not sure if you're familiar with what that is, but it's basically a games console. There have been a few of them before, four in fact, and this is the latest version brought out by Sony last year.

If I'm going to be completely honest, it's actually something we are buying for each other. What I mean is we're each paying half of the cost of the machine because it's actually quite expensive and neither of us can afford one on our own. The last time I looked, it was about 7,000 RMB, and that was just for the unit that include the disc drive. We need to get a second controller and the variety of games to go with it, which adds another 2,000 or 3,000 RMB to the price. In other words, 'Ouch!'

We've been talking about this for a little while now and have finally managed to save up enough money. It's something that we will both use a lot as we both enjoy gaming. We both want to start playing the new God of War game called Ragnarok; it's supposed to be superb and the next in the existing series.

So, as for the final suggested section, the why, it's probably because of that game. And also the fact that PS4 games now are just outdated. The quality and resolution of these next-generation games is just supposed to be beyond amazing. I can't wait!

Examiner: When do people normally send gifts to others? Speculate

Candidate: Obviously, birthdays are a good place to start, but also I think you should give gifts when you visit their home, especially if it's been a while. Another obvious one, especially for China, is the red pockets at the New Year.

Examiner: Do people give gifts or red packets at traditional festivals? Speculate

Candidate: Yes. My folks still give me red pockets each year at the Spring Festival, and I buy them moon cakes at the Mid-Autumn Festival. I don't think gifts are necessary for EVERY festival, but there are a few.

Examiner: Is it hard to choose a gift? Opinion

Candidate: I don't find it all that difficult to find presents for people, but then I only ever buy presents for people I know. It makes it simpler because I know the kinds of things they like and also the things that they don't have and might want.

Examiner: Will people feel happy when receiving an expensive gift? Speculate

Candidate: Some people do, but to be honest, I'm not one of them. Well, that's not entirely true. There's a small part of me that likes it, I just don't think it's the be-all and end-all. I've had very cheap presents that meant a lot to me, partly because it was so obviously thought out and I can say the same about expensive ones.

Lexical Resource	
Less Common Language	unit, resolution
Collocations/Idiomatic Language	a games console, be-all and end-all
Paraphrasing	buying for each other→each paying half, superb→amazing, hard→difficult
Discourse Marker	so, obviously, to be honest, well

■ An item on which you spent more than you expected

Part 2　　*Answer 1*（★★★★）　　　　　　　　　　　6ð 166

> **Describe an item on which you spent more than expected.**
>
> **You should say:**
>
> 　　**what it is**
>
> 　　**how much you spent on it**
>
> 　　**why you bought it**
>
> **and explain why you think you spent more than expected.**

I recently bought a <u>high-end</u> gaming computer. I was initially looking for a <u>budget-friendly</u> option, but after researching online and offline and visiting different stores, I ended up spending much more than expected.

The computer I bought is a near <u>top-of-the-line</u> model, with a fast CPU, a powerful graphics card, and plenty of storage. It cost me around 25,000 RMB, which was significantly more than the 10,000 RMB budget I had in mind.

I bought the computer because I'm an <u>avid</u> gamer, and I wanted a machine that could handle the latest games without any lag or stuttering. It took me a while to find all the different components, and it was suggested that I start with the graphics card, which is what I did. That was nearly 5,000 RMB on its own. Then it was just a case of getting the <u>motherboard</u>, CPU, memory and, of course, the case. Oh, and the hard drives, of course. I managed to get three <u>SSDs</u>, and then I put them into a RAID <u>configuration</u>, just in case there're any problems with them in the future.

After I bought it, I realized that I had spent a lot more money than I had initially intended. Despite this, I don't regret buying it because I believe that it was worth the extra money. <u>With any luck</u>, I won't have to upgrade anything for a few years to come. At least, I certainly hope not. But with the continuing expansion and development of all things, you never know.

Examiner: Do you often spend more than you expected? (*Evaluate*)

Candidate: Well, that's a little difficult to answer. It's because when I buy things that are expensive, I'll do some research on prices with different vendors 【卖家】 and figure out how much I need to spend, and therefore manage my expectations. On things that are cheap, I don't really mind how much I spend, so again, the problem doesn't exist.

Examiner: What do you think young people spend most of their money on? (*Speculate*)

Candidate: Games. Definitely games. Or I should probably say gaming. Most of my friends spend a bucket load of 【大量】 money buying equipment, or chests that will advance them in the game. They're generally quite small purchases, but the totals mount up very quickly.

Examiner: Do you think it is important to save money? (*Opinion*)

Candidate: Yes, I do. Most certainly. In the West, there's a spending mentality 【心态】, but here in China, it's much more about saving. It's essential for us that we've got some money in the bank for a rainy day 【穷困时期】 and aren't used to loading up credit cards for things that we don't really need.

Examiner: Do people buy things they don't need? (*Speculate*)

Candidate: I can't really speak for everyone else, but I don't. Not as a rule, anyway. There's very few things that I've bought that I don't use or admire on a regular basis. The PS5 for example, can I live without it? Yes. But would it bring immense 【巨大的】 joy to me and my friend? Oh, yes! So, is it needed? In my view, yes. Others may disagree, but to me it's important.

Lexical Resource	
Less Common Language	avid, motherboard, components, configuration, vendors, mentality, immense
Collocations/Idiomatic Language	budget-friendly, with any luck, a bucket load of, a rainy day, loading up
Paraphrasing	high-end→near top-of-the-line, important→essential
Discourse Marker	oh, well

Describe an item on which you spent more than expected.

You should say:

> **what it is**
>
> **how much you spent on it**
>
> **why you bought it**

and explain why you think you spent more than expected.

Well, what I'm going to describe for you today isn't when I bought one particular item, more like a group of items. I'm talking about my regular weekly trip to the supermarket.

It was the last time I went food shopping at the supermarket in my hometown. I didn't buy anything notably different from what I would buy normally. Well, that's what I thought anyway. I wanted some salmon and some crisps and a little bit of booze, but that was really the only item that was different to what I would typically buy in Beijing.

When I got to the checkout, I had a reasonably full trolley, so I knew it was going to be a little bit more than my typical weekly shop, but I was going to be in for a bit of a shock. 2,000 RMB! I nearly fell over. My regular shop is about 500 to 600 RMB, so 2,000 RMB is a hell of a jump. I was at a loss at that time to figure out what could add up to 1,500 RMB beyond what I would typically spend. I mean, the cart was reasonably full, but it wasn't busting at the seams.

It turned out that the salmon on its own was nearly 200 RMB, the bottle of booze I bought was 150 RMB, and all the other little extras turned out to be equally expensive. It was the spring holiday, so I thought, 'what the heck' and didn't worry about it too much, but needless to say, I spent a lot less on the next trip.

Examiner: Do you often spend more than you expected? ⟨Evaluate⟩

Candidate: I wouldn't say 'often', but it does happen sometimes, probably more than I'd like to admit. I try and figure out [搞清楚] how much things are before I buy them. It's just that occasionally I get it wrong.

Examiner: What do you think young people spend most of their money on? ⟨Speculate⟩

Candidate: That would depend on your definition of young. But I suppose with people in their 20s, it's going to go mostly on living costs. Food, travel, maybe a mortgage [抵押贷款]. I'm in my early 20s, and the thing I spend most of my money on is books and going out, but I have a feeling that's going to change soon, certainly if my girlfriend and I are going to get married.

Examiner: Do you think it is important to save money? ⟨Opinion⟩

Candidate: Absolutely. It's not just important, it's essential for our lives. If we weren't to have any savings, how could we pay for hospital bills in an emergency? My parents have drilled into me [向我灌输] that saving is probably one of the most important things someone can do during their life, and I've been saving all my red pockets for as long as I can remember.

Examiner: Do people buy things they don't need? ⟨Speculate⟩

Candidate: Oh yes, definitely. All the time. And I must admit I'm just as guilty as everyone else. But there's always the argument of do I really need that chocolate bar, or computer game, or extra beer. I suppose it depends on where you put the line between desire, want and need. For me, it gets a bit blurry [模糊的] sometimes.

Lexical Resource	
Less Common Language	booze, definition, mortgage, blurry
Collocations/Idiomatic Language	at a loss, busting at the seams, figure out, drilled into me
Paraphrasing	normally→typically, cart→trolley, young people→people in their 20s, important→essential
Discourse Marker	well, I mean, absolutely, oh yes, definitely

A toy you liked in your childhood

Describe a toy you liked in your childhood.

You should say:

    what kind of toy it was

    when you received it

    how you played it

and explain how you felt about it.

Probably my most loved toy when I was a kid was called Optimus Prime. He was the leader of the 擎天柱
变形金刚
transformer robots. You may have seen the movies that came out a few years ago.

I got it when I was about five or six years old, and it quickly became one of my favourites because it wasn't just one present, it was two. I could change the robot into a truck and play with the truck in a different way than the robot.

霸天虎
I would spend hours and hours playing with my little group of Deceptions and Transformers and 银河系
would have gigantic battles for the Galaxy in my bedroom. Quite often, my friends would come over, and we'd play together because they had different characters than I did. I can't remember exactly how many times I saved the earth.

I loved everything about Transformers at the time and also had the lunch box and the backpack, but my most cherished possession was that blue and red toy robot. I often took it with me to school and would occasionally get in trouble with the teachers for playing with it too much, but they would sometimes let me sit it on the desk in front of me.

I have very fond memories of it, and actually I'm sure it's still in my cupboard somewhere, although I haven't touched it for a while. I think I'd be a little bit embarrassed if I played with it again now, but it 怀旧之情   美好的旧时光
does bring up quite a lot of nostalgia for the good old days.

Examiner: Do you think parents should buy more toys for their kids or spend more time with them? (Opinion)

Candidate: Personally, I think more toys. These days, both parents need to work and sometimes until quite late. It can be difficult for the grandparents to keep up with small children and therefore if the children can spend time by themselves playing with their toys, I think it's beneficial for everyone.

Examiner: What kinds of toys are popular in your country? (List)

Candidate: I would venture〔小心地说〕to suggest the same toys as elsewhere in the world. Boys like cars and balls, and girls like dolls and toy houses. When they grow up into teenagers, the boys like computer games, as do some of the girls, to be honest, but girls are more likely to get into hobbies like shopping and art.

Examiner: How important are toys for a child's physical and mental development? (Evaluate)

Candidate: Crucial. I think that from a very young age, they need different stimuli. This may be touch and dexterity〔灵巧〕, like putting a shaped peg in a hole, or texture, like a cube with varying types of material on it. An infant needs all types of stimulation.

Examiner: Do you think that electronic toys can have a negative effect on children? (Opinion)

Candidate: If used in excess〔过度〕, yes. Just like anything, if you do it too much, it slips over from the good into the bad. But I don't think they're as bad as everyone thinks. For example, there's no scientific evidence that watching TV ACTUALLY is detrimental to〔有害的〕a person's eyes. It's just that it has been said for generations and is now thought to be true.

Lexical Resource	
Less Common Language	nostalgia, venture, dexterity
Collocations/Idiomatic Language	good old days, in excess, detrimental to
Paraphrasing	liked→loved, occasionally→sometimes, important→crucial
Discourse Marker	personally, to be honest

Describe a toy you liked in your childhood.

You should say:

    what kind of toy it was

    when you received it

    how you played it

and explain how you felt about it.

The toy I'd like to describe is a small plastic electronic piano. I remember that it was black, but the keys were white. It was only about a metre in length, so it wasn't full-size. I don't think my little eleven-year-old fingers could've handled that.

It was my mother who bought it for me. We were out shopping one day, and we walked past a music store. I asked if we could go in. We did, and had a look around. That's when I saw it and just wanted it straight away. It wasn't very expensive but, at the time, she said no, so we left. I was feeling very upset. The following day, however, when I got home from school, there was a present on my bed ... it was the piano I'd seen in the shop. I was over the moon, opened it straight away and began playing with it.

I played with it every day whenever I had free time after, and even before, school. I know I probably annoyed my parents, and even maybe my neighbours, with the constant sound of a child's attempt at playing such an instrument, but I didn't care. To me, it made a very interesting sound, and I was curious about how to develop this into my own music. I was always quite a creative little girl.

The main reason it was so important to me was, firstly, that it was a gift from my mother, and, secondly, maybe more importantly, it inspired me to learn more about music. I now not only play the piano but sing too. My music is a very important part of my character and my life, and I don't know what I'd do without it. It was all because of that little black piano from 10 years ago.

Examiner: Do you think parents should buy more toys for their kids or spend more time with them? (Opinion)

Candidate: For me, I think it's more important for parents to spend time with their offspring. Giving their children a mobile phone to play with or planting them in front of the TV is just laziness and, in my mind, doesn't count as raising their children. I can appreciate that it might not always be easy, but there's no substitute for a mother's love or a father's, for that matter.

Examiner: What kinds of toys are popular in your country? (List)

Candidate: That's a good question. When I was younger, I used to play with dolls. I particularly liked Barbie, although I didn't like Ken very much. I suppose this is a bit of a stereotype because I'm a girl, but a lot of my friends did the same. Another type of toy that I think is popular is Lego, you know, the building blocks. I never really played with it that much myself, but I can see the attraction for boys. I suppose these days though, most people want to play on their phones or PlayStation.

Examiner: How important are toys for a child's physical and mental development? (Evaluate)

Candidate: I think that they're very important for this. Like I mentioned earlier, playing with Lego not only increases a child's hand-eye co-ordination but also their spatial awareness. This can be invaluable to them while they're growing up and also in their adult years. I believe that teaching a child these things as early as possible is a good idea.

Examiner: Do you think that electronic toys can have a negative effect on children? (Opinion)

Candidate: Maybe. I suppose it depends on how they use it. Some of the games you can get on computers, and even phones, these days can be very violent and I don't think that's suitable for young children or even some teenagers. There are some games, however, that can be very intellectually challenging. For example, they might have puzzles in them that can help develop intelligence. So, I would say that some electronic devices can have a positive effect on kids.

Lexical Resource	
Less Common Language	planting, appreciate, substitute, PlayStation, intellectually
Collocations/Idiomatic Language	full-size, over the moon, building blocks, hand-eye co-ordination, spatial awareness
Paraphrasing	kids→offspring/children
Discourse Marker	for me, for that matter, you know, maybe

Something that was broken in your home

> **Describe something that was broken in your home.**
> **You should say:**
> 　　**what the equipment was**
> 　　**what the problem was**
> 　　**what you did after it was broken**
> **and explain how you felt about it.**

I'll describe for you a time when my TV was broken. My TV is an integral *(必需的)* part of my entertainment setup, and I use it regularly to watch movies, TV shows, and play video games. That day, I noticed that there was a problem with the TV – the picture was flickering *(闪烁)*, and the sound was distorted *(失真)*, so I couldn't settle down *(开始专心于)* into my regular gaming session.

I tried to troubleshoot *(检修)* the issue by checking the connections and checking the settings, but nothing seemed to work. I was so frustrated and disappointed that my TV was no longer working properly, especially as I wanted to play my favourite game at the time.

I decided to take the TV to a repair shop to have it fixed and was a little worried about the cost and how long it would take to get the TV back to its original condition. However, I felt that it was important to get the TV fixed as soon as possible, so I took it down to a little place I know that fixes things like this.

After a couple days, the TV was fixed, and I was able to use it again. Talk about relieved that I could use it again. I plugged in my PS4 almost immediately, booted up *(启动)* the system and played the Witcher 3 nearly all night. It was great to get my gaming fixed!

I've since bought a new one that has better sound and higher resolution and is a lot bigger. 55 inches, to be precise, so it's a lot more lifelike *(逼真的)*, and I can immerse myself in *(专心于)* my games even more than previously.

Examiner: Are you good at handling problems on your own? (Evaluate)

Candidate: For the most part, yes. I'm not one of these people that falls apart at the drop of a hat [崩溃] [立即]. I try and look at the problem logically and figure out what's wrong, and if I can fix it myself, I will. If I can't because I don't have the parts or tools, like my TV, I'll find someone to fix it for me.

Examiner: What are the common home appliances that people use these days? (List)

Candidate: Some of the typical equipment that is found in a home is a washing machine, a hob of some kind, probably gas, a TV and a WiFi router [路由器]. Beyond that, I think it gets specific to the type of home and who's living there. For my family, you can add a dishwasher and a sterilisation unit [消毒装置], which aren't going to be in every home.

Examiner: When an electronic item of yours does not work, would you repair it or buy a new one? (Speculate)

Candidate: Well, it would depend on what the electronic item was. Something like a smartphone or a laptop, I'd almost certainly get it repaired. The remote for the TV, I'd probably buy a new one.

Examiner: What can people do to protect their equipment from technical problems? (Speculate)

Candidate: Not plug them in, or use them. Seriously though, I think maintenance would be very high on the list of solutions. I would think that's why things like cars will last much longer if you service them regularly. I assume the same would apply to washing machines.

Lexical Resource	
Less Common Language	integral, flickering, distorted, troubleshoot, lifelike
Collocations/Idiomatic Language	settle down, booted up, immerse myself in, falls apart, at the drop of a hat, a sterilisation unit
Paraphrasing	common→typical, appliances→equipment
Discourse Marker	for the most part, beyond that, well, seriously though

> **Describe something that was broken in your home.**
>
> **You should say:**
>
> 　　**what the equipment was**
>
> 　　**what the problem was**
>
> 　　**what you did after it was broken**
>
> **and explain how you felt about it.**

It's interesting that you mention a TV because that's what I want to talk about. Initially, I thought it was some of the accessories [配件] that I'd bought to go with it, you know, surround sound speakers and the like. I thought maybe they weren't compatible [兼容的] because they were different brands, but it turned out to be the sound quality of the TV itself. Well, lack thereof. I thought I could have a go at [试一试] fixing it myself, so I put my repairman cap on and got my toolkit [工具箱].

After fiddling about with [摆弄] it on my own for about 2 hours, I finally gave up and called the real repair man. When I bought the TV a year ago, I also purchased an extended warranty [延长保修] to go with it. I'm happy I did, as when all this happened last month, the original manufacturer's warranty had just expired [过期]. He arrived the following morning and started to have a look at it. After all of about 2 minutes, it was fixed. It was as if he had magic hands or something. Two hours, I was playing around with it, and he came in and 'Abracadabra', it's fixed.

I was really happy that he'd fixed it, but also really annoyed at my own stupidity. There was a button on the setting in the TV's sound settings that needed to be active, which I hadn't turned on. That and some of the speaker wire wasn't connected properly. So, the magician repairman left after I signed his chitty [收据] and I promptly sat on the sofa like a couch potato for the next few hours catching up on [补上] some of my favourite TV series. Overall, a good weekend.

Examiner: Are you good at handling problems on your own? (Evaluate)

Candidate: Oh yes, definitely. Fixing problems, now that's a different matter. Seriously though, I do quite like a challenge, so when I come up against something that's new or difficult, I try and figure it out on my own first before asking for help. I firmly believe that you need to be able to stand on your own two feet and that if you crumble at the sight of something hard, you need to improve yourself.

Examiner: What are the common home appliances that people use these days? (List)

Candidate: Common ones? Well, you have the 'white' goods like the washing machine and the fridge, and then you have the 'brown' goods like the TV and computer. There are many specialist cooking appliances that some people have, like a blender or juice maker, but I wouldn't know how common they are in all households.

Examiner: When an electronic item of yours does not work, would you repair it or buy a new one? (Speculate)

Candidate: Nowadays, it really depends on how expensive it was to begin with, and how easy or cheap it would be to repair. For instance, the screen on my smartphone. I've already fixed it once because it cracked when I dropped it last year, and it's expensive to replace. My portable fan, however, that keeps me cool in the summer was only 20 RMB, so if that were to break, I'd probably just buy a new one. It wouldn't be worth the effort of trying to repair it.

Examiner: What can people do to protect their equipment from technical problems? (Speculate)

Candidate: As far as I'm concerned, not an awful lot. It will either work or not, and there's nothing in between. Apparently, there are things you can do to extend a battery's life, but I've never come across them myself. I've also heard of surge protectors for computers, but I'm not sure if that's already built into a PC or if it's an extra piece of equipment that you buy as an optional extra.

Lexical Resource	
Less Common Language	accessories, compatible, toolkit, expired, crumble, cracked
Collocations/Idiomatic Language	have a go at, fiddling about with, extended warranty, catching up on, stand on your own two feet, come across
Paraphrasing	item→equipment, handling problems→fixing problems
Discourse Marker	you know, well, definitely, nowadays, apparently

■ The last book you read

> **Describe the last book you read.**
>
> **You should say:**
>
>   **what type/kind of book it was**
>
>   **what it was about**
>
>   **where you read it**
>
> **and explain how you felt about the book.**

The last book I read was *The Alchemist* 〔《牧羊少年奇幻之旅》〕 by Paulo Coelho. This book is a novel that follows the journey of a shepherd boy named Santiago who embarks 〔开启〕 on a journey to fulfil his personal legend and find a treasure he dreams about. It's not my normal style of book, I prefer Sci-Fi, but a friend said that I should give it a go, so I did.

I read this book on my Kindle while I was travelling on a long flight the last time I went to the UK. It's about 11 hours as a direct flight to get there, so I had loads of time. I found the book to be a captivating 〔迷人的〕 and uplifting 〔振奋人心的〕 story that explores themes such as following your dreams, trusting the universe, and finding happiness. They're all things that we all want in life, but unfortunately, not all of us can find it. I'm still waiting myself, but then I've still got quite a lot of time.

The writing style of Paulo Coelho was thoroughly engaging and captivating, and the story was well-paced 〔节奏适中〕. I found the characters were endearing 〔迷人的〕 and relatable, and the journey of Santiago was both exciting and introspective 〔自省的〕. I felt genuinely inspired by the message of this book, which has encouraged me to pursue my own dreams and to trust the journey of life wherever that may take me.

Overall, I enjoyed reading *The Alchemist* and found it to be a well-written and thought-provoking 〔引人深思的〕 book. The book left a positive impact on me, and I would definitely recommend it to others who enjoy philosophical fiction.

Examiner:　Do you prefer paper books or E-books? (Compare & Contrast)

Candidate:　For me, it's E-books all the way. Previously, yes, I enjoyed the feel of the pages between my fingers, but these days, I can flick between pages most conveniently and download almost any book I can think of. So, yes, give me tech.

Examiner:　What kinds of books do children read? (List)

Candidate:　Children's books?! It kind of depends on the age group you're looking at. Infant, junior etc. It will vary depending on the kid, level of education, and age. So, anything from *Mr. Men* to *Harry Potter*.

Examiner:　In your country, who should teach children to read, schools or parents? (Opinion)

Candidate:　Both. I think that parents will teach their children how to read numbers and letters etc., before the children even go to school. Beyond that, the teachers will take over. But although teachers will help the children read, it's the parents that will encourage the homework and read to them in bed.

Examiner:　Do you think printed books will continue to exist? (Hypothesise)

Candidate:　I think they'll probably be around for the next few years, yes. I can't image them 完全消失 dropping off the face of the earth altogether, but I do believe that their days are somewhat numbered. Like I was saying earlier, I've moved over to E-Books now and have most of my friends. It's really only the older generation now that keeps the paper versions.

Lexical Resource	
Less Common Language	novel, captivating, uplifting, endearing, introspective, flick
Collocations/Idiomatic Language	embarks on, well-paced, thought-provoking, moved over, dropping off the face of the earth
Paraphrasing	printed→paper, children→kid
Discourse Marker	overall, for me, like I was saying earlier

Describe the last book you read.

You should say:

　　what type/kind of book it was

　　what it was about

　　where you read it

and explain how you felt about the book.

The last novel I read was a comedy aimed at late teens or maybe young adults. He was actually a British author. You might have heard of him, Terry Pratchett. Anyway, I love his stories and his ability to play with words and ideas. It's such a shame he's passed on now.

His first book of the *Discworld* series, *The Colour of Magic*, is about a foreigner coming to Ankh Morpork and hooking up with a wizard called Rincewind and then having adventures together. Quite often, the most stimulating parts of the book are where there's a play on words. The concept of 'Insurance' was new to the pub landlord in Ankh Morpok, and he kept misunderstanding and wondered why there were 'Ants' in the 'Sewer' – 'in-sewer-ants'. He only fully understood when his bar burnt down and was given a lot of money. He never did find out what happened to the ants.

Anyway, I mostly read these kinds of things in bed before I go to sleep. Being a student, I don't often have time during the day to read for pleasure. It's mostly classes, textbooks and the odd paper or two, so, for me, I like curling up under the covers with a good book that I can then allow my subconscious to continue with, in my dreams.

As for my feeling about the book, well, I loved it. I really like the whole series, even if it is a little tricky as a non-native English speaker at times. Personally, that's one of the things I like about it. The challenge to improve my English and understand the humour more accurately.

Examiner: Do you prefer paper books or E-books? (Compare & Contrast)

Candidate: I'm a real paper book fan. For me, the smell and feel of a new book is all part of the experience. I can understand the appeal of E-Books. They are easy, and you can download almost any text you can possibly think of, but it's just not the same, and I'm already ⌐厌倦 sick of staring at my smartphone all day.

Examiner: What kinds of books do children read? (List)

Candidate: Picture books mostly. I can't imagine them reading a good crime novel. I suppose it comes down to age and how old these children are, but you can't ⌐出错 go wrong with a ⌐立体的 pop-up picture book for the really young ones. The ⌐插图 illustrations are generally very colourful and made from quite ⌐结实耐用的 robust paper and plastic. They have to be, I suppose, or they'd get ⌐被撕成碎片 ripped to shreds in no time. For older kids, just starting school maybe, they're going to have colouring books and those that teach you how to do something.

Examiner: In your country, who should teach children to read, schools or parents? (Opinion)

Candidate: In my mind, it needs to be a ⌐团队努力 team effort. Parents are obviously going to start the process before the children even get to school, but once they've started, teachers can refine that process. Parents can then help with some reading practice at home and even at bedtime, reading together before everyone goes to sleep.

Examiner: Do you think printed books will continue to exist? (Hypothesise)

Candidate: For the time being, yes, I do, but I do think their days are numbered. I think we are all going to slowly ⌐转移 migrate over to electronic books eventually. Yeah, it's just a matter of when. Older people and those that aren't very good with technology will be the last to go, but when they're all gone and the new millennials are grandparents, I think printed material will ⌐销声匿迹 go the way of the dodo.

Lexical Resource	
Less Common Language	stimulating, subconscious, tricky, robust, migrate
Collocations/Idiomatic Language	passed on, hooking up with, curling up, sick of, go wrong, pop-up, ripped to shreds, team effort, go the way of the dodo
Paraphrasing	picture→illustrations, children→kids
Discourse Marker	anyway, personally, well, I suppose, in my mind, yeah

A story someone told you

> **Describe a story someone told you.**
> **You should say:**
>   **what the story was about**
>   **who told you that story**
>   **why you still remember it**
> **and explain how you feel about it.**

One story that sticks out in my memory was told to me by my grandmother. She told me a story about her childhood growing up in a small village during World War II. She spoke about the hardships and challenges she faced during the war, such as food and resource scarcity, as well as the threat of enemy soldiers passing through her village. She was very scared every day during this time.

Despite these difficulties, my grandmother shared with me how her community came together to support each other during these trying times. She spoke about the kindness and generosity of her neighbours and how they would share what little they had with each other, even in the face of extreme hardship.

I still remember this story so vividly because of the impact it had on me. It taught me about the power of community and the importance of looking out for one another, especially during difficult times. My grandmother's story also showed me that even in the face of adversity, there is always a way to find hope and positivity. I suppose it also showed that people really can come together in such times, rather than being driven apart.

Additionally, the story was a reminder of my grandmother's strength and resilience, as she was able to overcome these challenges and go on to live a long and fulfilling life. The story also gave me a deeper appreciation for my own life and the many blessings that I have.

Examiner: Do young children like the same stories as older children? (*Compare & Contrast*)

Candidate: No, I don't believe so. I think that the stories for younger children are too basic for older kids. It's only natural that as we all grow, we want more _{复杂} sophistication and can process new levels of creativity and imagination.

Examiner: How has technology changed storytelling? (*Speculate*)

Candidate: I'm not entirely sure that it has, not for children, at any rate. My mother always bought me books to read and then sat with me. I think that's pretty much what all parents do, even these days. It's possible that there are more stories available, because of things like the Internet, but the actual act of storytelling hasn't altered.

Examiner: How do people tell stories to children? (*List*)

Candidate: Well, sometimes from a book, sometimes just from their own experience or maybe their imagination. From what I know, that's how the *Harry Potter* books got started. It was an imaginary story that a mother told her children that then got published.

Examiner: Why do children like stories? (*Opinion*)

Candidate: I think it sparks their imagination _{激发他们的想象力}, and I don't think it's just children that like them. We all enjoy a good book, or movie or even just a tall tale _{奇闻怪事} from someone. I do believe though that it's not only good for youngsters' creativity, but also their language ability.

Lexical Resource	
Less Common Language	hardships, scarcity, trying, generosity, vividly, adversity, resilience, sophistication
Collocations/Idiomatic Language	sticks out, looking out for, come together, sparks their imagination, tall tale
Paraphrasing	hardships→difficulties, children→kids
Discourse Marker	additionally, from what I know

Describe a story someone told you.

You should say:

    what the story was about

    who told you that story

    why you still remember it

and explain how you feel about it.

I remember a time when a good friend of mine told me a tale of when he went on a trip to see the northern lights and stayed at the Ice Hotel in Sweden. It was about his stay there and his experience when travelling around and doing various winter activities.

It was a fascinating story and started with his flight from Stockholm to Kiruna, which is about 500 km inside the Artic circle. From the airport, it was a quick taxi ride to the Ice Hotel. Although he stayed there for four days, he only lived in the hotel for one night. He showed me the certificate that he got showing that it was −27 degrees Celsius. So, a little bit on the cold side! He also showed me the photos he took of the northern lights. To be honest, they didn't look as good as some others I've seen, but he explained that they were brighter in real life.

I think the reason I can recall it so easily is that he described everything with such clarity and passion; I felt that I was on the trip with him.

As for how I feel, I wish I could go on a trip like that. One of the items on my bucket list is staying there and having a vodka shot in the bar. And, of course, getting a good view of the lights. I'm really not sure when I will be able to venture out that way, but I hope it's soon.

Examiner: Do young children like the same stories as older children? (Compare & Contrast)

Candidate: I think they do, at least in part. For example, a story like *Harry Potter* is liked by junior
             奇幻故事
school level children as well as high school kids. Genres like Fantasy, Comedy or even
   科幻小说
Sci-Fi are somewhat universal and are loved by all.

Examiner: How has technology changed storytelling? (Speculate)

Candidate: I think it's changed quite a lot. 使用互联网
Access to the Internet has allowed people to find
all sorts of stories, both new and old, as well as the ability to download them to a
smartphone or pad to read or, these days, have it read to you.

Examiner: How do people tell stories to children? (List)

Candidate: I think nowadays, it is much more through video, you know, movies, TV, and even
                                         人际互动
social networks like Douyin. I think something's been lost with the personal interaction
between people and especially families.

Examiner: Why do children like stories? (Opinion)

Candidate: I think they find it fun. I always got enjoyment reading a book or watching a movie.
I'd often try and extend the story in my mind, to 'see what happens next'. I'd also
sometimes write my own stories about people I know, or maybe just make people up
as I go.

Lexical Resource	
Less Common Language	fascinating, clarity, shot, venture, fantasy
Collocations/Idiomatic Language	travelling around, bucket list, access to the Internet, personal interaction
Paraphrasing	story→tale, remember→recall
Discourse Marker	to be honest, as for how I feel, you know

■ A photograph of you that you like

> **Describe a photograph of you that you like.**
>
> **You should say:**
>
>   **where it was taken**
>
>   **when it was taken**
>
>   **who took it**
>
> **and explain how you felt about it.**

A photograph that I like was taken at Ritan Park on a gloriously sunny day. It was taken a few years ago, when I was visiting the park with my family. The photographer was my younger sister, who has always had a passion for photography. In the photograph, I'm sitting on a bench with a big smile on my face, surrounded by my family, lush green trees and beautiful flowers with a fantastic clear blue sky.

I love this photo because it captures a moment of pure joy and happiness. The warm sun on my face and the peacefulness of the park made me feel so relaxed and content. I also love the way my sister captured the beauty of the park in the background. It has the green of the grass, blue of the sky, but also some children playing that shows the warmth and activity of the park. It's a wonderful reminder of a happy day spent with my family because, over the last three years, they have been few and far between.

The fact that my sister took the photo makes it even more special to me. She has always been there to support me, and I love the fact that she captured this moment of happiness. Every time I look at this photograph, I'm reminded of the beautiful day we had at the park and how much I cherish my family. I'm hoping that we can have a lot more of these kinds of days in the future too.

Examiner: Why do some people like taking photos and some don't? [Speculate]

Candidate: That's an excellent question and, if I'm honest, I'm not sure whether I have a good answer for it. It might be that some people just aren't interested in photos, or it could be that they don't know how to use the technology. But I completely agree that there are definitely two camps.

Examiner: What do people use to take photos these days, cameras or phones? [Speculate]

Candidate: I think phones, for most people. It's easy, convenient, and of decent quality, certainly with today's smartphones. For some, though, they might want to use an SLR camera or something, you know, a professional camera for detailed, high-quality images.

Examiner: Would you like to take photos with strangers? [Opinion]

Candidate: In a word, no. I wouldn't want to take a photo with someone I don't know. I don't see the point and actually find it a little bit of an invasion of privacy. If they need me to move, so they get a nice shot, then fine. To include me, just seems a little strange.

Examiner: What kind of picture would you like to hang in your bedroom? [List]

Candidate: Calming ones. Maybe of family and friends, or a coastal scene, something like that. I'm not one for designer art. If I find a picture or painting that I like, I'll hang it; if I don't, I won't.

Lexical Resource	
Less Common Language	passion, lush, captures, content, cherish
Collocations/Idiomatic Language	few and far between, high-quality, invasion of privacy, coastal scene
Paraphrasing	photo→image, strangers→someone I don't know
Discourse Marker	that's an excellent question, you know, in a word

Describe a photograph of you that you like.

You should say:

    where it was taken

    when it was taken

    who took it

and explain how you felt about it.

That's actually quite a funny topic for me. I was in Yunnan, which is a most south-westerly place in China, a few years ago and is known for the range of wildlife it has.

————哎呀
Crumbs, it was nearly fifteen years ago. Anyway, I was about five years old and was travelling there with my parents and we were at a wildlife reserve looking at all the different animals. We went into the reptile house, and my mum thought it would be a good idea if I wore a snake. Yup, you heard correctly, she wanted me to put a snake around my neck. I was always a good little girl, and the snake
                                                      黏糊糊的————
didn't look that big, so I went along with it. I remember it felt so cold and, well, kinda slimy, and was actually quite afraid, but my Dad comforted me and said that he'd do it too.

So, there we were with snake scarves while my mum took lots of photos. I will never forget that day,
                           吓呆的————
like I said, I was quite literally petrified, I couldn't move with this animal slithering over my shoulders, but both my parents thought it was very funny. Looking back now, I do think it's a great photo because I look both cute and scared at the same time.

I'm glad I did it then, because now I'm older you would catch me doing it again. What's the
        ————愚我一次，其错在人；愚我两次，其错在我。
expression 'Fool me once, shame on you; fool me twice, shame on me.' I think that's the one that's most appropriate.

Examiner: Why do some people like taking photos and some don't? (Speculate)

Candidate: I think it's mainly because some people really want to have a memory of that time so that they can 回忆 look back on it later in life, whereas others are maybe afraid, or shy, of having their photo taken. They might take a photo of the environment, but not with them in it.

Examiner: What do people use to take photos these days, cameras or phones? (Speculate)

Candidate: Definitely smartphones. They are used by nearly everyone these days and can be used almost anytime and anywhere. They're also of much better quality than some of the old digital cameras from a few years ago and are getting better year on year.

Examiner: Would you like to take photos with strangers? (Opinion)

Candidate: Well, yes and no. I think if I was on holiday somewhere, England for example, I'd very much like to have some 快照 snaps with the locals so that I can remember it. If I was here, in China, I don't think I'd be as happy to do it. 请注意 Mind you, saying that, if they were English people having a holiday here, that'd be OK.

Examiner: What kind of picture would you like to hang in your bedroom? (List)

Candidate: I think maybe one of my idols, or someone I particularly admire. I'm a big fan of the singer, Harry Styles, so a big 肖像 portrait of him would be nice. Otherwise, maybe just a beautiful scenic picture that I can look at and feel calm.

Lexical Resource	
Less Common Language	reptile, slimy, petrified, snaps, idols, portrait
Collocations/Idiomatic Language	went along, year on year, 'Fool me once, shame on you; fool me twice, shame on me.', look back on
Paraphrasing	photos→snaps, idols→someone I admire
Discourse Marker	crumbs, anyway, yup, well, mind you

■ A piece of good news you heard/received

> **Describe a piece of good news you heard/received.**
>
> **You should say:**
>
>   **what the news was about**
>
>   **how you received this news**
>
>   **who you shared it with**
>
> **and explain why you think it was a good piece of news.**

A good piece of news I heard recently was about the development of a new cure for a rare disease. This news was shared by a reputable news outlet on the Internet. I learned about this cure on a Wednesday morning while reading my daily news updates.

The cure in question was developed by a team of international researchers, and it showed promising results in treating a rare disease that affected a small percentage of the population. This news was particularly exciting because the disease in question had been previously considered incurable, and many people had suffered from it for years.

The news was reported in great detail, explaining the science behind the cure and the results of the clinical trials. It was heartening to see how the cure had helped patients who had previously been unable to receive treatment. It was also inspiring to learn about the collaboration between the scientists and the medical community, working together to find a solution for the disease.

In my opinion, this news was a good piece of news because it brought hope and light to people who had been struggling with this rare disease. The development was a testament to the power of collaboration, hard work and persistence in the face of seemingly insurmountable challenges. It also showed how scientific advancements can lead to improved quality of life for people all over the world.

Overall, this piece of news was a positive reminder of the incredible progress and achievements that are possible when people come together for a common goal.

Examiner: Do you think children should start watching news from a young age? [Opinion]

Candidate: Absolutely, because from an early age, they need to understand the outside. They can watch news from TV, which is a good source of information. Watching news also can expand kids' vocabulary and broaden their horizons.

Examiner: How do people in your country get news? [Speculate]

Candidate: Basically, people in China get news from their mobile phone and Internet. A lot of people on their way to school or home would like to browse news in WeChat, Toutiao, or other websites. You know, it is a convenient way to get news. Actually, almost old people still like to read a newspaper, maybe the electronic devices are too difficult for them to use.

Examiner: Do you think the TV/radio should only broadcast good news? [Opinion]

Candidate: No, I don't think the news should only be good. I think it's important to know about what's going on in the world, whether it's good or bad. However, I would like to see some more good news as it always seems to be one disaster after another. It's a bit depressing when it's just that.

Examiner: What kinds of good news do people like to hear? [List]

Candidate: Well, the good news the people like to hear, of course, first is from the job. They got the pay rise and promotion because it means they can earn more money than before, and it can help their family to have a high-quality life. As for the students, they want to hear some good news about their grades. If they get a high mark, they will be happy, and their parents will be glad.

Lexical Resource	
Less Common Language	reputable, heartening, collaboration, insurmountable, browse, depressing
Collocations/Idiomatic Language	in question, in the face of, pay rise and promotion
Paraphrasing	heartening→inspiring, suffered from→struggled with, children→ kids, happy→glad
Discourse Marker	in my opinion, overall, absolutely, basically, you know

Describe a piece of good news you heard/received.

You should say:

   what the news was about

   how you received this news

   who you shared it with

and explain why you think it was a good piece of news.

Describing the best piece of news that I have received so far, it would have to be my Gaokao results that I received last year. These are the results that all Chinese students get at the end of high school and are really important. I was really pleased because I got the results that I expected and could therefore go to the university I wanted.

I knew the date of when the results would be ready, so I first looked online and then, after a few days, went to my school and collected them. Both my mother and father were there with me when I first found out my score. I was really pleased for that. I think if I had just been on my own, I wouldn't have been able to sign on. Also, when I went to the school, they came with me and having my family there to support me was a huge help.

As for who I shared this news with, well, everyone! As I said, my parents were with me so they were the first people that knew, and they were also over the moon. When I got home, I contacted a lot of my close friends to ask them what score they got to see if we can attend the same university. A lot of them also got the results they needed, so we all ended up going to the same place together. I feel sorry for the classmates that didn't get what they wanted, but I'm sure they'll be okay.

I'm hoping my next piece of good news that I receive will be from my university teachers saying that I have got a first in my degree. I hope my parents will be there with me to see that too.

Examiner: Do you think children should start watching news from a young age? (Opinion)

Candidate: Frankly, no, I don't. Most of the news is depressing, and they can't do anything about it. Maybe when they're teenagers so that they can get an idea of how the world works, but not before then. It's just unnecessary. Why expose the very young to the distresses of the world until you have to?

Examiner: How do people in your country get news? (Speculate)

Candidate: Probably like everyone else. I scan my mobile each morning and then sometimes again at lunchtime and in the evening for current affairs. I know some people watch the news on TV at certain times, and even some still read newspapers, but I don't think it's that many nowadays.

Examiner: Do you think the TV/radio should only broadcast good news? (Opinion)

Candidate: In my opinion, no. For a start, they wouldn't have enough to fill the time they have allotted. Secondly, it would just seem to be fake. You can always twist the news into something positive for someone, even if there's a war. So, no, I'd rather have reality than a view of the world through rose-coloured glasses.

Examiner: What kinds of good news do people like to hear? (List)

Candidate: I think, any and all types. Good news, is just that, good! Whether it's something personal, like a wedding, or the birth of a child or whether it's bigger, you know, worldwide, like landing on Mars. I don't know of anyone that actually enjoys BAD news.

Lexical Resource	
Less Common Language	pleased, depressing, distresses, allotted, twist
Collocations/Idiomatic Language	over the moon, ended up, through rose-coloured glasses
Paraphrasing	good news→best piece of news, news→current affairs
Discourse Marker	frankly, in my opinion, for a start

A company where you live that employs a lot of people

> **Describe a company where you live that employs a lot of people.**
>
> **You should say:**
>
> > **what it does**
> >
> > **how many people it employs**
> >
> > **what kind of people work there**
>
> **and explain how you feel about it.**

One company that comes to mind is Amazon, which is one of the largest corporations in the world. It's an e-commerce giant that offers a vast range of products and services to customers around the world. From what I know, it started off as a book website selling both new and second-hand books and expanded from there. These days, it employs hundreds of thousands of people globally and is headquartered in Seattle, Washington.

The company employs a diverse group of people, including software engineers, product managers, customer service representatives, and delivery drivers, among others. Amazon has created numerous job opportunities and has a positive impact on the local economy by providing employment and income to the residents.

I think it is a positive thing that companies like Amazon employ a large number of people and contribute to the local economy whether this be a city, or a nation. By providing employment and income, these companies help individuals and families lead a better life, allow them to grow, and create a more stable society. Furthermore, companies like Amazon also invest in new technologies and innovations, which helps drive progress and improve the quality of life for everyone. The latest of these is using drones as delivery devices, which I think is really cool.

Overall, I think companies like Amazon that employ a large number of people are crucial for the growth and development of communities, and I admire their positive impact on society.

Examiner: Should big companies be punished more seriously if they break the law? (Opinion)

Candidate: I don't think so, no. I see no reason why, just because they're a big company, they should have extra punishments. The law is the law; everyone can benefit or be punished at the same level. What is important though, is that they ARE punished if they break the law. No person or company should be 凌驾于法律之上 above the law.

Examiner: Should big companies donate more to charities? (Opinion)

Candidate: Yes, I believe they should. These giant multinationals make 极大的 humungous profits, you know, in the hundreds of billions of dollars, and yet in every country that they operate in there are still people living on the streets, jobless and hopeless. If they donate more to charities that can help these people, I think that would be a good thing.

Examiner: What are the good things about working for a big company? (List)

Candidate: Stability for one, promotion prospects for another. A large company is much less likely to 破产 go bust than a small start-up, for example. Also, with a large company, you're more likely to be able to climb the ladder and even reach the top, which wouldn't happen in a small enterprise, unless it's your own, of course.

Examiner: Do people in your country like to work for big companies or small companies? (Speculate)

Candidate: I think that the answer to that has probably changed with my generation. Taking my grandparents and parents for example, I'd say that they all wanted, and do, work for big companies. For me, and my friends for that matter, I would prefer to work for a small 对……有更大的影响力 company so that we have more influence over the decisions and development of it.

Lexical Resource	
Less Common Language	headquartered, drones, crucial, prospects
Collocations/Idiomatic Language	comes to mind, started off, go bust, climb the ladder, have more influence over
Paraphrasing	company→corporation/giant/multinationals, big→large/giant/humungous
Discourse Marker	from what I know, furthermore, overall

> **Describe a company where you live that employs a lot of people.**
> **You should say:**
> > **what it does**
> > **how many people it employs**
> > **what kind of people work there**
> **and explain how you feel about it.**

I live in the northwest of Beijing near Zhongguancun, which is where there are a lot of big technology companies like Intel. So, I'll talk about that one as I know a bit about it, not all that much, but I'll try and tell you what I know.

Intel, basically, is a microchip maker. It predominantly manufactures processors for Laptops and PCs, although it also makes GPUs and other forms of chips. It must be one of the largest companies in the world, because everything from a washing machine to a car needs processor chips these days.

I don't know the exact number of employees that it has, but it's maybe over a hundred thousand worldwide. It has a variety of headquarters around the world, but I think the biggest is in Ireland. Probably for tax reasons.

As for the types of people it has, well, I would assume all types. You'll need high-level engineers for a start, then salespeople and After-sales service agents, not to mention the legal and marketing teams they must have in each region. So, I would say a little bit of everyone must be part of this massive organisation.

To be honest, I've always liked Intel. I can't put my finger on exactly why, but I just have this feeling that they're behind the scenes somewhat making sure everything works. Lots of people know about Apple and Microsoft because everybody uses the software. A lot of people forget that without the hardware, the software wouldn't run.

Examiner: Should big companies be punished more seriously if they break the law? (Opinion)

Candidate: I suppose that really depends on what you're comparing it to. If it's smaller companies, then yes, I do. Sometimes larger companies believe that they can do anything they want and that they're untouchable. 〔不可受惩罚的〕 Sometimes they need to be knocked down a peg 〔灭威风〕 or two.

Examiner: Should big companies donate more to charities? (Opinion)

Candidate: I think it depends on what the company does and what charities they donate to, if any, in the first place. Many large companies already donate to charity for tax purposes, but it's not really a big thing in some countries. At least, not as far as I know.

Examiner: What are the good things about working for a big company? (List)

Candidate: For me, one of the big reasons would be the social side of things. With a small company, you might not be able to make any new friends, but the chance is much greater in a large one. On top of that, 〔除此以外〕 you have the ability to work in different departments of a big company and maybe even in different countries.

Examiner: Do people in your country like to work for big companies or small companies? (Speculate)

Candidate: Here in China, I think most people prefer to work for a large corporation rather than an SME. 〔中小企业〕 I agree with them in the fact that it's probably a lot more stable. A small enterprise might go bust, 〔倒闭〕 whereas I really can't imagine a company like the Bank of China, or Sinopec going pop. 〔破产〕 Moreover, as I just mentioned, you can also get a lot of different experiences in large companies as you can transfer 〔转岗〕 between various departments or even possibly other countries. That's not something I can see happening within a small company.

Lexical Resource	
Less Common Language	microchip, processors, hardware, software, untouchable, transfer
Collocations/Idiomatic Language	high-level, put my finger on, behind the scenes, knocked down a peg or two, go bust, going pop
Paraphrasing	big→massive, company→enterprise, going bust →going pop
Discourse Marker	well, to be honest, on top of that, moreover

An article on health you read in a magazine or on the Internet

> **Describe an article on health you read in a magazine or on the Internet.**
>
> **You should say:**
>
>   **what it was**
>
>   **where you read it**
>
>   **why you read it**
>
> **and explain how you felt about it.**

The article I read was about the benefits of mindfulness and meditation for mental health. I came across it while browsing through an online health magazine. I have always been interested in learning more about ways to improve my mental well-being, so when I saw the title of this article, I decided to give it a read.

It discussed the growing body of research that suggests mindfulness and meditation can help alleviate symptoms of anxiety and depression, reduce stress levels, and improve focus and overall mood. The author also shared some simple tips for starting a mindfulness practice, such as setting aside a few minutes each day for deep breathing and paying attention to the present moment without judgement.

I found it to be informative and well-written, with a good balance of scientific evidence and practical advice. I appreciated that it was accessible and easy to understand, even for someone like me who doesn't have a background in psychology or health.

I left feeling inspired and motivated to incorporate mindfulness and meditation into my daily routine. The article reinforced my belief that taking care of our mental health is just as important as taking care of our physical health, and that simple practices like mindfulness can have a significant impact.

Overall, I think this was a valuable and interesting article on health, and I would definitely recommend it to others who are interested in learning more about mindfulness and meditation.

Examiner: Do you think people are healthier now than in the past? (Compare & Contrast)

Candidate: Overall, the answer to this question depends on various factors, such as the region, socio-economic status, and lifestyle habits of individuals. However, in many parts of the world, people today have access to better healthcare, clean water, and nutritious food compared to people in the past, which has led to a significant improvement in health outcomes. So, the fast answer is yes.

Examiner: How can you tell whether a website is reliable or not? (Evaluate)

Candidate: Evaluating the reliability of a website is crucial, particularly when it comes to health-related information. First off, I think you need to check the domain. If it ends in '.gov', or '.edu', they're more likely to be more trustworthy than a regular '.com' address. Beyond that, I'd look to see if it's up to date by finding the dates of posts or the copyright info.

Examiner: What activities can a school organise for children to keep fit? (List)

Candidate: There are lots of things that can be sorted out for kids in schools, PE class, for a start. I don't know of a school that doesn't do this. Even in universities, part of our curriculum is PE. And if we don't pass, we don't graduate. I hated the running, but the badminton was good fun.

Examiner: What can governments do to improve people's health? (Opinion)

Candidate: I think that if the government can encourage healthier lifestyles through either education in schools, like we just spoke about, or perhaps through advertising and public announcements and initiatives. Although a government can't really force people into being healthy, I certainly think it can point people in the right direction about making their health better.

Lexical Resource	
Less Common Language	mindfulness and meditation, alleviate, incorporate, trustworthy, initiatives
Collocations/Idiomatic Language	came across, setting aside, have access to, sorted out
Paraphrasing	accessible→easy to understand, inspired→motivated, website→'.com' address, reliable→trustworthy
Discourse Marker	overall, when it comes to, first off, beyond that, for a start

---

Describe an article on health you read in a magazine or on the Internet.

You should say:

    what it was

    where you read it

    why you read it

and explain how you felt about it.

Well, it was a while ago, but one article I read was talking about whether people who deliberately damage their health through smoking or overeating should pay more for their healthcare, especially in countries where there is some kind of welfare.

I can't remember exactly how I found it. I think maybe it was just on a popup^{弹窗} that I clicked accidentally and then just got hooked into^{被迷住了} it while I was surfing online.

I found it interesting because some of my friends smoke and are a bit tubby^{矮胖的}. Not precisely obese, but definitely on the fat side. It gave some good points on the argument that individuals SHOULD pay extra for healthcare based on the idea that they already know that habits like smoking damage their health and yet they don't stop. The same went for^{同样的情况也发生在} eating too much. Some people are excessively^{极度} obese and weigh 150 kilos or more, when, for their body shape, they should be half that, and yet, again, they don't diet or do any exercise. They simply go to the hospital every time their knee hurts.

Overall, I agreed with the article. Doctors are busy enough without excessive appointments being made from people that just don't take care of themselves. Although you pay to go and see the doctor, you can quite often claim^{索要} quite a lot of it back. For people that destroy their health deliberately, I don't think that they should be able to. They should just pay the full amount.

Examiner: Do you think people are healthier now than in the past? (Compare & Contrast)

Candidate: As a general rule, yes. I think that health care has improved, as well as diet and food quality, especially over the last 50 years or so. I think a lot of it comes down to 可归结为 education. A lot of people know how to look after themselves better and are therefore healthier as a result.

Examiner: How can you tell whether a website is reliable or not? (Evaluate)

Candidate: I think it's quite a difficult thing to do. Making sure that it's current is probably a good start, and then see if it's a well-known company or simply a blog that somebody has set up. It's becoming more challenging these days to find decent sites for research, or anything else for that matter, just because it's so easy to publish a website these days that everyone and their dog are doing it. 所有人都在做

Examiner: What activities can a school organise for children to keep fit? (List)

Candidate: Well, they're already doing a lot through PE classes, sports clubs and even events like inter-school sports days. I suppose they could also encourage their students to cycle or walk to school rather than getting a bus or being driven, but I think that should only apply to the older kids.

Examiner: What can governments do to improve people's health? (Opinion)

Candidate: I know some countries have suggested a tax on sugary food and fast food, which I think is a great idea. Beyond that, I think that they can continue health education to youngsters so that when they grow up, they already have ideas of healthy living 灌输 instilled in them.

Lexical Resource	
Less Common Language	popup, tubby, excessively, claim, decent, instilled
Collocations/Idiomatic Language	got hooked into, the same went for, comes down to, everyone and their dog are doing it
Paraphrasing	tubby→obese/on the fat side, activities→events, children→kids/youngsters
Discourse Marker	overall, as a general rule, well, beyond that

A film that made you think a lot

> **Describe a film that made you think a lot.**
>
> **You should say:**
>
> > **what it was**
> >
> > **when you saw it**
> >
> > **what it was about**
>
> **and explain why it made you think a lot.**

The movie that made me pause for thought was *The Shawshank Redemption*. I saw this film for the first time about five years ago, maybe six, and I was deeply moved by the story. It's a film about hope, friendship, the power of the human spirit and just plain common decency.

The story revolves around Andy Dufresne, a banker who is sentenced to life in prison for a crime he didn't commit. He befriends another prisoner named Red, who becomes his closest ally in the tough environment of Shawshank Prison. Despite the harsh conditions, Andy never gives up hope and continues to look for ways to improve his situation. Through his determination and resourcefulness he manages to turn his life around and helps others in the process.

I watched this film on iQIYI and was immediately drawn in by the compelling story and the great acting performances. I'm a big fan of Morgan Freeman. I was also struck by the themes of resilience, perseverance, and the human capacity for change. The film touched me deeply and made me think a lot about the importance of never losing hope, no matter how difficult the circumstances or how long it takes.

To summarise then, *The Shawshank Redemption* is a powerful film that left a lasting impression on me. It is a film that celebrates the human spirit and the power of hope, and I would highly recommend it to anyone looking for a thought-provoking and inspiring movie experience.

Examiner: Where do people generally watch movies nowadays? (List)

Candidate: Cinemas are still popular these days. For the most part, people, including myself, are heading back to the big screen venues. I think there has been a shift, though, to streaming services to either TVs or mobiles and now that a large number of movie theatres have closed down, it's not always as convenient to go out.

Examiner: How important are actors in the success of a movie? (Evaluate)

Candidate: I think that they are extremely important, but not necessarily the be-all and end-all. The story, the effects, the marketing, and possibly even the director will all make their own contributions. Sometimes even if the actor is famous and well-liked, their movies can bomb. Will Smith, Tom Cruise, Jackie Chan have all made.

Examiner: Do you think that technology improves the quality of a movie? (Opinion)

Candidate: Definitely, without a doubt. Whether it's increased resolution, you know, making 4K or now 8K movies, or things like 3D movies, or even CGI that is used to create events, or even people these days. If you look at movies from the 80s and 90s, there is a visible difference in the quality versus those of today.

Examiner: What kinds of films are popular in China? (List)

Candidate: Sci-Fi movies are gaining popularity these days. I'm not sure if you know it, but there was a film called *The Wandering Earth* that was incredibly popular here in China. I think they've already made the sequel. For me, it makes a refreshing change from all the Marvel Super Hero movies we've had over the last few years.

Lexical Resource	
Less Common Language	befriends, harsh, resourcefulness, compelling, resilience, thought-provoking, resolution, sequel
Collocations/Idiomatic Language	revolves around, be-all and end-all, bomb
Paraphrasing	film→movie, think a lot→pause for thought
Discourse Marker	to summarise then, definitely, for me

Describe a film that made you think a lot.

You should say:

    what it was

    when you saw it

    what it was about

and explain why it made you think a lot.

A recent film that I enjoyed watching and that made me pause for thought, was *Interstellar*.

There is a cinema quite close to where I live, so I often go and watch new movies there. On this occasion, which was probably about three years ago now, I went with some of my friends to see it together. I remember distinctly that it was a weekend during the summer because we had to plan to meet as we weren't in Uni at the time.

The movie is in the sci-fi genre. I really enjoy this type of movie because I like to think that we are not necessarily alone in space. The plot of the movie is about trying to find somewhere else for the human race to live because the Earth has run out of resources, and lots of people are now starving and dying. During the film, they do find some planets that they think are habitable but, in the end, they're not, and most of the people that travel through space die. It wasn't a particularly 'feel good' movie, which I sometimes find refreshing.

It made me think a lot because, as I said earlier, I really enjoy science-fiction movies. This movie was heralded as a proper science, science fiction movie. What I mean by that is that a lot of the scenes showing black holes were what scientists believe they actually look like. I have actually seen this movie many times already, but I never get bored of it. All of my friends agree with me and, in fact, we have seen it together repeatedly.

Examiner:　Where do people generally watch movies nowadays? [List]

Candidate:　I think that although a lot of people still enjoy going to the cinema, there are many more, certainly in China, that download it to their mobile phones or tablets to watch them. This not only is cheaper, but also means you can watch the movie anywhere. On the other hand, watching it this way, in my opinion, does not give you the full visual and sound experience.

Examiner:　How important are actors in the success of a movie? [Evaluate]

Candidate:　Oh, absolutely essential. Many people will go and watch a movie just because it has their favourite actor in it. Even these days, with more animation films appearing, people will still go to it to hear their voices. I think the actors are even more important than the directors because even though the directors might be famous, they are not in front of the camera and, therefore, less known.

Examiner:　Do you think that technology improves the quality of a movie? [Opinion]

Candidate:　Yes, of course. These days technology is crucial to a movie and the better the technology, the better the movie. Things like the introduction of 3D movies, such as *Avatar* and high-definition〔高分辨率的〕 movies, improve the quality of what you see. Also, with inventions like CGI, directors and actors can do a lot more different things without which it might not be possible. *Interstellar* would be a classic example of this because, without technology, that kind of movie would not be able to be made.

Examiner:　What kinds of films are popular in China? [List]

Candidate:　I think the movies that are popular around the world are also popular here. There seem to be phases of different styles that are popular at a particular time. Recently it's all been animation; the last couple of years it's all been Sci-Fi. There'll probably be a new fad〔流行〕 just around the corner〔即将来临〕.

Lexical Resource	
Less Common Language	genre, habitable, refreshing, high-definition, animation, fad
Collocations/Idiomatic Language	run out of, was heralded as, just around the corner
Paraphrasing	think a lot→pause for thought, film→movie, important→essential, improve→better
Discourse Marker	on the other hand, oh, of course

■ An interesting song

> **Describe an interesting song.**
> **You should say:**
>   **what the song is**
>   **what story the song tells**
>   **whether the song is popular**
> **and explain why you think it is interesting.**

The song that I find interesting is *Imagine* by John Lennon. It was written and performed by the late Beatle, John Lennon, in the early 1970s. The song tells the story of a world without borders, wars, and religions. It speaks of a world where people can live together in peace, love, and harmony.

The song was released in 1971, I believe, and since then has become one of the most popular and recognisable songs of all time. People from all walks of life and cultures across the world have come to love and admire this song for its message of hope and unity.

What I find interesting about it is the message it conveys. The lyrics describe a world free from all the hatred, division, and suffering that we see around us. It inspires us to believe that a world of peace and love is possible if we all work together towards that goal. It encourages us to put aside our differences and work towards a common goal of creating a better world for everyone.

In my opinion, *Imagine* is a timeless classic that will continue to inspire people for generations to come. It serves as a reminder that we can all make a difference in the world if we work together towards a common goal. It is a testament to the power of music to inspire change and bring people together.

Examiner: What are the differences between the songs young and old people like to listen to? [Compare & Contrast]

Candidate: Younger people tend to be more drawn to contemporary genres of music, such as hip-hop, pop, electronic dance music (EDM), and rock. They may also be more likely to explore new and emerging artists and sub-genres. On the other hand, older people may have a stronger preference for music that was popular during their formative years, such as classic rock, or pop from the 80s.

Examiner: Why do you think pop music is so popular? [Speculate]

Candidate: Pop music is known for its catchy and memorable melodies that are easy to sing along to. These hooks and earworms can get stuck in people's heads and create a strong connection to the music. You know, it's also in the name; 'pop' is short for 'popular'.

Examiner: Has your taste in music changed since you were younger? [Compare & Contrast]

Candidate: Not really, no. I might listen to different artists, but the overall style is the same. I haven't turned into a metal-head, or a heavy rocker over the last few years. I still enjoy modern pop, and a little bit of country music occasionally too.

Examiner: What are the differences between a live concert and an online concert? [Compare & Contrast]

Candidate: Well, the atmosphere, I think, would be the biggest difference. Being in the concert hall or stadium in person is so much better than watching on a computer, even if you do have good earphones to use. Also, it's more difficult to enjoy the concert with your friends when it's online. It's not exactly as if you can get five people around one computer screen very easily.

Lexical Resource	
Less Common Language	released, lyrics, division, timeless, testament, catchy, metal-head
Collocations/Idiomatic Language	from all walks of life, put aside, hip-hop, formative years, hooks and earworms
Paraphrasing	tells→describes, live→in person
Discourse Marker	in my opinion, you know, well

> **Describe an interesting song.**
> **You should say:**
>   **what the song is**
>   **what story the song tells**
>   **whether the song is popular**
> **and explain why you think it is interesting.**

See You Again is the song that I like to listen to while I'm having a walk, taking the bus or even just relaxing at home. Charlie Puth is the singer-songwriter, and the melody had successfully got me carried away when I first listened to it. As the movie *Fast and Furious 7* is about reunion and brotherhood, it makes me reminisce of old times.

I really like the rap part of this song, which depicts what friendship means and how much it matters. It reminds me of my friend James, who came with me to watch the movie last year. He's in England now, so I don't get to catch up or hang out with him nearly as much as we used to, which saddens me. When we were together, we were like two peas in a pod, you know, completely inseparable. We use video conferencing as much as possible, but I still worry about and miss him, so the lyrics of this tune have made me well up a few times, when I'm thinking of him.

This song, to me, is like love at first sight. It's full of emotion and motivation, and memories, so it's very hard to explain what it really captures me mostly. I've listened to it well over a hundred times, but I'm not tired of it yet. I'm trying to learn how to sing it, especially the rap part, so that when I next go to KTV, I can sing it for my other friends! Hopefully, they won't all run away screaming, as I must admit, I don't have the best voice in the world.

Examiner: What are the differences between the songs young and old people like to listen to? (Compare & Contrast)

Candidate: These days, young people generally like pop music, or rap. Although, saying that, country music is very popular now too, probably because the lyrics can be understood clearly and it might trigger memories for people. Older people, however, might listen to more classical music that is calmer for their nerves.

Examiner: Why do you think pop music is so popular? (Speculate)

Candidate: Well, it's probably partially due to its name. As you know, pop music is short for 'popular' so that's the first reason. Secondly, I suppose it's designed that way. Musicians try to write and sing songs that they hope people will like and therefore become popular. It's a bit silly to write a song that no one's going to want to buy.

Examiner: Has your taste in music changed since you were younger? (Compare & Contrast)

Candidate: I suppose a little bit, yes. I like all kinds of music, but it depends what mood I'm in as to what I listen to. There are lots of new types of song coming out every week, so I can just file them into the separate groups, and if there's a new type of song come out, I'll see if I like it and then add it to the collection.

Examiner: What are the differences between a live concert and an online concert? (Compare & Contrast)

Candidate: Honestly, I don't really know. I've never logged in to an online concert. Thinking about it though, I'd assume that the audio quality won't be as good. The sound will only be as good as your laptop speakers. I would also say that the cost should be significantly less, but like I said, I wouldn't actually know about that considering I've never bought an online concert ticket.

Lexical Resource	
Less Common Language	reunion, reminisce, inseparable, captures, trigger
Collocations/Idiomatic Language	got me carried away, catch up, hang out with, like two peas in a pod, well up, love at first sight, short for
Paraphrasing	audio→sound
Discourse Marker	saying that, however, well, honestly

Chapter 4 Activities & Events
活动与事件类

■ A tradition in your country

| Part 2 | *Answer 1*（★★★★） | 🎧 210 |

> **Describe a tradition in your country.**
> **You should say:**
> > what it is
> >
> > who takes part in it
> >
> > what activities there are
> **and explain how you feel about it.**

One tradition in China that I find interesting is the Chinese New Year celebration, also known as the Spring Festival. It's by far the most important holiday in China and is celebrated by Chinese families all over the world these days. It usually falls between January 21st and February 20th and marks the start of the lunar calendar year.

During the celebration, families come together to eat traditional food, exchange gifts, and participate in various activities. One of the most famous activities is the reunion dinner, where families gather for a big feast to catch up and bond with each other. 叙旧增进感情 Another popular activity is decorating the house with red lanterns, paper cut-outs, and other decorations, as red is believed to bring good luck and fortune.

People also participate in dragon and lion dances, where performers dress up in elaborate 精心制作的 costumes and perform energetic dances to the beat of drums and cymbals. 鼓铙 Firecrackers 鞭炮 are also set off 引爆 to scare away evil spirits 驱邪 and bring good luck for the coming year, although this is mostly banned in big cities now.

I find the Chinese New Year celebration to be fascinating because of its rich history and cultural significance. It is a time for families to come together, renew their relationships, and welcome the New Year with hope and joy. The vibrant 充满活力的 and colourful celebrations, along with the delicious food, are a testament 证明 to the strong cultural traditions and values that are deeply rooted 深植于 in Chinese society today. Overall, I feel a great appreciation for this tradition and the way it brings my family together to celebrate our heritage 遗产 and values.

Examiner: How do people value traditional festivals? (Evaluate)

Candidate: I think a lot of people value traditional holidays and events as a part of their cultural heritage and identity. I think it also brings a lot of people together, not just the immediate families [直系亲属] but also the neighbours and people in the community. For example, everyone says Happy New Year to everyone at that time, not just their parents.

Examiner: What is the difference between festivals now and those in the past? (Compare & Contrast)

Candidate: Well, not a lot really, otherwise they wouldn't be traditional festivals. The Spring Festival has been celebrated for thousands of years, literally. It dates back to [追溯到] the 14th century BC. You can say the same thing about the Mid-Autumn Festival, which goes back to the BCs as well. So, it's because these celebrations started in the past that they're now traditional.

Examiner: Do you think western festivals like Christmas are replacing traditional festivals in your country? (Opinion)

Candidate: No, I don't think so. I like to think that they're adding to, rather than substituting [取代] them. Christmas has no doubt expanded in popularity here, but it's never going to be more important than the Spring Festival. It's interesting that the Spring Festival is now celebrated among a lot of western countries too, which is a turn-up for the books [意想不到的结果].

Examiner: Do you think it is wrong for children not to celebrate traditional festivals? (Opinion)

Candidate: Indeed, I do. We need to teach each generation about the culture and traditions of their home so that they can understand where they come from. If they don't want to celebrate them later in life, well, that's up to them, but to begin with, they must be allowed to celebrate along with everyone else.

Lexical Resource	
Less Common Language	elaborate, vibrant, testament, heritage, substituting
Collocations/Idiomatic Language	catch up and bond with each other, set off, deeply rooted in, dates back to, a turn-up for the books
Paraphrasing	festival→celebration, replacing→substituting
Discourse Marker	well, indeed, to begin with

> **Describe a tradition in your country.**
> **You should say:**
>   **what it is**
>   **who takes part in it**
>   **what activities there are**
> **and explain how you feel about it.**

Well, one tradition that I'm particularly fond of is the giving of mooncakes during the Mid-Autumn Festival.

This festival isn't quite as big as Chunjie, or the Chinese New Year, but I'd put it as number two on the list, and it's been knocking around for in the region of 2,000 years. The idea is that a maiden lives in the Moon with her rabbit companion, and if people worship that white plate in the sky, their wishes may come true.

Mostly it's a time for family and everyone getting together and having a nice meal. I've always enjoyed it because it's six months away from New Year, which means it kinda balances the year for me. I don't get to see my family that often, and I think if I had to wait a full year to get together, I'd be a lot unhappier.

There are lots of things to do. Besides the giving and receiving of mooncakes, we generally get together over the 3-day holiday and light lanterns and, in my family's case, sit outside on our balcony and have dinner under the moonlight.

Overall, during this festival, we can contemplate the traditions of our country and consider family values and togetherness. I think it's important to keep these kinds of traditions alive, so that we can pass them on to future generations and remember the stories of our youth. If we don't, I believe that we'll lose our roots and eventually drift into obscurity.

Examiner: How do people value traditional festivals? (Evaluate)

Candidate: I think for some important traditional festivals, people give them great value and will celebrate them every time. And for others, it depends. Also, it seems that among young generation, traditional festivals are less celebrated than older generation. They may think festivals are days for them to have days off and go out for fun.

Examiner: What is the difference between festivals now and those in the past? (Compare & Contrast)

Candidate: On the one hand, the way to celebrate them has changed. People tend to get together to watch a movie and have dinner at festivals now, while in the past, specific customs would usually be held. On the other hand, the audience changes. In the past, almost everyone would celebrate festivals, while now young people show less interest in it.

Examiner: Do you think western festivals like Christmas are replacing traditional festivals in your country? (Opinion)

Candidate: No, I don't think so. To be accurate, I would say festivals like Christmas extend the choice of the celebrations in my country. People are still celebrating our traditional festivals all the time. Globalisation means to communicate or combine, not to replace. Western festivals are novel, so they might attract attention.

Examiner: Do you think it is wrong for children not to celebrate traditional festivals? (Opinion)

Candidate: Yes. I think traditional festivals are an important part of our own culture. If kids don't celebrate them, they would gradually forget about it and cause its disappearance. So, in order to protect our own cultural treasures and know more about ourselves, it is essential to let the children celebrate traditional festivals.

Lexical Resource	
Less Common Language	worship, contemplate, obscurity, accurate, extend, have days off
Collocations/Idiomatic Language	knocking around, in the region of, white plate
Paraphrasing	contemplate→consider, see them→get together, festivals→celebrations, children→kids
Discourse Marker	well, on the one hand, on the other hand, to be accurate

■ An occasion when someone gave you advice

| Part 2 | *Answer 1*（★★★★） | 🎧 214 |

> **Describe an occasion when someone gave you positive advice about your work/study.**
>
> **You should say:**
>
> who the person is
>
> what he/she said
>
> how the advice/suggestion affected you
>
> **and explain how you felt about the advice/suggestions.**

A time that stands out in my mind when someone gave me positive advice about my work was when I was feeling overwhelmed ⌐—不知所措的 and unsure about my future as a software engineer. I was constantly comparing myself to my peers and feeling like I was falling behind. One day, I had a meeting with my mentor, who was a senior engineer at the company I was working at. During our conversation, he told me that everyone progresses at their own pace and that what mattered most was the effort I put in and my growth as an engineer.

He encouraged me to focus on learning new technologies and developing my skillset ⌐—综合技能, rather than worrying about where I stood in comparison to others. He also emphasised the importance of taking breaks, finding balance, and not burning out ⌐—筋疲力尽. This was a welcome change from the negative self-talk I had been indulging in ⌐—沉溺于, and it made a huge impact on my confidence and motivation.

His advice affected me in a positive way because it gave me a fresh perspective and allowed me to focus on my own journey rather than comparing myself to others. I began to feel more fulfilled in my work and less stressed, which improved my overall productivity and happiness.

To summarise, I am incredibly grateful for ⌐—感谢 the positive advice my mentor gave me, and it is something that I still think about today. His words helped me to appreciate the journey and the process of becoming a better engineer, rather than just focusing on the destination. I believe that his words helped me to grow as an engineer and as a person, and I will always be thankful for that.

Examiner: What advice do parents give to teenagers about making friends? (*Speculate*)

Candidate: Well, I suppose that in terms of recommendations, parents will often tell them to find out if their new friends have similar interests and are honest. There are a lot of unscrupulous people in the world who want to take advantage of others, and parents will try to steer their children away from them.

Examiner: How do experts give advice to others? (*Speculate*)

Candidate: Through online platforms, although it's difficult these days to find actual experts. I suppose real experts will offer supporting evidence for their advice, or maybe they are recognised experts in their field, like Bill Gates as an expert in technology, or Warren Buffet as a financial expert. If this were the case, more or less anything they said about a topic could be considered as advice.

Examiner: What kinds of advice do parents give to their children? (*Speculate*)

Candidate: Oh, I think they give advice about all sorts of things. They don't focus on any one particular thing. So, everything from advice on friendships, like we mentioned earlier, to advice on study habits, to how to find a job. There's not one particular area that stands out.

Examiner: Whose advice is more helpful, parents' or friends'? (*Compare & Contrast*)

Candidate: I think that depends on the topic. On top of that, I think it depends on the situation too. What I mean is, let's say I'm having trouble studying for my IELTS exam; I could ask my friends or my folks. The advice they would give is different because my friends have taken the IELTS test whereas my parents haven't, but having said that, my parents have taken many more tests than my friends, so to me in terms of value, both are equal even if they're different.

Lexical Resource	
Less Common Language	overwhelmed, skillset, unscrupulous
Collocations/Idiomatic Language	burning out, indulging in, grateful for, take advantage of, more or less, stands out
Paraphrasing	advice→recommendations, parents→folks
Discourse Marker	well, in terms of, on top of that

> **Describe an occasion when someone gave you positive advice about your work/study.**
>
> **You should say:**
>
>   who the person is
>
>   what he/she said
>
>   how the advice/suggestion affected you
>
> **and explain how you felt about the advice/suggestions.**

When I was an adolescent, I never listened to people giving me advice because I am different from them and have my own way of doing things. Now I am a university student, I am more open to receiving advice. Actually, last week, my tutor〔导师〕asked me if I was learning a lot about IELTS, and I said 'No, not really'. We sat down and had a long chat about this, and at the end of it, he advised me to go to the library and look for some books that could help me do better in this exam.

When I got to the library, I found there was a very large section on English and the IELTS exam, so I spent the rest of the day looking for a book that was suitable for me. I eventually found one that seemed to be better than the other and spoke to both my teacher and my course tutor about it. They agreed, so I chose the 9 Fen Daren speaking book by New Channel. The new version is written by James Foster.

As for how I felt about receiving this advice, I would say, pleased because it turned out to be good advice. This week, I should have gone back there to find some more books, but as I was very tired, I just got onto my bed and passed out〔昏睡〕. However, I really believe that if someone gives you the advice, you should actually do it rather than just say you're going to do it. English for me is quite difficult but, using my determination〔决心〕, I'm sure that I can improve.

Examiner: What advice do parents give to teenagers about making friends? (Speculate)

Candidate: First, the one they choose should be kind. Only a kind person won't hurt others. Second, honest. Without honesty, a person is unreliable. Third, friendship is built upon two persons; so, it is important that these two can truly understand each other and get along well with each other. Without these, it is hard to make friends.

Examiner: How do experts give advice to others? (Speculate)

Candidate: I think for experts, they will not only tell others about the advice or what they should do, but also explain why they should act like this. What's more, experts may take specific cases to persuade others. So usually, their advice is based both on theory and practice, which ensures that they take effect when adopted.

Examiner: What kinds of advice do parents give to their children? (Speculate)

Candidate: The starting point of this advice is usually kind and beneficial to their children. They would give advice based on their own experience and their knowledge about their own children. This advice would cover all aspects of life, from how to make friends, to how to study well, and to even how to raise children.

Examiner: Whose advice is more helpful, parents' or friends'? (Compare & Contrast)

Candidate: I think it's hard to say because both of them are beneficial. Their advice is from different perspectives. My folks have a long experience of life, which could help me to avoid the mistake they have made. Friends know you better than your parents in daily life. They can understand your inner thoughts and provide comfortable suggestions. The combination would be the best.

Lexical Resource	
Less Common Language	adolescent, tutor, determination, persuade
Collocations/Idiomatic Language	passed out, get along well with, take effect, folks
Paraphrasing	friends→friendship, beneficial→helpful, parents→folks
Discourse Marker	however, first, second, third, what's more

A time you taught something new to a younger person

Part 2　*Answer 1*（★★★★）　　　　　　　　　　6∂ 218

> **Describe a time you taught something new to a younger person.**
> **You should say:**
> > **what you taught**
> > **when it happened**
> > **who you taught**
> **and explain how you felt about the teaching.**

A time I taught something new to a younger person was when I volunteered as a mentor for a local after-school program. This happened about a year ago, and I taught a group of elementary school students how to code using Scratch. I think it's important for the younger generation to learn about computers as soon as possible as they will need it later in their lives.

I was really excited to share my knowledge with the kids and help them learn something new. The students were eager to learn and were very enthusiastic about the project. I started by explaining the basics of programming and how to use Scratch to create interactive games and animations. Then, I walked them through the process step-by-step and encouraged them to try out new things on their own.

Teaching the children was a truly fulfilling experience. Seeing their faces light up with excitement and their eyes widen with wonder as they learned something new was amazing. I was also happy to see their progress as they built their projects and solved problems on their own. It gave me an enormous sense of achievement and pride.

Overall, teaching these kids was a great opportunity for me to give back to my community and inspire the next generation of coders. It also allowed me to improve my own teaching and communication skills. I felt proud to have made a positive impact on the students' lives, and I am very grateful for the experience. I'm hoping that I can do it again in the future for another group of potential software engineers.

Examiner: What can children learn from their teachers or parents? (Opinion)

Candidate: Well, in my opinion, they learn more from their parents. Obviously, they learn different things from each of them at different times, but as an easy answer. From teachers, they'll learn academics; from parents, they'll learn life.

Examiner: How can people be motivated to learn new things? (Speculate)

Candidate: That's an interesting question. People are motivated by different things, and I don't think you can force someone to learn something. It needs to come from inside. But if you can 诱使 entice someone into wanting to understand something new, that's a good start.

Examiner: What skills do adults need to have? (List)

Candidate: Wow, another difficult question. OK, skills. I would say that adults need the ability to adapt to different situations, and to understand where the boundaries are within each. They also need to know when to learn and when to 传递知识 pass that knowledge on. Beyond that, I've no idea.

Examiner: What skills should be taught to children? (List)

Candidate: Ha, you don't let up, do you? I'm assuming a skill is not necessarily anything academic. I'm thinking more about mental and physical abilities. So, skills of making friends, skills of understanding relationships together with skills in playing sports, 手眼协调 hand-eye coordination and the like.

Lexical Resource	
Less Common Language	mentor, animations, adapt, entice
Collocations/Idiomatic Language	walked them through, light up, give back to, grateful for, pass that knowledge on, hand-eye coordination
Paraphrasing	kids→children, code→programming
Discourse Marker	overall, well, obviously, wow, ha

Describe a time you taught something new to a younger person.

You should say:

    what you taught

    when it happened

    who you taught

and explain how you felt about the teaching.

My niece, my big brother's little girl, is about five now and has recently started going to school. I, as a good aunty, wanted to help her with her English. She doesn't really learn that at the moment, but she does sometimes look at Western letters and numbers, you know, A through Z and zero to nine.

So, I bought a book where you can trace out the numbers with something like a whiteboard marker and then wipe it clean so that you can do it over and over again. Whenever I see her, which is most weekends, we sit down together before lunch or dinner or something, and do maybe four or five of the letters and the same in the numbers, sometimes more. She's getting really good at it now. We've completed the book at least twice already and are working rigorously on the third attempt.

It's wonderful practice for me as I plan on becoming a teacher in the future, maybe primary, maybe junior school. I'm not sure yet. So, I have a willing student that I can use to get some practice on and make the decision about all that when I return from my studies in the UK in about two years. Teaching is something that I've always wanted to do, and will be following in my father's footsteps. Somewhat sentimental, I know, but there you go.

Examiner: What can children learn from their teachers or parents? (Opinion)

Candidate: Everything. Who else are they going to learn from, especially in their early years? Parents are a kid's first teachers. How to walk, how to speak, how to eat and the like. It's only later when they're five or so that they'll start learning things from proper teachers. You know, Maths, Art and stuff.

Examiner: How can people be motivated to learn new things? (Speculate)

Candidate: I suppose that a lot of it comes down to a couple of things. Firstly, whether they enjoy the idea of learning something new and, second, whether it's inside their comfort zone. If the answer is 'Yes' to both of these, then the impetus will come. If not, it won't.

Examiner: What skills do adults need to have? (List)

Candidate: Well, that's not an easy question to answer. From my perspective, as a prospective teacher, I need to know how to deal with young children and teach them the basics of academic skills like reading and writing. This will be completely different from, say, a chef, who needs to be able to create mouth-watering food for a restaurant.

Examiner: What skills should be taught to children? (List)

Candidate: I think all kids should be instructed in basic social skills as well as academic ones. They can be guided on how to find their feet when dealing with other children and should understand the meaning of friendships. I truly believe that having a good command of social interaction is just as important as getting an A in History, or some other less prominent subject. That, and decision-making skills, are important too.

Lexical Resource	
Less Common Language	wipe, rigorously, sentimental, impetus, prospective, instructed
Collocations/Idiomatic Language	trace out, comes down to, comfort zone, mouth-watering, find their feet, having a good command of
Paraphrasing	motivated→impetus, taught→instructed
Discourse Marker	you know, so, well

A time that someone didn't tell you the whole truth

> **Describe a time that someone didn't tell you the whole truth about something.**
> **You should say:**
>> **when this happened**
>> **what the situation was**
>> **who you were with**
> **and why the person didn't tell you the whole truth.**

The story I'd like to tell you about a time when someone lied to me is actually quite amusing.

A long time ago, well, about two years, in a city far, far away, actually, just down the road from here, there was a boy who was about to become a man … and the force … changed. Ha-ha. It was on my birthday a couple of years ago. Over here, an 18th birthday is a very important one, as it means that you're becoming an adult and entering the next stage in your life.

I was away from home at the time and was missing my family and some of my old friends from high school and was hoping that they'd be able to come and see me for my special day. The day before, my mum called me and said that they couldn't come and that they were stuck at home. Needless to say, I was gutted. I remember thinking that on one of the most important days of my life, I was going to be alone, you know, playing billy no mates.

I didn't sleep well the night before, and felt lonely and isolated that morning. I went to my regular little restaurant near my uni for some breakfast, thinking that the world was a horrible place, and life just wasn't fair. When I got there, I noticed that there weren't any people there. It was a bit strange as there's usually a few people eating.

Suddenly, people jumped out from everywhere. Both my folks were there as well as all of my friends, both past and current. It was fantastic!

I think the reason why they weren't honest with me is pretty obvious. I'm glad they weren't, as the surprise made it all the more special.

Examiner: Do you think it's important to teach children to be honest? (Opinion)

Candidate: Yes. If children lie once and don't get punished, they will lie more times. If kids lie many times, they will lie till they grow up. They will not only lose credit of themselves but also do harm to others who trust them. So, it's extremely critical to tell them the importance of honesty.

Examiner: Why do people lie sometimes? (Speculate)

Candidate: On the one hand, they want to make a better 'I'. They hide their disadvantages and wrong doings from others to leave a perfect impression like richness. On the other hand, they want to protect a good 'he or she'. We can call this kind of fib a white lie. People use it to avoid greater sorrow and give others temporary comfort.

Examiner: Can you tell if someone is lying? (Opinion)

Candidate: Yes, sometimes I can. If someone is nervous when he or she is talking to me, I will doubt the reliability. For example, they avoid making direct eye contact with me or they are uncomfortable to place their hands in one place. But if a liar can disguise himself or herself well, it will be hard to tell whether what they say is true or fake.

Examiner: Do you think it is more important to win a game or follow the rules in sports? (Compare & Contrast)

Candidate: Definitely, to follow the rules is more important. Rules are the foundation of a game, without which win or loss makes no sense at all. In sports, everyone should bear in mind that fairness of the game and respect to each other count a lot. What's really terrifying is the loss of credibility rather than the loss of a game.

Lexical Resource	
Less Common Language	amusing, disguise, terrifying, credibility
Collocations/Idiomatic Language	gutted, playing billy no mates, fib, white lie, bear in mind
Paraphrasing	family→folks, important→critical, children→kids, fib→lie
Discourse Marker	well, you know, on the one hand

> **Describe a time that someone didn't tell you the whole truth about something.**
>
> **You should say:**
>
> > **when this happened**
> >
> > **what the situation was**
> >
> > **who you were with**
>
> **and why the person didn't tell you the whole truth.**

I remember a time when a close friend of mine didn't tell me the whole truth about a situation we were in together. It was a few years ago, and we were supposed to go on a trip together with a group of friends. My friend had planned everything and was in charge of making all the reservations and arrangements.

A few days before the trip, I received a call from another friend who informed me that the hotel we were supposed to stay in had been fully booked, and that my friend had already made alternative arrangements without informing me. When I asked my friend about it, he hesitated at first but eventually admitted that he had been unable to secure the original reservation and had been too afraid to tell me.

I was a bit upset that my friend didn't tell me the whole truth, but I understood why he felt that way. He was afraid of disappointing me and ruining our plans, and didn't want to risk damaging our friendship.

In the end, the alternative arrangements turned out to be just as good, and we still had a great time on the trip. But the experience taught me the importance of open and honest communication in any relationship. I realised that sometimes it's better to tell the whole truth, even if it may be difficult or unpopular than to hide or downplay the facts.

Overall, I feel that my friend's lack of honesty was a small blip in an otherwise strong and trusting friendship. We learned from the experience and moved on, and our friendship is stronger than ever.

Examiner: Do you think it's important to teach children to be honest? (Opinion)

Candidate: Of course. Honesty is a basic quality for everyone to have. We must teach people from a young age which can let a person form correct thinking. Only then can we learn to trust each other and live more harmoniously.

Examiner: Why do people lie sometimes? (Speculate)

Candidate: Some of the lies are kind for some people, protecting them from sadness. But some lies are bad and dangerous for people. All in all, whether lies are good or bad for people, we shouldn't lie to others. Everyone has the rights to know the truth.

Examiner: Can you tell if someone is lying? (Opinion)

Candidate: Generally, yes. But not necessarily always. For me, I like watching people, so when they start shifting their feet or don't look at me, there's usually something up. I'll compare their body language with what they're actually saying and how they're saying it and see if it all matches. If it does, they're probably telling the truth. If it doesn't, it's probably because they're not telling the truth, or at least not the whole truth.

Examiner: Do you think it is more important to win a game or follow the rules in sports? (Compare & Contrast)

Candidate: I think it's important to follow the rules, but I also believe in pushing the boundaries of those rules. Believing that everyone is going to play fairly in all sports is just too naive, especially if the level of said sport is high. You know, like at the Olympics, or the football World Cup or something. There have been far too many scandals from all over the world about doping, switching nationalities and the like. It's difficult for us ordinary people to follow the rules when many of the top-level people don't.

Lexical Resource	
Less Common Language	alternative, unpopular, downplay, harmoniously, naive, scandals, top-level
Collocations/Idiomatic Language	blip, pushing the boundaries, and the like
Paraphrasing	children→young age
Discourse Marker	overall, of course, all in all, you know

■ An occasion when you forgot something important

> **Describe an occasion when you forgot something important.**
>
> **You should say:**
>
> **when it was**
>
> **what you forgot**
>
> **why you forgot it**
>
> **and explain how you felt about it.**

I recall an occasion when I forgot something essential. It was during my final exams in college, and I had an important exam the next day. I was feeling quite confident about the exam as I had been preparing for it for weeks. The night before the exam, I made a checklist of all the things I needed to carry with me the next day. I went through the list multiple times to make sure I hadn't missed anything.

However, when I reached the exam hall the next day, I realised that I left my ID card at home. I was so shocked and frustrated that I had forgotten something so important. I couldn't understand how I had missed it on my checklist. I tried to find a solution, but there was nothing I could do. Without an ID card, I wasn't allowed to enter the exam hall.

I felt terrible about the whole situation. Not only had I let myself down, but I had also let down my family and friends, who had been supporting me throughout my studies. I felt like all my hard work had gone to waste.

Looking back on that day, I still feel a twinge of disappointment and frustration. But I also learned a valuable lesson about the importance of double-checking and being extra careful, especially when it comes to important events. It taught me to take extra precautions and to not take anything for granted.

Examiner: What kinds of things do people forget easily? [List]

Candidate: Trivial ┌──琐碎的 things or things that suddenly change from the routine. When you are asked to write a long paper and your teacher tells you to read a certain writer's specific book, you might miss the name of the writer or the book. Also, you might miss the bus if the time is suddenly changed and different from the one you usually take.

Examiner: What kinds of people are more forgetful? [List]

Candidate: Older people are easier than younger to forget things. This phenomenon cannot be improved because it is human nature. When people are not in the right condition, for example, they are drunk or sick, they tend to have a bad memory. But when they get out of the illness, they will return to their normal states.

Examiner: How can people improve their memory? [Speculate]

Candidate: First, they can keep memorising something constantly. Repetition helps a lot when it comes to memory. Second, they can create their own way to help store things, like specific symbols or abstract concepts. Third, they might turn to ┌──诉诸 medical treatment. And this way is not usually recommended and seems not to be so necessary.

Examiner: What do you think of people using calendars to remind themselves of things? [Opinion]

Candidate: I think it is a good way to do so. Almost everyone cares about the date. So to connect to-do things ┌──待办事件 with the calendar can function as a daily reminder. Every time you check the date, you will be reminded. Also, the calendar will ensure you the specific time of the things, which will help them a lot.

Lexical Resource	
Less Common Language	precautions, trivial, abstract
Collocations/Idiomatic Language	a twinge of, turn to, daily reminder, to-do things
Paraphrasing	important→essential, forgot→hadn't remembered, forgetful→a bad memory, certain→specific, memorise→store
Discourse Marker	however, looking back, first, also

Describe an occasion when you forgot something important.

You should say:

    when it was

    what you forgot

    why you forgot it

and explain how you felt about it.

Oh dear, this topic brings back some bad memories. I got into such trouble because of this.

In a nutshell, I forgot my girlfriend's birthday. Yup, I was in the doghouse for DAYS because of it. It was a little earlier this year, near the end of term. I was completely overwhelmed by the sheer number of assignments and exams I had at that time and really didn't know my ar ... from my elbow, if you'll excuse the vernacular.

I knew in the back of my mind that it was approaching, but I thought I had another week. I had a test first thing in the morning that my better half knew about, so she wasn't upset at me for not calling. At lunchtime, though, I had an ear-bashing like no other.

At first, I got angry at her because I didn't really understand what on earth was happening, but then the penny dropped, and I began the long road of grovelling and apologising. And what a long road it was, full of crevasses, mountains, fire and brimstone.

I finally managed to get back in her good books, but she definitely made me work for it. She was right to be upset, though, I shouldn't have forgotten, and it has taught me to put her birthday in my phone so that I NEVER forget it in the future. Oh, smartphones are great. It's probably saved my life. It's certainly saved my relationship. I've already put down Valentine's Day, 20th May and all the other dates that are important to women. I suppose I am well-trained!

Examiner: What kinds of things do people forget easily? (List)

Candidate: Oh, I can never remember to pick up my keys, so I think that's fairly common. I think you could probably add wallet and phone to that list. Overall, I think it's the little things that always change places. Big things like my laptop, I'll never forget, but because I put my keys on my table, in my coat, etc. I'm forever forgetting to take them with me when I go out.

Examiner: What kinds of people are more forgetful? (List)

Candidate: I suppose those who tend to be more absent-minded. So, those who have a high-level of concentration of very specific things to the exclusion of all else. Perhaps more obviously, the very elderly could be added to the list. Although having said that, my grandma has an excellent memory.

Examiner: How can people improve their memory? (Speculate)

Candidate: That's not an easy question to answer. I've heard of brain excersies and techniques that you can do to make recall better. I can't remember the official name for them, but it's things like creating a memory tower, memory association. To be honest, I've never really understood that, because to remember a thing, you have to remember a different thing that's related. Why not just remember the first thing?

Examiner: What do you think of people using calendars to remind themselves of things? (Opinion)

Candidate: Oh, one of the lessons that I learnt is the calendar on my phone is my best friend. I can honestly say that it's the best invention since sliced bread. In my opinion, using technology to help you in daily life is just a sensible thing to do. After all, it's what it's there for.

Lexical Resource	
Less Common Language	vernacular, concentration, exclusion
Collocations/Idiomatic Language	in the doghouse, didn't know my ar ... from my elbow, my better half, ear-bashing, on earth, the penny dropped, fire and brimstone, get back in her good books
Paraphrasing	forget→never remember, forgetful→absent-minded, improve their memory→make recall better
Discourse Marker	in a nutshell, yup, at first, oh, overall, I suppose, although, to be honest, in my opinion

A time you used your smartphone to do something important

> **Describe a time you used your smartphone to do something important.**
> **You should say:**
>   **what happened**
>   **when it happened**
>   **how important the smartphone was**
> **and explain how you felt about the experience.**

I remember a time when I used my mobile to do something very important. It was about two years ago, and I was at the airport waiting for my flight. I had been travelling for work and had a connecting flight, but my flight was delayed by several hours. It was a pain, but not entirely surprising, at least, not to me.

As I sat in the airport, I realised that I had left my passport at the hotel where I was staying. I had to fly to another country for a meeting the next day, and I was panicking because I thought I wouldn't be able to make it. That's when I used my smartphone to save the day.

I quickly used my phone to connect to the Internet and book a new hotel room for the night. I also used it to call the hotel where I had stayed and ask them to send my passport to the new hotel. I was able to use it to access all the information I needed to resolve the situation and ensure that I was able to make it to my meeting the next day. Talk about a skin-of-the-teeth day.

In that moment, my smartphone was essential. Without it, I would have been stranded at the airport, would have missed my meeting and would have been at my wit's end. I felt relieved and grateful that I had access to my smartphone, and I was reminded of how technology can be a lifesaver in times of need.

Examiner: What do you usually do with a mobile phone? [List]

Candidate: Normally, their essential functions. First, I use a mobile phone to contact and communicate with others. Second, I use a mobile phone to entertain. 娱乐 There are a lot of applications which enable me to listen to songs, paint, play games and so on. Third, I use it to purchase goods online and pay whenever I go in my daily life.

Examiner: What are the differences between young people and old people when using a mobile phone? [Compare & Contrast]

Candidate: For old people, mobile phones are most used to contact other persons. They seldom use it for entertainment. However, for young people, its functions really vary. Besides communication, they use it for almost anything, like searching for information, buying food or clothes, and having fun.

Examiner: Which one is more important, using a mobile phone to make phone calls or to read messages? [Compare & Contrast]

Candidate: I think to make phone calls is more important. For one thing, there are other forms of reading messages like a letter. The content of both of them is the same. For another, to make phone calls is better to have a clear and effective conversation, which means they just talk and can respond at any time.

Examiner: Do you think there should be a law to stop people from making phone calls in public? [Opinion]

Candidate: No, I don't think so. On the one hand, phone calls usually mean important or urgent things to happen. If forbidden, 被禁止 these are missed, which would cause devastating consequences. On the other hand, it is a fact that some people may talk too loud on the phone, so it is better to set a limit of the sound instead of stopping it completely.

Lexical Resource	
Less Common Language	panicking, stranded, entertain, forbidden
Collocations/Idiomatic Language	save the day, skin-of-the-teeth, at my wit's end
Paraphrasing	smartphone→mobile, important→essential, people→persons, stop→forbidden
Discourse Marker	in that moment, on the other hand

Describe a time you used your smartphone to do something important.

You should say:

    what happened

    when it happened

    how important the smartphone was

and explain how you felt about the experience.

For me, this is a challenging topic. The reason is that I use my mobile for numerous essential things. Please give me a moment to think.

OK, one occasion that comes to mind is having to transfer some money to my girlfriend so that she could pay her restaurant bill. It was one of those times when she was being particularly ditzy and had forgotten her credit cards. She called me all panicked, and I had to send her over some cash through WeChat.

It must have been about two weeks ago, and she's still thanking me for it because she was so embarrassed at the time. For me, it's done and dusted, and I've already forgotten about it. After all, she's my better half; it's my job to look after her.

Needless to say, without my phone, I couldn't have helped her as quickly as I could, and I would have ended up taking a taxi to go and meet her, which would have been problematic to say the least.

Like I said, I don't really think about it anymore. It's something that I needed to do to help someone I love. I'd do it again if the need arose, and although it was vital to her, to me, not so much. So, all in all, I don't really feel anything about it anymore.

Examiner: What do you usually do with a mobile phone? ⟨List⟩

Candidate: What, you mean other than sit on it? Seriously though, I do the everyday things that everyone else does, make phone calls, surf the Internet, message people through WeChat. I do use the health app quite a lot, which may be a little unusual, as I enjoy cycling and occasionally use the map app as well.

Examiner: What are the differences between young people and old people when using a mobile phone? ⟨Compare & Contrast⟩

Candidate: First off, messaging. Older people quite often make phone calls rather than WeChat people, and they mostly will use a computer to surf the Internet rather than their smartphone. They also won't play nearly as many games as my generation does. I can't really think of any others, but I think I've covered the main things that aren't the same.

Examiner: Which one is more important, using a mobile phone to make phone calls or to read messages? ⟨Compare & Contrast⟩

Candidate: I don't think one can be classed as more important than the other. I believe they are of equal importance. They're just a different way of communicating. Sometimes a message is sufficient; other times, you'd need to speak to someone in real time.

Examiner: Do you think there should be a law to stop people from making phone calls in public? ⟨Opinion⟩

Candidate: That's already happened, hasn't it? If it's not law, it's undoubtedly a strong suggestion, especially on trains, in parks and places like that. I think it's a good idea. There are far too many people that seem to shout into their phones anywhere, anytime. In my opinion, it's essential to keep quiet places, well, quiet.

Lexical Resource	
Less Common Language	ditzy, embarrassed, panicked, sufficient
Collocations/Idiomatic Language	comes to mind, done and dusted, my better half, ended up
Paraphrasing	a time→occasion, important→vital/essential, usually→everyday, differences→not the same
Discourse Marker	for me, needless to say, to say the least, all in all, first off

■ A time when you felt bored

> **Describe a time when you felt bored.**
>
> **You should say:**
>
> > **when it was**
> >
> > **who you were with**
> >
> > **what you were doing**
>
> **and explain why you felt bored.**

It was a hot summer afternoon earlier this year, and I was stuck at home with nothing to do. I was feeling bored and didn't know how to spend my time. I was all alone and had no one to talk to. The TV shows and movies that I normally enjoyed didn't seem appealing anymore, and neither did my playstation games. *(游戏机)*

I felt bored because I had no stimulation *(刺激)*, no one to interact with, and no sense of purpose. The monotony *(单调乏味)* of the day was dragging on *(困难地度过)*, and I felt like I was stuck in a rut *(一成不变)*. I was just going through the motions, but nothing seemed to bring me joy or excitement.

I was stuck in this situation for what felt like hours, until finally, I decided to take a walk in the park. The fresh air and new surroundings were just what I needed to shake off the boredom. It was invigorating *(使精力充沛)*, and suddenly, the world seemed like a much more interesting place. The change of scenery was enough to jumpstart *(快速启动)* my creativity, and I felt like I could tackle anything that came my way. I had a real pep in my step *(步履轻盈矫健)*.

I think it's important to have variety and stimulation, if not a little excitement, in our lives. When we're stuck in a monotonous routine, it can be easy to feel bored and unmotivated. But with a little creativity and a change of scenery, we can turn things around and rediscover the joys of life.

Examiner: When do people feel bored? (Speculate)

Candidate: Boredom emerges when people have nothing to do. For example, a retired worker will feel bored because he is too old to work and there are no other things he can do. Besides, when people do not develop an interest or when there is no company, they will feel bored.

Examiner: What can people do when they feel bored? (Speculate)

Candidate: If they don't want to talk with others, they can watch TV series, play online games, or read a book, or go out for exercise. If they want a companion, they can turn to their friends and talk or travel with them. And a pet will be either an excellent choice. People can have their company all the time.

Examiner: Do people get bored with daily routines? (Speculate)

Candidate: Yes. Once stuck in a rigid or set routine, people feel jaded and want to make a change. We can imagine, from the moment you open your eyes to the moment you close your eyes to sleep, you repeat the same work, face the same people, eat the same meals, it is hard not to go crazy.

Examiner: Is it easier for young people to feel bored than for the old? (Compare & Contrast)

Candidate: No, I don't think so. Nowadays, there are a variety of entertainments and technologies for young people to rescue them from boredom. They can play all forms of games and talk with their friends through various applications. However, for old people, they are less energetic, and they may not be able to use technologies well, which makes them more bored.

Lexical Resource	
Less Common Language	stimulation, monotony, invigorating, rigid, energetic
Collocations/Idiomatic Language	stuck in a rut, jumpstart, pep in my step, joys of life, jaded
Paraphrasing	stimulation→excitement, bored→jaded
Discourse Marker	besides, nowadays, however

> **Describe a time when you felt bored.**
> **You should say:**
>   when it was
>   who you were with
>   what you were doing
> **and explain why you felt bored.**

Oh, over the last three years, pick a time; there have been too many to count. One particular occasion when I was really climbing the walls was when there was some major building work in my compound in Beijing. I live on my uni campus, and it must have been during last spring or summer, I noticed lots of my classmates and some of the teachers on the roads that go through the campus. It had been decided to erect a dividing line between the teacher's accommodation and the student dorms.

Within a day, virtually everything had been separated, and many play areas were closed and locked. This meant I couldn't play basketball, couldn't go to the cafeterias, couldn't even go to the little exercise yard. There was quite literally nothing to do. Yes, I had some homework to do, but I didn't really want to.

I think it was the second or third day after the change, and I remember waking up, having some breakfast and thinking, 'another mind-numbing day'. Nothing seemed to get me going. In the end, I just stayed in bed all day, slept, watched a bit of TV, slept again. You know how it is.

After a few weeks, they all came down again, which was wonderful. Looking back, I wish I had tried to be more active because I've gained more than a few pounds that I now need to work off, but hindsight is always 20/20, isn't it?

Examiner: When do people feel bored? (Speculate)

Candidate: Basically, anytime they've got nothing to do. It's not when people are tired and want to rest, just that when they want to do something but can't. Recently, I wanted to go and play basketball, or even just go for a walk, but I couldn't because it was difficult to get outside.

Examiner: What can people do when they feel bored? (Speculate)

Candidate: I think that it would depend on the person. Some people are good at finding things to occupy their mind. Me, not so much. Although having said that, I can occasionally find myself a TV series to go through, you know, have a real marathon session.

马拉松式的

Examiner: Do people get bored with daily routines? (Speculate)

Candidate: Well, I can't speak for others but I quite enjoy having a regular schedule. I'm not a fan of change, in anything, so when I can organise my time so that it remains constant and regular, I'm generally a happy bunny. Obviously, things do change, and some people enjoy that, 'a change is as good as a rest', they say. Nope, a change is unwelcome and should not be allowed.

Examiner: Is it easier for young people to feel bored than for the old? (Compare & Contrast)

Candidate: That's an interesting question. It's not something I've ever thought of before. What do I think? I have to say, yes, they do. I would say that the younger people are generally more active and need to be doing things. The older people, especially those in their 70s or 80s want to slow down anyway.

Lexical Resource	
Less Common Language	compound, erect, mind-numbing, occupy, marathon
Collocations/Idiomatic Language	climbing the walls, mind-numbing, get me going, hindsight is always 20/20
Paraphrasing	time→occasion, daily routines→regular schedule, the old→those in their 70s or 80s
Discourse Marker	oh, looking back, although having said that, well, nope

■ An occasion when you received bad service

> **Describe an occasion when you received bad service.**
> **You should say:**
>   **what happened**
>   **when and where it happened**
>   **who you were with**
> **and explain why the service was bad.**

I received awful（糟糕的）service at a restaurant during a family dinner. The restaurant was known for its delicious food and friendly staff, so we were looking forward to the meal. However, the experience was far from what we expected.

We were seated at a table, and it took quite a while for a server to come over and take our order. When he finally arrived, he seemed rushed（草率的）and uninterested in taking our order. Our drinks arrived late, and the food was cold and undercooked. When we brought this to the attention of the waiter, he was unapologetic（不愿道歉的）and seemed annoyed by our complaints.

The service continued to be subpar（低于标准的）throughout the meal, with the waiter neglecting to check on us and neglecting to refill our drinks. When it was time for the bill, there were errors and overcharges, which took a long time to resolve. By the time we left the restaurant, we were all disappointed and frustrated with the service.

I was with my family, including my parents and younger siblings（兄弟姐妹）, and it was meant to be a special evening. However, the bad service ruined the evening for us. We left feeling unsatisfied and not at all impressed with the restaurant.

So, to summarise then, the service we received was terrible because the staff was uninterested and unprofessional. They seemed rushed and neglected their duties, which resulted in a poor customer experience. Additionally, the food was not up to the standard（不符标准的）we were expecting from a restaurant of that calibre（质量）. Overall, the bad service left a negative feeling, and I certainly wouldn't recommend the restaurant to anyone now.

Examiner: Who should be responsible for bad services? (Opinion)

Candidate: Well, the person who is giving the bad service. So, like I explained just now, the waiter. I think the buck should stop with the manager though, it's up to him to make sure that the staff is trained well.

Examiner: Why do some people choose to remain silent when they receive bad services? (Speculate)

Candidate: Perhaps they don't want to cause a fuss. Or they may just figure that they want to get out of there as soon as possible. Personally, I think it's always better to say something, for the main reason that unless someone says something, the service may never improve in the future.

Examiner: What kinds of services are bad services? (List)

Candidate: That's a large list. I think you can receive bad service from any and all companies or industries where people deal with the public. This could be in a shop, a hotel, a restaurant, or a gym, to name a few. I suppose it's up to the client to measure whether the service received is actually bad, though.

Examiner: As a boss, what would you do to prevent bad service? (Hypothesise)

Candidate: The first thing I'd do is make sure my staff are trained to give good service. Education, I think, is paramount in the service industry because it can eliminate and dodge negative situations before they even happen. A second thing I'd do is make sure I only hire staff who understand that good service is key to the success of my business. If they don't get that, I wouldn't employ them.

Lexical Resource	
Less Common Language	rushed, unapologetic, subpar, siblings, calibre, paramount, eliminate, dodge
Collocations/Idiomatic Language	far from, the buck should stop with, cause a fuss
Paraphrasing	bad→awful/terrible, server→waiter, subpar→not up to the standard, hire→employ, understand→get
Discourse Marker	so, overall, well, personally, to name a few

---

Describe an occasion when you received bad service.

You should say:

    what happened

    when and where it happened

    who you were with

and explain why the service was bad.

Oh, that's an easy topic, especially today. It's all about my trip to the hairdresser and, needless to say, my hair. I mean, look at it! I'm so upset, not to mention angry.

I thought I'll pop down 〔匆匆去〕 to get my hair done before today's exam. I was a bit nervous about today, still am, in fact, and I thought I'll do something to take my mind off 〔暂时忘记〕 things. So, my bright idea was to get a new style haircut, a massage and a facial 〔面部护理〕. What could go wrong?!

It was only yesterday that all this occurred at my regular hairdresser, which is only around the corner from where I live. I gave him a photo of what I wanted, and he said, 'No problem'. Usually, they're great, but this idiot, every time I said I didn't like something, he just laughed and said don't worry about it. At the end of the day, I really wasn't happy with it, but I couldn't get a second opinion 〔第二意见〕 from my mother, as I was on my own.

I spoke to the hairdresser and said that it's not the same as the picture, and he just said that it was. I talked to the manager, said I wanted it changed, and she just wanted to charge me more money. I was furious 〔狂怒的〕, but also exhausted 〔筋疲力尽的〕. I felt utterly humiliated 〔脸面丢尽〕, and I wasn't going to get anywhere with these people, so I just stomped 〔跺着脚走〕 home. I didn't even bother with the massage and facial.

I'll tell you one thing; I'm NEVER going back to that hairdresser.

Examiner: Who should be responsible for bad services? Opinion

Candidate: The management of whoever is giving you the inferior service. In my experience, people who are in the service industry aren't trained very well in whatever they're doing. The powers that be just hire completely inexperienced staff and expect them to learn on the job with little or no guidance until something bad happens. Having said all that, the server does bear some responsibility because they should be proactive in learning how to serve people correctly in their chosen occupation.

Examiner: Why do some people choose to remain silent when they receive bad services? Speculate

Candidate: I think that mostly it's because they don't want to cause a scene or make the server feel bad. I can understand these reasons, but I don't agree with them myself. I think that if you remain quiet with bad servers, they won't have the opportunity to learn from any mistakes. You don't have to jump up and down and scream at them to make a point about bad service.

Examiner: What kinds of services are bad services? List

Candidate: A waitress giving you the wrong meal, or a shop assistant knowing nothing about the products that they sell. The list can go on. I think that any service where the customer feels unhappy, for whatever reason, can be considered 'bad'.

Examiner: As a boss, what would you do to prevent bad service? Hypothesise

Candidate: Well, the first thing I'd do is make sure that all staff had adequate initial training to do the job and then subsequent programs at regular intervals. Another thing I'd introduce is customer feedback forms so that customers can give anonymous feedback about any particular server. A mentor program might be worth having a look at too, so that new staff have someone to guide them each day and ask questions if necessary.

Lexical Resource	
Less Common Language	facial, furious, exhausted, stomped, inferior, subsequent, anonymous
Collocations/Idiomatic Language	pop down, take my mind off, second opinion, utterly humiliated, the powers that be, at regular intervals
Paraphrasing	happened→occurred, bad→inferior
Discourse Marker	needless to say, I'll tell you one thing, having said all that, well

■ An ambition that you have had for a long time

> **Describe an ambition that you have had for a long time.**
>
> **You should say:**
>
>   **what it is**
>
>   **what you did for it**
>
>   **when you can achieve it**
>
> **and explain why you have this ambition.**

One ambition that I have had for a long time is to become a successful software engineer. I have always been fascinated [入迷的] by technology and the idea of building things that can make a positive impact on people's lives. The thought of being able to create innovative software solutions that can improve people's daily lives is what drives me to pursue this ambition.

To achieve this, I have dedicated myself to continuously learning and improving my skills. I have taken online courses, participated in coding competitions, and worked on personal projects to gain hands-on experience. I have also sought out mentorship [指导] from experienced software engineers and have consistently sought feedback on my work to identify areas for improvement.

I believe that I can achieve this desire within the next five years if I continue to work hard and stay dedicated. I am confident that my efforts will pay off [取得成功], and I will be able to secure a successful software engineering role at a top tech company.

The reason why I have this ambition is that I believe that technology has the power to change the world for the better [向好的方向发展]. I want to be a part of this change and make a meaningful contribution to society through my work as a software engineer. Additionally, I find the field of software engineering to be endlessly challenging and exciting, and I am motivated by the prospect of continuously learning and growing in my career.

Overall, becoming a successful software engineer is a goal that I have had for a long time, and I am determined to make it a reality. I believe that with hard work, dedication, and continuous learning, I can achieve this ambition and make a positive impact on the world through my work.

Examiner: Why do people have ambitions? ⟮Speculate⟯

Candidate: I think everyone wants to better themselves, so 'ambitions' are the goals we set ourselves to make us improve our lot. I think we all have them. It would be incredibly boring if we didn't.

Examiner: What are the kinds of ambitions children often have when they're young? ⟮List⟯

Candidate: I think it would depend on the types of things they like and who they look up to. Quite often, they want to imitate their parents and become a teacher or a doctor. Sometimes they might get ideas from TV, like becoming an astronaut or a superhero.

Examiner: Should parents interfere with their children's ambitions? ⟮Opinion⟯

Candidate: I don't think 'interfere' would be the correct word. I think parents should guide their children in all things, but I don't believe that parents should try and change their children's goals and ideals. Most kids' ambitions will change and develop over time anyway. One week they want to be Superman, the next a vet, the next a teacher.

Examiner: Why do people have ambitions at work? ⟮Speculate⟯

Candidate: Probably for the same reason that people have them in their personal life. It's like I said earlier, people want to improve their lives. This means that people want to get promoted and earn more money. Without ambition, I don't think this would be possible. They don't necessarily have to want to be the CEO, but similarly, they don't want to stay at the bottom of the ladder either.

Lexical Resource	
Less Common Language	fascinated, mentorship, lot, vet
Collocations/Idiomatic Language	make a positive impact on, pay off, for the better, make a meaningful contribution to, improve our lot, look up to
Paraphrasing	ambition→desire/goal, better→improve
Discourse Marker	additionally, overall

Describe an ambition that you have had for a long time.

You should say:

   what it is

   what you did for it

   when you can achieve it

and explain why you have this ambition.

One ambition that I'd like to talk about that I've had for a while but haven't achieved yet is to climb a mountain. In particular, I'd like to climb Mount Qomolangma. For me, I don't want to have all the same ambitions as everybody else. I'd like to have a few that are different and also more challenging.

This is something that very few people have achieved, and this is why I want to do it. It would be a new thing for me because I've never done anything like this before, and probably requires quite a lot of training, although I'd need to look into this more. I know that you can go to the first base camp without any training, but then going up to the peak, because of the lack of oxygen and altitude sickness, I would rather make sure my body is prepared for what it might encounter.

I've had this ambition since I watched a documentary about the Nepalese Sherpas and how they go up and down this mountain on almost a daily basis, and just found it fascinating. It also showed how the villages around Mount Qomolangma have changed because of the tourism industry and that because there are many more people who wish to climb the mountain, their economy has grown.

As for why I still have this ambition, money is the main factor, and also, to be honest, I'm a little scared. Lots of people die at the peak of Mount Qomolangma, and there are avalanches and things like this, so firstly, I think I need to pluck up some courage in order to do it. Having said that, I hope I can do it in the next few years because if I get too old, I'll probably never do it. So, it is something that is definitely achievable that I must push myself to do.

Examiner: Why do people have ambitions? (Speculate)

Candidate: I think it's part of human nature for people to have the desire to better themselves. I think it's important for people to have goals and ambitions but not necessarily achieve them all. Otherwise, later in life, you will have nothing to strive for.

Examiner: What are the kinds of ambitions children often have when they're young? (List)

Candidate: I suppose most people, when they're small, want to be famous or rich. Others might know what kind of job they want to do when they grow up, for example, be a fireman or be a doctor, but I think these ambitions change quite a lot as they grow up.

Examiner: Should parents interfere with their children's ambitions? (Opinion)

Candidate: Yes, I believe they should. Children don't have the knowledge or experience to know how to go through life and how to set goals. It's the responsibility of their folks to show and teach them what good ambitions are versus bad ones. Only then will children be able to grow and understand what is good for them.

Examiner: Why do people have ambitions at work? (Speculate)

Candidate: In my opinion, I think people would get bored if they stayed in the same job all their working life, so if they try and learn and then achieve new levels in the company, they not only will earn more money but also have a sense of self-satisfaction.

Lexical Resource	
Less Common Language	peak, oxygen, documentary, avalanches
Collocations/Idiomatic Language	look into, altitude sickness, pluck up some courage, strive for
Paraphrasing	goals→ambitions, young→small
Discourse Marker	for me, having said that, in my opinion

■ A trip that you plan to go on in the near future

> **Describe a trip that you plan to go on in the near future.**
> **You should say:**
> 　　**where you want to go**
> 　　**what you will do**
> 　　**who you would like to go with**
> **and explain why you would like to go there.**

Well, the holiday I would like to go on would be a round-the-world trip. I know in countries like the UK and America, students often take a gap year between finishing their high school education and starting university, I like to do the same. I want to visit as many countries as possible and maybe turn it into a working holiday as well.

I will finish my school year in July and would like to start my trip maybe in August. I feel that this would be a good time to go, partly because of the weather, which I hope will be nice in the southern hemisphere and also because it would give me a full year to relax and enjoy myself before hitting the books again at uni.

As for who I'd go with, I'd probably go on my own because a lot of my friends don't have the same idea or plan as I do and they're not really as outgoing or adventurous as I am. I do have some friends in some of the countries I will visit, so it'll be nice to see them and stay with them maybe, but it wouldn't be the same as actually travelling with them.

Regarding the 'why' of doing this holiday, I suppose the simplest answer is, because I can. But the other main reason is because if I don't do it now, I don't know when I'll have the opportunity to do it. I'd rather do it now and take the bull by the horns, as it were.

Examiner:　Where do Chinese people like to travel to? (Speculate)

Candidate:　Many of us travel to Europe and America for holidays, if we can afford it, that is. I suppose others may go a little nearer to home, like Japan or Korea, or even somewhere like Hong Kong. It probably depends on the reason for the trip.

Examiner:　Why do some people prefer to stay at home during holidays? (Speculate)

Candidate:　If I'm honest, I don't always go away during holidays. Sometimes, I just don't fancy it. Maybe others feel the same way. For me, it's more about being able to relax at home, go to the beach if I want to, enjoy some sun and then spend some more time with my family.

Examiner:　What kinds of activities do people like to do on holiday? (List)

Candidate:　Again, it depends on the people and what they're interested in. Lots of people like going sightseeing, hiking or some kind of sports like skiing in the Alps. Others prefer a more relaxing holiday and just go out to eat, maybe do some shopping or lie on the beach and get a tan. I tend to do the latter, as I want to relax on a holiday rather than be too active.

Examiner:　Do people in your country like to have holidays? (Opinion)

Candidate:　I believe so. Obviously, I can't speak for everyone, but I think it's considered a part of life that we work, but we can also play. Otherwise, Jack is a very dull boy! I also think we NEED holidays sometimes, you know, to recharge the old batteries. Thinking about it a bit more, I don't think anyone would actually say 'No' to having a holiday.

Lexical Resource	
Less Common Language	hemisphere, adventurous, fancy
Collocations/Idiomatic Language	hitting the books, take the bull by the horns, Jack is a very dull boy, to recharge the old batteries
Paraphrasing	trip→travel/visit, activities→sightseeing, hiking or some kind of sports
Discourse Marker	well, if I'm honest, again, obviously, thinking about it a bit more

---

Describe a trip that you plan to go on in the near future.

You should say:

> **where you want to go**

> **what you will do**

> **who you would like to go with**

and explain why you would like to go there.

Well, with any luck, I'll be going to the UK in the not-too-distant future. It depends on how well I do on this test.

The plan is to go to the UK to get my Master's degree. I've already got my Bachelor's, so I plan to get the next level up. I've got a couple of options on where I can go. Firstly is Manchester, which is in the north of England, with a backup of Southampton, which is all the way in the south, on the coast. So very different places, but basically the same course.

Most Master's in England, well, you probably know, are only one year, so my thinking is that although the price is twice as much, I can do it in half the time as the Master's here would take at least two years, if not three. So, I figure that depending on the regulations at the time, I can do my Master's, then get a job over there for a while, come back and not only will I have a better level of education, I'll also have some work experience. But, like I said, it depends on what the laws say. I don't want to get into any trouble.

I chose England mainly because the education is world-renowned for its excellence and the second reason is that I can travel a little bit. I might study in England, but it also gives me the opportunity to visit Europe and broaden my horizons a bit. It's really an opportunity I can't pass up, but like I said at the beginning, I've got to do well in this exam first. Fingers crossed!

Examiner: Where do Chinese people like to travel to? (Speculate)

Candidate: Now that people are freer to travel again, pretty much anywhere. Other countries in Asia are always popular, mainly because they're close and obviously the domestic travel market is always good. A lot of my friends go to Hainan Island during the ^(寒假) winter break as it's a lot warmer than Beijing.

Examiner: Why do some people prefer to stay at home during holidays? (Speculate)

Candidate: Well, first off, I think because of the money. It can be quite expensive to travel, especially abroad. Secondly, I suppose it would depend on the length of the holiday. Some of our holidays are only a couple of days, whereas others are a few weeks, so where you go and what you do is ^(取决于) governed by those ^(约束条件) constraints. I suppose a final group just don't want to go anywhere. I'm sometimes like that. I might ^(匆匆出去) pop out for a meal or go and see friends, but I would just as easily relax at home and do nothing.

Examiner: What kinds of activities do people like to do on holiday? (List)

Candidate: I suppose that it would depend on the type of holiday they're having. If they go to somewhere that is famous for beaches, it's likely that they want to swim a lot and get a ^(晒黑) tan. If they go to a mountainous area in winter, they likely want to ski or ^(玩滑板) board. I think all of them would go shopping and enjoy some meals out, though, so that's common to all of them.

Examiner: Do people in your country like to have holidays? (Opinion)

Candidate: In my opinion, yes, of course, they do. Who doesn't? We have to do the occasional ^(调休) make-up days if the short holidays get extended, but that's OK. I'd prefer to have a longer break and then an additional day's work than just get a single day off. But people in my country are just like everyone else, we study or work hard and then want to relax, so having a break is a lovely way to do that.

Lexical Resource	
Less Common Language	backup, regulations, world-renowned, excellence, constraints, tan, board
Collocations/Idiomatic Language	with any luck, not-too-distant-future, pass up, winter break, pop out, make-up days
Paraphrasing	regulations→law, holidays→break
Discourse Marker	well, so, fingers crossed, first off, in my opinion

■ A time when you were stuck in a traffic jam

> **Describe a time when you were stuck in a traffic jam.**
>
> **You should say:**
>
> > **when it happened**
> >
> > **where you were stuck**
> >
> > **what you did while waiting**
>
> **and explain how you felt in the traffic jam.**

I was stuck in a traffic jam during my daily commute [通勤] to work. It was a typical weekday morning, and I was on my way to the office when suddenly, the traffic came to a standstill. I was on the highway, and it seemed like there was an accident ahead, causing a massive backup [堵塞] of vehicles.

I was trapped in the traffic jam for over an hour, and it was incredibly annoying. The cars were moving at a snail's pace [蜗牛般的速度], and I felt like I was going nowhere. The weather was hot, and the air conditioning in my car wasn't working properly, making the situation even more unbearable.

To pass the time while waiting, I tried to stay occupied. I listened to music, made some phone calls, and even tried to catch up on [补做] some work-related emails. However, I couldn't shake the feeling of frustration and annoyance.

The traffic jam made me feel stressed and anxious, as I was already running late for a meeting and was worried about the impact it would have on my day. I felt trapped, as there was nothing I could do to change the situation, and I was completely at the mercy of [受制于] the traffic.

So, to finish, being stuck in a traffic jam was an irritating [烦人的] and stressful experience. It made me feel trapped and powerless, and the situation was made even more unbearable by the hot weather and the faulty [有故障的] air conditioning in my car. However, I tried to make the best of [充分利用] the situation by staying occupied and staying productive while waiting.

Examiner:　How can we solve the traffic jam problem? ⌈Speculate⌋

Candidate:　The first thing is to stay calm. During a traffic jam, annoyance or anger cannot make any

　　　　　　sense and even make the situation worse. The second thing is to schedule the route. In

　　　　　　this way, you can either set off in advance or choose a route which might have better

　　　　　　traffic. So to solve it well, careful planning and a relaxed state of mind are critical.

Examiner:　Do you think developing public transport can solve traffic jam problems? ⌈Evaluate⌋

Candidate:　Yes, I think, to some degree, it can. Public transport has a larger capacity, which means

　　　　　　the number of private vehicles on the road would reduce. But the speed tends to

　　　　　　be slow, and there would be an extremely long queue waiting to get on the public

　　　　　　transport, which would cause another form of jam.

Examiner:　Do you think highways will help reduce traffic jams? ⌈Evaluate⌋

Candidate:　No, I don't think so. The cause of traffic jams may not have a close relationship with the

　　　　　　type of roads. It is more related to the way of how people get on the way and how they

　　　　　　schedule their time. What's more, for many people, highways are not so necessary for

　　　　　　them to commute or just go out.

Examiner:　What are good ways to manage traffic? ⌈Speculate⌋

Candidate:　First, if possible, more roads should be built, or the structure of the traffic network

　　　　　　should be updated to meet the streaming cars. Second, public transportation should be

　　　　　　recommended. Even though it has a slower speed, it may save time than waiting in a

　　　　　　traffic jam. At last, a good mood is essential when you are already in a jam.

Lexical Resource	
Less Common Language	commute, backup, irritating, stressful, faulty, capacity
Collocations/Idiomatic Language	at a snail's pace, catch up on, at the mercy of, make the best, make any sense, set off
Paraphrasing	stuck→trapped
Discourse Marker	so, what's more, first

Describe a time when you were stuck in a traffic jam.

You should say:

    when it happened

    where you were stuck

    what you did while waiting

and explain how you felt in the traffic jam.

It was on the way here actually. Today's been a bit of a 可怕的经历 nightmare 到目前为止 so far. We, my father and I left REALLY early this morning because I wanted to get here with enough time to 冷静 chill out and relax before coming into this room.

I don't know if you know Beijing very well, but at 8 am in the morning on the 3rd Ring Road, it turns into the world's largest car park. To be honest, it's not THAT bad, it just feels that way. To my understanding, the rush hour everywhere is the same, it really doesn't matter what country you're in.

It was worst coming out of the Guomao Exit in the east, probably because there are so many people coming into that area to come to work. I've done the route many times over the years, and would normally leave earlier, you know, probably around 6.30, but as my exam today wasn't until 午餐时间 lunch-ish, I didn't see the point. I figured if I get here for around 10, I'd have over an hour to prepare myself mentally.

Did it work that way? Oh, 糟糕 heck. I only got here about 20 minutes ago. I was 爬行 crawling along all the way, a real 蜗牛般的速度 slug's pace. I could have walked it faster. As for what I did while I was waiting, well, I swore a lot, shouted at the world, but, in reality, there was nothing I could do. I just had to try and calm down and be patient, because I knew if I 紧张 wound myself up too much, I'd be completely useless now.

Examiner: How can we solve the traffic jam problem? (Speculate)

Candidate: Perhaps by getting rid of all the cars, but I really don't think that's going to happen anytime soon. Seriously though, there are already imitations here in Beijing, and I know that London, for example, has a payment system in place which would discourage some drivers from using their car. I don't think there's only one way to do it. I think it would take multiple solutions. Car sharing might be a good one for here.

Examiner: Do you think developing public transport can solve traffic jam problems? (Evaluate)

Candidate: I'm not sure I say solve, but it can certainly relieve some of the pressure. The convenience of cars, and the need for delivery trucks will always be needed. I think though we can organise something like the park and ride systems that are in the UK. There are already some of them 分布在 dotted about Beijing; I just think we need more.

Examiner: Do you think highways will help reduce traffic jams? (Evaluate)

Candidate: As I said earlier, I don't think there's just one answer. Expansion of roads, public transportation, among other things can all help. So, the short answer to your question is yes, but there's a much longer answer to this too. I'm not sure we'd have enough time to go through it all.

Examiner: What are good ways to manage traffic? (Speculate)

Candidate: I would say 错列的 staggered working times, so that there is no 'rush hour'. This would help 减轻 alleviate some of the traffic jams. The other thing I'd recommend would be to optimise the traffic lights system. The number of times that I seem to get stuck there for no particular reason, is something that I think can be easily resolved, certainly with all the AI apps that are around these days.

Lexical Resource	
Less Common Language	nightmare, crawling, relieve, expansion, staggered, alleviate
Collocations/Idiomatic Language	so far, chill out, rush hour, lunch-ish, heck, wound myself up, dotted about
Paraphrasing	crawling→slug's pace, chill out→relax/calm down/be patient, solve→resolved, solutions→answer, relieve→alleviate
Discourse Marker	to be honest, you know, seriously though, as I said earlier

A foreign language (except English) that you want to learn

> **Describe a foreign language (except English) that you want to learn.**
>
> **You should say:**
>
> > **what it is**
> >
> > **where you would learn it**
> >
> > **how you would learn it**
>
> **and explain why you want to learn it.**

The foreign language that I would like to learn is Spanish. Spanish is one of the most widely spoken languages in the world, and it would be an incredibly useful skill to have. I think it's number three behind English and Chinese, which means I could communicate with many Europeans and South Americans.

I would like to study it in a language school or through online classes as it would provide me with a structured and immersive 沉浸式的 learning experience, and I would be able to learn from experienced and qualified teachers. Online classes would offer more flexibility and convenience, and I would be able to learn at my own pace and on my own schedule.

I would start by learning the basics, such as grammar, vocabulary, and sentence structure. I would then practise speaking and listening to the language, using online resources and language exchange programs. I would also try and immerse myself in the culture by watching Spanish movies and TV shows, listening to Spanish music, and reading Spanish books and newspapers. One of my favourite types of music and dance is the Tango.

So, to sum up everything then, the reason I want to learn Spanish is that I believe language is one of the most important tools for connecting with people from different cultures. Learning Spanish would allow me to communicate with Spanish-speaking people from all over the world, and it would open up a whole new world of possibilities for me. Additionally, knowing it would be a valuable asset in my personal and professional life, and it would enhance my global competitiveness.

Examiner: Is it popular to learn English in your country? ⌐Opinion⌐

Candidate: Absolutely. It's compulsory in most schools and universities, so almost everyone learns it at some point. Obviously, some students take it further than others, me, for example. I'd like to study in the UK, so I need to have quite good English in order to be able to do that.

Examiner: What are the difficulties of learning a new language? ⌐List⌐

Candidate: Oh, the hardships are too numerous to count. I'm not sure if we have long enough. I think probably top of the list would be how large the difference is between your native tongue and the new language. For example, English and Chinese are a long way apart, but something like Chinese and Japanese are much closer together.

Examiner: What's the best way to learn a new language? ⌐Speculate⌐

Candidate: For me, I need to dive in and see if I can tread water. Perhaps I'll start with online classes, like I mentioned earlier, and then as I can understand the basics, move on to watching TV programs, finding a language partner, and just making sure that I can maintain the use of it. As they say, 'if you don't use it, you lose it'.

Examiner: What can people do to learn a second language? ⌐List⌐

Candidate: I think there are lots of things people can do. Book some classes, download some material from the Internet, or even just find a friend who speaks that language. If you want to go to the extreme, you could move to that country for a while and immerse yourself.

Lexical Resource	
Less Common Language	immersive, competitiveness, asset, compulsory, numerous
Collocations/Idiomatic Language	native tongue, dive in, if you don't use it you lose it
Paraphrasing	learn→study, difficulties→hardships, language→tongue
Discourse Marker	so, to sum up everything then, additionally, absolutely

> **Describe a foreign language (except English) that you want to learn.**
>
> **You should say:**
>
> > **what it is**
> >
> > **where you would learn it**
> >
> > **how you would learn it**
>
> **and explain why you want to learn it.**

Spanish. That's the other language I would like to study beyond English. After all, the three most spoken languages are English, Chinese and Spanish. Obviously, there are lots of others, but would they really benefit me in the future?

I'm reasonably sure I can organise classes through my current university because I've already got some friends that have them. I just don't know if it's an official class or something that an external *外部的* person or company has organised. I'm hoping I can just join my friends as we're all about the same level.

From what my friends have said, there's also the opportunity to get together with Spanish-speaking students that already study at the university. Kind of a language exchange program. Personally, I think this is the best way to learn a language. You've got to sit down with some natives and have a chat. I can help them with some of their Chinese, and they can do the same with my Spanish.

Like I mentioned earlier, the three major languages are English, Chinese and Spanish. To me, it just seems logical to learn these languages above any other. Sure, I can study Japanese or even Korean, but would that help me in a global environment *全球环境*? My answer is no. I think I'd be better off *更好* with what I've chosen. I'd like to keep my options open when it comes to language and communication, and certainly, for now, that's the one I'd go for. I suppose I can always learn more languages in the future; I do kind of have a knack for *有诀窍* them.

Examiner: Is it popular to learn English in your country? (Opinion)

Candidate: Oh, definitely. It's one of the 义务的 compulsory subject areas during our education and has been for quite a while now. Studying abroad has been very popular over the last 20 years or so too, and it's why I'm here today, so yes, it's very common.

Examiner: What are the difficulties of learning a new language? (List)

Candidate: I think the first 难关 hurdle people need to 克服 get over is their own lack of confidence that they can successfully study a new language. Lots of people I know attempt a new language and give up after a few weeks just because they feel that they can't do it. Once you're past this stage, I think the next big difficulty is the grammar. Learning all the rules of the language is far harder than memorising the vocab, for me anyway.

Examiner: What's the best way to learn a new language? (Speculate)

Candidate: I think the top method of acquiring a new language is to 使自己沉浸于 immerse yourself in whatever language you're trying to learn. Find some events or places you can interact with people speaking that language, watch some of their TV, listen to radio programs and just use it daily. If you have the opportunity to go to that country, that'd be good too.

Examiner: What can people do to learn a second language? (List)

Candidate: To start with, go and do some classes, even if it's just a few. I believe that this can give you a base on how it can sound and be structured. From there, find a language partner so that you can practice new words or phrases with them and continue your self-study. Like I just said, immersing yourself in that language as much as possible is always a good idea, and making sure that you study, even a little bit, everyday.

Lexical Resource	
Less Common Language	reasonably, external, compulsory, hurdle
Collocations/Idiomatic Language	global environment, better off, have a knack for, get over, immerse yourself in
Paraphrasing	most spoken→major, difficulties→hurdle, learn→acquiring
Discourse Marker	obviously, sure, for now, oh, definitely, to start with, like I just said

■ A healthy lifestyle you know

> **Describe a healthy lifestyle you know.**
> **You should say:**
> 　　**how you know about it**
> 　　**what it is**
> 　　**what one would do living this lifestyle**
> **and explain why it is healthy.**

Well, the healthy lifestyle I will talk about today is a balanced diet combined with regular exercise. I know about this lifestyle through reading various health articles and books, as well as observing people who live this way.

A balanced diet consists of consuming a variety of nutrient-dense 营养密集的 foods, including fruits and vegetables, whole grains, lean 脂肪少的 protein sources, and healthy fats. It is important to limit or avoid processed foods, sugary drinks, and excessive amounts of salt and unhealthy fats. To live this lifestyle, one would focus on making healthy food choices, such as eating a rainbow of 五颜六色的 colourful fruits and vegetables, and portion control.

Regular exercise is also an important component of a healthy lifestyle. This can include activities such as walking, running, cycling, swimming, and strength training. To live this lifestyle, one would aim to get at least 30 minutes of moderate physical activity most days of the week.

This has numerous health benefits. A balanced diet provides the body with the nutrients it needs to function optimally, and it can reduce the risk of chronic diseases such as heart disease, stroke, and certain types of cancer. Regular exercise can also improve cardiovascular 心血管的 health, boost energy levels, and enhance mental wellbeing. 心理健康

In order to live this lifestyle, I would focus on making healthy food choices, such as eating a variety of nutrient-dense foods, and incorporating 使并入 physical activity into my daily routine. By adopting a balanced diet and regular exercise, I can improve my overall health and reduce the risk of chronic diseases.

Examiner: How should schools teach students to live healthily? (*Speculate*)

Candidate: I'd like them to use some scare tactics, but I don't think it's ever going to happen. It's all very well just saying, 'Don't smoke!' or 'Don't drink alcohol!', but I think if students were to actually see a lung covered in cigarette tar, or a liver damaged by cirrhosis, it would make them think twice.

Examiner: What can doctors do to help people solve health-related problems? (*Speculate*)

Candidate: I think they could suggest different techniques depending on what the individual's health issues are. For example, when I hurt my ankle my doctor suggested that I swim rather than run, and the health benefits of swimming are better. Or at least they're not as potentially damaging to the ankles or knees as jogging.

Examiner: What kinds of lifestyles are unhealthy? (*List*)

Candidate: Oh, loads. One of the depressing things about life is that all the fun things are generally bad for you. Chocolate, MacDonald's, TV and comfy sofas. Seriously though, I think anything excessive is unhealthy, even if people think it's a healthy thing to do. Let's take running as an example. Going for a run of a few kilometres each day would probably be good for you, as long as you use the right equipment. Running 25 kilometres every night probably isn't.

Examiner: What do people in your country do to maintain health? (*Speculate*)

Candidate: Keep a healthy diet and do, at least some, exercise. I think that we're quite good at moderation. So yes, we'll eat a few unhealthy foods, and lounge around sometimes, but not that often. Similarly, we don't overdo the sports and diets to lose weight.

Lexical Resource	
Less Common Language	nutrient-dense, lean, optimally, cardiovascular, incorporating, excessive, moderation, overdo
Collocations/Idiomatic Language	a rainbow of, chronic diseases, mental wellbeing, scare tactics, think twice, loads, lounge around
Paraphrasing	describe→talk about, running→jogging, maintain→keep, moderation→not overdo
Discourse Marker	well, seriously though, yes

Describe a healthy lifestyle you know.

You should say:

    how you know about it

    what it is

    what one would do living this lifestyle

and explain why it is healthy.

A healthy regime is something that we all think we can do, yet few of us actually keep it going. I maintain a relatively healthy balance between diet and exercise but am always on the lookout for ways to improve it. Some of the information I've found seems to me to be a little dramatic and even excessive, like the carbs only diet, but you've always got people online that swear by it. For me, though, from all my sources, whether online, my parents or teachers, or even the doctor, I try to figure out what's best for me. So, although there are people that have a healthier routine than me, what I do works for my body and my sanity.

There's nothing particularly special about it. There's no specific routine to it. I just believe in a balance between healthy and junk food and doing exercise rather than sitting at a desk all day.

As a student, much of my day is sitting in class at a desk, listening to my teachers. This means that I'm in a fixed sedentary position for about six hours a day, sometimes more. I generally try and play some sport at least twice a week and will usually cycle to and from class to keep this from affecting my body too much. Regarding diet, I do really enjoy MacDonalds sometimes, but realise that I can't have it too much. Once a week is enough, I think, but don't force that limit on myself. Sometimes, I'll have it twice in a week, then feel a little guilty and skip it for the next week in the knowledge that I can have one the week after.

I think this program is healthy because, firstly, I don't go to extremes one way or the other. I try and balance my calorie intake and try and keep a varied exercise program going. I think, perhaps more importantly, I keep my sanity by not making the rules absolute.

Examiner: How should schools teach students to live healthily? (Speculate)

Candidate: Leading by example, I think, would be a good start. By making sure that school canteens only had healthy food, they could show their pupils what's good to eat and what's not. I would also suggest that there are specific classes on the subject. Not just as part of biology or something, but an actual healthy eating class. It wouldn't have to be all semester, but, you know, maybe a few weeks.

Examiner: What can doctors do to help people solve health-related problems? (Speculate)

Candidate: Get out into the communities more. Most people only go and see a doctor when they have a medical problem. Many of these are caused by unhealthy lifestyles, so I think if the doctors can dish out some good old-fashioned preventative medicine, it would be better for everyone concerned. Breaking your leg and going to A&E is one thing, having high blood pressure and smoking too much is another.

Examiner: What kinds of lifestyles are unhealthy? (List)

Candidate: Well, one where someone studies all day and plays computer games all night is bad for you, for a start. A lot of my classmates do this, and I've told them a million times it's not good for them. I do occasionally join in, but only seldomly. We know that smoking and excessive alcohol are bad for you, yet there are still many people who do this. I think partly because they're addictive, but I believe that with enough willpower, you can beat them.

Examiner: What do people in your country do to maintain health? (Speculate)

Candidate: Kind of what I do, I suppose. As I said in the previous part, you just can't go to extremes in things. People will always go on a diet sometimes, and I think as you get older, it's more difficult to find the motivation to exercise because you're either tired from work or just don't know anyone that plays what you like anymore. There's always the gym, I suppose. There are many unhealthy people, but I guess that's the same in any country.

Lexical Resource	
Less Common Language	regime, carbs, sanity, sedentary, willpower
Collocations/Idiomatic Language	on the lookout for, swear by, in the knowledge that, go to extremes, leading by example, dish out, go on a diet
Paraphrasing	lifestyle→routine/program, students→pupils, unhealthy→bad for you
Discourse Marker	well, as I said in the previous part

Chapter 5 Places
地点类

■ A house or an apartment you would like to live in

Part 2	*Answer 1* （★★★★）	🎧 262

> **Describe a house or an apartment you would like to live in.**
>
> **You should say:**
>
> > **what it is like**
> >
> > **where it would be**
> >
> > **why you would like to live in this house/apartment**
>
> **and how you feel about this house/apartment.**

The house I would like to describe this afternoon actually belongs to one of my English friend's parents. To me, it is enormous, like properly huge. It has three floors, six bedrooms, two bathrooms upstairs and a shower room downstairs, as well as lots of other rooms. It is situated in an area of about two acres of land, and you could see for miles in any direction.

I think the original house is about 400 years old, but since then it has been extended twice and is located in Wincanton, which is in South West England. I would love it if I could have a house like that in my hometown of Beijing. We have courtyard houses and hutong, but they're nothing like Bayford House. Oh, that is the name of the house, by the way.

For me, I'd enjoy living there for two reasons. The first is just the size of the place. Wherever you walk, you just have a sense of space. Secondly, the history. The fact that this house has been standing in one shape or another for four centuries is just incredible.

As for the last section, as to how I feel about this house, I would have to say wonder, and probably a little bit green with envy because I know I'll never be able to live in it, although one of the things I do think about is that it might take a long time to clean and keep tidy. So I suppose, it's not all positive.

Examiner: What kinds of apartments are the most popular? (List)

Candidate: Here in China, I think the types of flats that are most common are the regular hutong. The cities here don't have a lot of space anymore and therefore are built up rather than out. Typically, these are one or two-bedroom apartments with a kitchen, lounge and bathroom.

Examiner: What are the differences between houses that young people and old people like? (Compare & Contrast)

Candidate: I suppose the main difference between young and old people is not really a matter of what, more like a matter of where. Old people, and by that I mean 70 plus, prefer living in quiet areas of a city or maybe even the countryside, whereas the younger generation prefer city centres, where they can go out and enjoy themselves.

Examiner: What are the differences between apartments and houses? (Compare & Contrast)

Candidate: I think the main difference between these two comes down to structure. An apartment, although part of a larger building, is typically only on one floor, whereas a house will have two or more. Saying that, though, I have seen apartments with stairs to the floor above. So, thinking about it a little more, maybe it's that houses are stand-alone units, but apartments aren't.

Examiner: Do people usually rent or buy a house in your country? (Speculate)

Candidate: In my hometown of Beijing, these days, most people rent because they simply can't afford to buy. Over the last few years, prices, both in and around Beijing, have gone through the roof. Pun intended. Personally, I would rather purchase an apartment, but I don't know if I'd be able to afford it.

Lexical Resource	
Less Common Language	enormous, acres, incredible, courtyard, hutong, incredible, lounge
Collocations/Idiomatic Language	green with envy, comes down to, stand-alone, gone through the roof, pun intended
Paraphrasing	apartments→flats, like→love/enjoy
Discourse Marker	to me, by the way, for me, as for the last section, saying that, though

> **Describe a house or an apartment you would like to live in.**
>
> **You should say:**
>
> > **what it is like**
> >
> > **where it would be**
> >
> > **why you would like to live in this house/apartment**
>
> **and how you feel about this house/apartment.**

I'm not that fussy when it comes to accommodation. As long as it is fairly spacious with good quality modern appliances and furniture, I don't really care if it is a house or a flat.

As for the question of 'where', I would really like to live in a coastal city, something like Sydney in Australia. I've been to Australia a number of times and just fell in love with the environment and the people. The city centre is a bit pricey for my tastes, but some of the surrounding areas, you know, the suburbs, are a lot less expensive.

I'd like to live in this kind of apartment mainly because I believe it would be more tranquil than living slap bang in the middle of a city, but still close enough to all the mod cons that a big city can provide. A three-bedroom, two-bathroom flat with a nice sized lounge would be a little slice of heaven for me. I neither want nor need anything much bigger, as that would be plenty of space for all my family as well as any guests that might come to stay.

What I'd really like to do is have this apartment during the winter months of Beijing and then come back here during the summer. That would just be perfect. All I have to do now is find a very well-paying job so that I can earn the money to do it.

Examiner: What kinds of apartments are the most popular? List

Candidate: I don't think, certainly in my experience, that they're all different kinds of flat. I've only ever seen multi-storey buildings with one, two or maybe three-bedroom apartments. I suppose some of them are taller than others because in some parts of Beijing you could only build five floors. I'm not sure if that rule has now changed.

Examiner: What are the differences between houses that young people and old people like? Compare & Contrast

Candidate: Oh, how long a list do you want? Because I can think of quite a few. I suppose the top couple^{两个} would be size and noise level. Younger people, like me, want big places so that we can relax more and have a feeling of space. Old people, like my parents or even my grandparents, prefer smaller places that are also quiet.

Examiner: What are the differences between apartments and houses? Compare & Contrast

Candidate: In my opinion, it would come down to size. A house is going to be much bigger than an apartment. I've seen some of the old-style courtyard houses around the centre of Beijing, and they are simply gorgeous^{美丽的}, not to mention huge. I'd prefer a courtyard house over a flat any day if I could afford one.

Examiner: Do people usually rent or buy a house in your country? Speculate

Candidate: I think people typically rent these days mainly because the prices of houses or flats here in Beijing are sky-high^{高昂的}, and only the stupidly rich can afford them. Well, I can afford anything larger than a shoe box anyway.

Lexical Resource	
Less Common Language	fussy, spacious, pricey, tranquil, gorgeous
Collocations/Idiomatic Language	as long as, slap bang, mod cons, well-paying, sky-high, larger than a shoe box
Paraphrasing	apartment→accommodation/flat
Discourse Marker	oh, in my opinion

■ A place in your country that you would like to recommend to visitors

> **Describe a place in your country that you would like to recommend to visitors.**
>
> **You should say:**
>
> **what it is**
>
> **where it is**
>
> **what people can do there**
>
> **and explain why you would like to recommend it to visitors.**

When it comes to talking about a fascinating part of my country, I would have to say that my hometown of Beijing is, by far, the most interesting. It is located in the North of China and, as you probably know, is the capital city. I have lived in Beijing all my life and grew up in Haidian District, although now I study north of the 5th Ring Road near Changping. So, as for knowing about it and what it has to offer, well, I'm a local.

Beijing is famous for many things, both new and old, modern and ancient. For example, you have things like the Summer Palace and Forbidden City, which go back hundreds if not thousands of years as well as new buildings like the Bird's Nest and the new CCTV building. I suppose the things that make it famous are that the government is based here, and government officials will come and meet in the Great Hall of the People to discuss and vote on important matters of state.

For me, I think what makes it most interesting is that there are so many differences depending on where you go, from the old-style courthouses and hutong in the very centre, to the modern business buildings in the CBD, then to the more historical and mountainous areas that basically make up the Beijing border. I don't think there's anything quite like it anywhere else in the world, at least, none that I've seen so far.

Examiner: Is it important to take photos while travelling? (*Opinion*)

Candidate: I think so, yes. Without them, it's very easy to forget people, places, or times 彻底地 down the line. These days taking photos is a lot simpler than it was, say, 20 years ago, and it's also much easier to store them.

Examiner: Can you trust other people's travel journals on the Internet? (*Speculate*)

Candidate: Well, personally, I think you have to take them 有保留地 with a pinch of salt. Different people have different ideas about what is good or bad about a place and may be looking for something completely different to you. I think it would also depend on how long the other person has stayed in that place, because the longer the stay, the more they would understand.

Examiner: What factors affect how people feel about travelling? (*List*)

Candidate: I suppose the top two things, certainly for me, would be price and weather. Price 许多 because I don't have oodles of money and would need to travel 节省费用 on a budget, and weather because I would want to go somewhere with nicer weather than where I currently am.

Examiner: Will you go to a foreign country to travel because of the distinct landscape? (*Opinion*)

Candidate: Definitely, yes. Most of the reasons I travel abroad is to see different features and scenery in a particular place. For example, I would love to go and see the 大峡谷 Grand Canyon in America.

Lexical Resource	
Less Common Language	fascinating, oodles, remotely
Collocations/Idiomatic Language	down the line, with a pinch of salt, on a budget
Paraphrasing	by far→so far, new and old→modern and ancient, factors→things, go to a foreign country→travel abroad
Discourse Marker	well, for me, definitely

> **Describe a place in your country that you would like to recommend to visitors.**
>
> **You should say:**
>
> > **what it is**
> >
> > **where it is**
> >
> > **what people can do there**
>
> **and explain why you would like to recommend it to visitors.**

The place I'm going to talk about today is a coastal city called Weihai. It's relatively small by Chinese standards, and I think it is only a 三线城市 third-tier city, but for my family and I, it is a wonderful escape from the 熙熙攘攘 hustle and bustle of Beijing city life.

It's located in Shandong Province, which is on the East Coast of China. It's 接近 not a million miles away from Korea. To fly, it takes a little over an hour, by one of the fast trains it would be around 5 hours and to drive it is about 9 hours. I know that because I've done all three.

The main attractions of Weihai are the beaches and the fresh seafood. I'm not really a big fan of 螃蟹和龙虾 crabs and lobster, but I do like fish occasionally, so for me, it's the fact that I can feel the sand between my toes and get a bit of a tan. I often take my 潜水工具 snorkelling gear down to the beach too. That way, I can see some of the ocean wildlife all around me while I have a swim.

I would suggest this to people for a couple of reasons. One, it's 偏僻地 off the beaten track, 可以这么说 so to speak, and it's not nearly as crowded or busy as some of the larger cities like Qingdao, Shanghai or Beijing. Two, because people are a lot more friendly there than in the big cities and you're much more likely to be able to interact with people, and therefore get a more accurate feeling about the country.

Examiner: Is it important to take photos while travelling? (Opinion)

Candidate: Oh, it's not just important, it's essential. If you don't take any photos when you're visiting new, you can't then share them with your friends or family when you return. Also, the fact that they are now so easily stored on a computer means that you can remind yourself of the trip at any point in the future.

Examiner: Can you trust other people's travel journals on the Internet? (Speculate)

Candidate: Honestly, it's not something I've ever really thought about, but I suppose my answer would be yes. I believe that you could rely on other people's experiences of a place in order to get some kind of idea as to whether you want to go or not.

Examiner: What factors affect how people feel about travelling? (List)

Candidate: The biggest issue I think people would think about is whether they actually enjoyed the trip. If someone was going on a weekend away and had a nightmare getting there and then, after arriving, had difficulties with the hotel or food or weather or something, I think they would be pretty unhappy about the whole thing. However, if someone had an easy trip to the airport, a comfortable flight and an excellent hotel on the beach with beautiful sunny weather, I think it's reasonably safe to say they would be a happy 知足常乐的人 bunny.

Examiner: Will you go to a foreign country to travel because of the distinct landscape? (Opinion)

Candidate: Geographical features, no. Quantity and quality of sunshine and general hotness, yes. To me, one mountain is the same as any other, and I could also say that about many of the beaches I have visited as well. I would go to a foreign country because, in my own country, I wouldn't be able to see or do something. For example, I went to Sweden a few years ago because I wanted to see the Northern Lights. You can't do that in Beijing.

Lexical Resource	
Less Common Language	third-tier, crabs and lobster, snorkelling gear
Collocations/Idiomatic Language	hustle and bustle, not a million miles away, off the beaten track, so to speak, going on a weekend away, a happy bunny
Paraphrasing	important→essential, trust→rely on, distinct landscape→ geographical features
Discourse Marker	oh, honestly, to me

■ A quiet place you like to go to

> **Describe a quiet place you like to go to.**
> **You should say:**
>   **where it is**
>   **how you knew it**
>   **what you do there**
> **and explain how you feel about the place.**

Speaking of a quiet place, I want to talk about a small public garden which is near my grandmother's place.

About a month ago, on my way to visit my grandparents, I found a small garden with its construction just finished. A lot of different kinds of trees and flowers were planted there, and a few benches were provided for visitors. Luckily, it is far away from the downtown area, and as it's only just finished, few people know about it. As a result, it's really a quiet and nice place to get some rest and simply chill out alone.
^{冷静}

Since that day, I have been there several times every month, especially when I am upset or need to clear my head. I feel pretty relaxed and free when I stay there because I can enjoy some quality time with myself and not get disturbed. Most of the time, I sit on the benches, listen to my favourite pop songs, or walk along the tree-lined path. Different kinds of plants are growing there, which is another
^{树木成排的}
reason I love that place. Compared to the city centre, the environment in that small garden is much better. The clean air helps me clear my mind and forget some of my negative feelings. Besides, it was an excellent opportunity for me to get close to nature in my daily life.

I hope more facilities could be built in that place so that I could do some physical exercise there, while I suppose that more and more people would find my beautiful little spot and make it a good public place to socialize and communicate with their neighbours. Although that might not be quiet enough
^{社交}
anymore, I believe that will improve the relationship within the community.

Examiner: Is it easy to find quiet places in your country? ⟨Opinion⟩

Candidate: To be frank, no, you can't. It's a question of population. There are just so many people living and working in Beijing that it's incredibly difficult to find any peace and quiet. Recently, I've taken to using noise-cancellation earphones as this helps me block out the outside world almost totally.

Examiner: Why do old people prefer to live in quiet places? ⟨Speculate⟩

Candidate: I assume that the biggest reason is sleeping quality. As we know, it will become harder for people to sleep deeply as we grow older, so elderly people always need to live in a much quieter place to ensure they get enough good rest at night. At the same time, most old people want to lead a peaceful life after retirement and find opportunities to restart some hobbies without disturbance in a quiet place.

Examiner: How would you deal with noisy neighbours? ⟨Hypothesise⟩

Candidate: Well, I think most people don't deliberately disturb others. It is just sometimes people have different living habits, and they do not realize they are bothering their neighbours. I would rather talk to them politely first, and I believe that most people are nice and would respect my needs. But if they don't listen to reason and still persist in their old ways, I'd seek help from our community or even the police.

Examiner: Why do some people like to use noise as background sound when they are working or studying? ⟨Speculate⟩

Candidate: I don't know, but I'm one of those people. I often have the TV on when I'm trying to do my assignments. I think it's because if I want a little break for 30 seconds or a minute, I can just turn my head and watch some TV but then go straight back to my computer afterwards. It seems less cumbersome to do an assignment that way.

Lexical Resource	
Less Common Language	tree-lined, socialize, noise-cancellation, assume, disturbance, deliberately, persist, cumbersome
Collocations/Idiomatic Language	chill out, clear my head, get close to nature, block out
Paraphrasing	rest→chill out, socialize→communicate, old people→elderly people
Discourse Marker	since that day, to be frank, well

> **Describe a quiet place you like to go to.**
>
> **You should say:**
>
>   **where it is**
>
>   **how you knew it**
>
>   **what you do there**
>
> **and explain how you feel about the place.**

Well, it might sound somewhat strange, but a quiet place I like going to is actually my bathroom. I know, I know, you're probably thinking that I should be saying a park or something like that, but the fact is I don't know of any parks near where I've moved to, and there's normally so many people around in the city centre that it probably wouldn't be quiet anyway. So, I'm sticking with my 坚持 bathroom.

I think I can probably skip the 'where it is' and 'how you knew it' because I think that's going to be 跳过 fairly obvious. I'll concentrate more on the 'what you do' and 'how you feel'.

I have a bubble bath every Sunday afternoon around 5 o'clock, or at least as many as possible. For me, after a long week, I can't think of anything I would rather do than sit in my bath and soak all of my troubles away. It has a jacuzzi function, but that's not exactly quiet, so the 'quiet' bit is when I dip 按摩浴缸 my head underwater so that it covers my ears. That generally blocks out all the sound from within my flat as well as any from outside. Literally, the only thing I can hear is my blood pumping. 按照字面意思

I adore my bath and the bubbles that go with it, and no, I don't play with a rubber duck. Although having said that, I might buy one, ha-ha. Seriously though, it is a place where I feel at peace and can regenerate the batteries for the following week. 恢复精力

Examiner: Is it easy to find quiet places in your country? ⸤Opinion⸥

Candidate: The fast answer to that is no. The slightly slower one is that it would kind of depend on what time of day you went to a place as well as the time of the week. For example, I know of a hot pot restaurant called Xiabu Xiabu that at 2 o'clock on a Saturday afternoon is absolutely heaving _{挤满人的}, but at 11 o'clock on a Tuesday morning is a ghost town.

Examiner: Why do old people prefer to live in quiet places? ⸤Speculate⸥

Candidate: I think it's because the more elderly among us are just sick to death _{极厌倦} of noise. My grandfather absolutely hates it. Having worked in a factory for 30-odd _{左右} years with banging, clanging and any other loud noise you can think of, he just doesn't want to hear it anymore.

Examiner: How would you deal with noisy neighbours? ⸤Hypothesise⸥

Candidate: Generally, at least according to my experience, people don't know they're being particularly noisy. In the past, I've gone over to the people next door and rang their bell. I just asked them to be a bit quieter. To date _{到目前为止}, they've all turned the TV down or the music or whatever it was, and everybody is happy. Something like a crying baby, you can't really do anything about except wait.

Examiner: Why do some people like to use noise as background sound when they are working or studying? ⸤Speculate⸥

Candidate: Do you know? I have absolutely no idea. Personally, I think the whole idea is ridiculous _{可笑的}. When I study, or need to write a paper or something, I need absolute quiet so that I can concentrate completely and totally.

Lexical Resource	
Less Common Language	skip, concentrate, soak, jacuzzi, dip, pumping, adore, heaving, odd, ridiculous
Collocations/Idiomatic Language	sticking with, regenerate the batteries, ghost town, sick to death of, to date
Paraphrasing	old→elderly, neighbours→people next door
Discourse Marker	literally, generally, do you know

■ A café you like to visit

> **Describe a café you like to visit.**
>
> **You should say:**
>
> > **where it is**
> >
> > **what kinds of food and drinks it serves**
> >
> > **what you do there**
>
> **and explain why you like to go there.**

I love visiting a café called Lush, which is located in the heart of the city. The café is surrounded by beautiful greenery and a peaceful atmosphere, making it the perfect place to escape the hustle and bustle of the city. The café serves a variety of delicious foods and drinks, including freshly brewed coffee, tea, smoothies, and baked goods. I am a big fan of their pastries and always indulge in a croissant or a muffin when I visit.

When I go there, I like to sit outside on their patio and enjoy the lovely weather. The patio is surrounded by a variety of colourful plants and flowers, creating a tranquil and serene environment. I also enjoy reading a book or working on my laptop in the café, as it provides a quiet and peaceful setting for me to be productive.

The staff there are incredibly friendly and accommodating, which adds to the overall positive experience of visiting the café. They are always willing to make recommendations and help with menu choices. The café also offers free Wi-Fi, making it easy for me to stay connected while I enjoy my time there.

Overall, I love visiting Lush because of its peaceful atmosphere, delicious food and drinks, and friendly staff. It's the perfect place to unwind, relax, and enjoy some quiet time to myself. I highly recommend it to anyone looking for a tranquil and comfortable café experience.

Examiner: What kind of people would like to go to a café? (List)

Candidate: From what I know, study groups and students. Cafés are a popular spot for students to study or work on group projects. The atmosphere is often quiet and conducive to productivity, and you can always find a few in almost any café in the world.

Examiner: Why do young people like studying in a café instead of at home? (Speculate)

Candidate: I think they go there mainly for a change of scenery and it can help reduce boredom and distractions. It can also help to avoid the distractions of home life, such as televisions, social media, or household chores. Another reason is just that they want to be around other people, or maybe meet up with their friends.

Examiner: Do old people like to drink coffee? (Speculate)

Candidate: I think it really depends on the person and maybe the habits of their culture. Here in China, older people either drink tea or water, whereas in the West, the United States, for example, coffee is the beverage of choice. I also think it depends on the time of day. Many seniors will have a coffee in the morning, but not in the evening.

Examiner: Do Chinese people like to drink coffee? (Speculate)

Candidate: Like I just said, no, not really. Let's put it this way, no one in my family except me has ever had coffee. My parents tried it once but just didn't like it. As a general consideration, though, I think coffee intake is on the increase.

Lexical Resource	
Less Common Language	greenery, patio, serene, accommodating, unwind, conducive, beverage, intake
Collocations/Idiomatic Language	in the heart of, hustle and bustle, meet up with, on the increase
Paraphrasing	tranquil→serene, unwind→relax, like→love, old people→seniors
Discourse Marker	overall, like I just said, let's put it this way

---

Describe a café you like to visit.

You should say:

   where it is

   what kinds of food and drinks it serves

   what you do there

and explain why you like to go there.

The café that I enjoy going to is actually my local Starbucks. It's about a 5-minute walk from the campus of my university and is on the corner of the 4th Ring Road and Zhongguancun East Road in the Haidian District of Beijing. It's actually not that far from here, maybe 10 minutes in a taxi.

Like nearly every other café, it serves coffee and a selection of snacks. My favourite is the vanilla latte they have. I'm not really a big fan of their food, but at a push, I will have their Crepe Monsieur, which is just a fancy way of saying a ham and cheese sandwich. There is a range of cakes and suchlike, but they never really whet my appetite.

For the most part, I meet my friends there, get out of the dorm and actually use some decent Wi-Fi for a change. I think that the reason the Wi-Fi at my university is so bad is that there are so many people using it at the same time. It just goes so slowly sometimes, and it's just unusable. I can't access domestic pages, let alone any international ones.

Beyond the change of pace and scenery, there aren't any particular reasons I trot over there, but as long as they are close and they keep doing exquisite lattes, I will be a customer there probably for a long time to come. And you know, I'm delighted they didn't shut down. It seems that they dodged the bullet, which pleases me enormously. I really didn't want to have to find another place to replace it.

Examiner: What kind of people would like to go to a café? (List)

Candidate: If I ever go to a café during the week, I mostly see older, maybe retired people there reading a book. I do see the odd *(少量的)* businessman, or woman for that matter, and a few students dotted about. So, thinking about it, I'd say it's quite a variety of people that visit cafés.

Examiner: Why do young people like studying in a café instead of at home? (Speculate)

Candidate: Well, I can't really speak for everyone else, but for me, I enjoy going to a café to study because it's quieter than my home. My grandma seems to be either preparing or cooking food all hours of the day, and I think people half a world away *(世界的另一端)* can hear her chop carrots. With my little brother always playing computer games, sometimes I just have to get out.

Examiner: Do old people like to drink coffee? (Speculate)

Candidate: Sometimes, but as far as I know, not often. I think it's mainly because they don't really want to have too much caffeine *(咖啡因)* in their diet for health reasons. For instance, none of the seniors that are in my family or that I know of would ever have a coffee before they go to bed because they just wouldn't sleep.

Examiner: Do Chinese people like to drink coffee? (Speculate)

Candidate: I think it's a growing trend here, but I certainly wouldn't make the generalisation that Chinese people like coffee, not like the Americans do. I enjoy coffee occasionally, but I wouldn't identify *(认定)* myself as a coffee lover or anything like that, and I really couldn't speak for the rest of the population.

Lexical Resource	
Less Common Language	domestic, exquisite, odd, identify
Collocations/Idiomatic Language	at a push, whet my appetite, trot over, dodged the bullet, speak for, make the generalisation
Paraphrasing	food→snacks, a selection of→a range of, like→enjoy, old people→seniors
Discourse Marker	so, well, sometimes

■ A place in a village that you visited

Part 2   *Answer 1*（★★★★）   6∂ 278

> **Describe a place in a village that you visited.**
>
> **You should say:**
>
>   **where it is**
>
>   **when you visited this place**
>
>   **what you did there**
>
> **and how you feel about this place.**

One place in a village that I recently visited was called The Village Green. It is located in a small,
风景如画的
picturesque village surrounded by rolling hills and countryside. I went there last summer during my
holidays.

郁郁葱葱的
It's a community park that serves as the central gathering place for the village. It features a large, lush
green lawn, shaded by mature trees and surrounded by benches and picnic tables. The park is well-
景观美化   极好的   修剪整齐的   矮树丛
maintained, and the landscaping is stunning, with colourful flower beds and well-manicured shrubs.

It was on a sunny afternoon, and I spent several hours relaxing on a bench, watching the world go by.
热闹的   散步
The park was bustling with activity, with families playing games, couples strolling hand in hand, and
叙旧
friends catching up over picnics.

In the centre of the park, there was a small stage, and a local band was playing live music. The
观看来往的人群
atmosphere was lively, and I enjoyed listening to the music while people-watching. I also enjoyed
observing the many different species of birds that had gathered in the trees.

I feel very positive about this park. It is a lovely and peaceful place that is well-loved by the local
证明
community. The park is a testament to the importance of community space and the role it plays in
bringing people together. The Village Green is a must-see for anyone travelling to the village, and I
highly recommend it.

Examiner: Is there anything special about the villages in China? (Opinion)

Candidate: I would say so, yes. Many Chinese villages are steeped in centuries of history and cultural traditions. They are often closely tied to the local environment and include distinctive customs, festivals, and religious practices. These do differ though, depending on where you are in China.

Examiner: What do people usually do when going to a village? (Speculate)

Candidate: I think a lot of people go there to the differences between city life and country life. Whenever I have been to the countryside and the little villages therein, the first thing I do is buy fresh meat and vegetables directly from farms rather than going to a supermarket. The taste is much better.

Examiner: Do you think people will live in the village in the future? (Hypothesise)

Candidate: Urbanisation is a trend that has been happening in many countries, including China, where people are moving from rural areas to cities in search of job opportunities and improved living standards. However, some people still choose to live in villages, either because they have a strong attachment to their hometowns, or because they prefer the more relaxed and less hectic pace of rural life.

Examiner: Why do people want to go to the countryside? (Speculate)

Candidate: I think the main reason is to do with health. Being in a rural environment has been shown to have a positive impact on physical and mental health. Fresh air, outdoor activities, and a less hectic pace of life are all factors that contribute to improved well-being. I know that whenever I can get out of the city, I always feel better for it.

Lexical Resource	
Less Common Language	picturesque, lush, landscaping, bustling, strolling, testament, urbanisation, attachment
Collocations/Idiomatic Language	catching up, must-see, steeped in, in search of, hectic pace, have a positive impact on
Paraphrasing	picturesque→stunning, villages→rural areas
Discourse Marker	I would say so, however

> **Describe a place in a village that you visited.**
>
> **You should say:**
>
>   **where it is**
>
>   **when you visited this place**
>
>   **what you did there**
>
> **and how you feel about this place.**

I recently had a trip to England to see some of my friends there who are currently studying at university. We took a trip to a little place called Bayford, near a not much larger place called Wincanton and had lunch in the local pub.

It was only a couple of weeks ago that I was there, and I have finally managed to get over the jet lag. It takes longer and longer the older I get, but anyway, I digress.

As to what we did there, I think you've probably already got a pretty good idea. Yep, we had a good old-fashioned traditional Sunday lunch, and it was thoroughly delicious. We had some traditional ale with our meal in a pint glass, the size of which was a little bit of a surprise. Then, we had some more ale, and then some more, because the first two felt lonely.

We staggered out of there thoroughly content, absolutely stuffed and more than a little drunk. It didn't matter because none of us was driving, and the B&B that we had booked was 100 metres away. I don't actually remember how long it took us to walk that 100 metres, but it was quite a long time. I'm not sure if it was the food, the people, or the booze, but that little pub in that little village is now my favourite place on earth. Quaint, I would suggest, is the word you would use to describe it; tiny is another one. But all the people in there, you could only fit about 20, were all very friendly and the barkeep, I think, was very happy to have some different clientele.

Examiner: Is there anything special about the villages in China? (Opinion)

Candidate: Not especially. 没什么特别的 One village in China is pretty much the same as another one. They all have farms, little houses or bungalows 平房 and animals everywhere. I suppose comparing it to English villages, they would certainly be classed as different, but I wouldn't necessarily say special.

Examiner: What do people usually do when going to a village? (Speculate)

Candidate: Chill out, I expect, you know, relax. Village and country life can certainly be physical, 耗体力的 but it does mean you can turn your brain off. 放空大脑 I suppose it would depend on whether that village is your hometown or whether you are going there as a tourist or visitor.

Examiner: Do you think people will live in the village in the future? (Hypothesise)

Candidate: I think there will always be people living in villages, but I do think those people will not necessarily be villagers. For a lot of people who grow up in a village, they want to live in a city because it's more exciting than where they come from. Those who have worked in a city all their life want to go to a village for the exact opposite reason.

Examiner: Why do people want to go to the countryside? (Speculate)

Candidate: Well, I suppose it depends on what you mean by 'go to'. If you mean to visit, or just travel there for a short time, it's probably just to unwind and de-stress from city life. If you mean move to, from the city, I suppose actually it would be for the same reason. So, the answer would be to get away from the rat race 激烈竞争 of city life.

Lexical Resource	
Less Common Language	digress, old-fashioned, staggered, booze, quaint, fit, clientele, bungalows
Collocations/Idiomatic Language	get over, jet leg, stuffed, turn your brain off, rat race
Paraphrasing	chill out→relax/unwind/de-stress, go to→visit/travel
Discourse Marker	anyway, I digress, not especially, well

The home of someone you know well and you often visit

> **Describe the home of someone you know well and you often visit.**
>
> **You should say:**
>
> > **whose home it is**
> >
> > **how often you go there**
> >
> > **what it is like**
>
> **and explain how you feel about the home.**

The home I am going to describe is my best friend's home. I visit her place quite often, about once a week.

Her home is located in a quiet neighbourhood and is a two-story building with a cosy and welcoming atmosphere. The interior of the house is decorated with bright colours, such as yellow and green, that give it a cheerful and warm vibe. The living room is spacious and has a comfortable sofa, a TV, and various paintings hanging on the walls. The kitchen is well-equipped and has a big table, where we often sit and chat over a cup of tea or coffee.

Upstairs, there are three bedrooms and a bathroom. My friend's room is the largest and is decorated with posters of her favourite bands and movies. Her bed is soft and comfortable, and she has a small desk, where she often studies or works on her laptop.

The backyard is also a highlight of the house. It has a beautiful garden with various plants and flowers, and a small pond, where koi fish swim. In the summer, my friend and I often have barbecues or simply relax in the sun on the patio.

I love visiting my friend's home because of the warm and inviting atmosphere. The home is a true reflection of her personality, and I always feel at ease and comfortable when I'm there. Whether we're watching a movie in the living room, cooking in the kitchen, or having a picnic in the backyard, I always have a great time at her place. It's like a second home to me, and I cherish the memories we've made there.

Examiner: What are the differences between buildings in the city and in the countryside?
(Compare & Contrast)

Candidate: The major element that isn't the same is height. Many of the buildings in cities, whether they are residential or business, are tall, like, really tall, 30 stories or more. In the countryside you don't really see anything much more than about 5 or 6 stories. Another difference would be design. These days modern cities are trying to vary their architecture, whereas the rural areas tend to keep the same style.

Examiner: Do you prefer to live in the city or in the countryside? (Compare & Contrast)

Candidate: My preference would be the city. There's just so much more to do in a city, even a small one. I'd be bored out of my mind if I lived in the country as everything would be based around my home. It would be a hassle to go out and see my friends for an evening as they'd be so far away.

Examiner: What safety risks are there in residential buildings in cities? (List)

Candidate: Honestly, I've got no idea. I've never looked into it. Let me think, earthquakes could be in there somewhere, as well as fire. I do often see fire extinguishers in all the public areas on each floor. Oh, something I did hear about the other day was access for the disabled, you know, the ramps and the like so that they can easily access the building.

Examiner: Is it expensive to decorate a house or an apartment where you live? (Hypothesise)

Candidate: Again, this isn't something I really know about. I've never had to do it, and when my parents last did it a few years ago, it wasn't a question that I asked. I think it could depend on the appliances that you buy and the quality of the curtains and furniture. I don't think that the labour is particularly expensive, but again there's probably different quality levels of that too.

Lexical Resource	
Less Common Language	cosy, interior, vibe, patio, cherish, hassle, ramps, appliances
Collocations/Idiomatic Language	bored out of my mind, looked into
Paraphrasing	differences→not the same, prefer→preference, access for the disabled→ramps
Discourse Marker	like, honestly, let me think, oh, you know

> **Describe the home of someone you know well and you often visit.**
>
> **You should say:**
>
> > **whose home it is**
> >
> > **how often you go there**
> >
> > **what it is like**
>
> **and explain how you feel about the home.**

The house I would like to describe this afternoon actually belongs to one of my English friend's parents. To me, it is enormous, like properly huge. It has three floors, six bedrooms, two bathrooms upstairs and a shower room downstairs, as well as lots of other rooms. It is situated in an area of about two acres of land, and you could see for miles in any direction.

I think the original house is about 400 years old, but since then it has been extended twice and is located place called Wincanton, which is in South West England. I would love it if I could have a house like that in my hometown of Beijing. We have courtyard houses and hutong, but they're nothing like Bayford House. Oh, that was the name of the house, by the way.

For me, I enjoy visiting there for two reasons. The first is just the size of the place. Whichever room you go into, you just had a sense of space. Secondly, the history. The fact that this house has been standing in one shape or another for four centuries is just incredible.

As for the last section, as to how I feel about this house, I would have to say wonder, and probably a little bit green with envy because I know I'll never be able to live in it, although one of the things I do think about is that it might take a long time to clean and keep tidy. So I suppose, it's not all positive.

> *Look at this:* *Please look at A house or an apartment you would like to live in – Part 2 – Answer 1 on page302. What do you notice? Does it entirely answer the question? In some cases, it is possible to use one answer for different topics. I did it deliberately. Take a look at the Summary on pages 326—327.*
>
> 注意：请查看第 302 页的你想居住的房子或公寓 – Part 2 – Answer 1 。你注意到什么？该答案能完全地回答问题吗？在某些情况下，一份答案适用于几个不同的话题。我刻意使用了一样的答案。请参考第 326—327 页的小结。

Examiner: What are the differences between buildings in the city and in the countryside?
(Compare & Contrast)

Candidate: Well, I would say size and shape. Many houses in rural areas are a single story, and sometimes have high ceilings, although not always and typically the kitchens are at the back of the house. Another thing that is very different is the outside toilet. In modern buildings, even in the countryside, they're mostly indoors now, but many of the older homes still have them outdoors.

Examiner: Do you prefer to live in the city or in the countryside? (Compare & Contrast)

Candidate: I've never lived in the countryside, so I couldn't really say. Some of my friends tell me that it's very peaceful there, but sometimes hard work as they need to look after their animals or assigned land. I think, for the time being, I'd like city life, but when I retire, maybe I'll move out and live in the sticks.

Examiner: What safety risks are there in residential buildings in cities? (List)

Candidate: I suppose the biggest risk is whether the building is going to fall down. In the city, if you live on the 15th floor, there's a long way to fall. In the country, you don't have that problem. I would also suggest that there may be more crime in cities, so the residential areas need more security.

Examiner: Is it expensive to decorate a house or an apartment where you live? (Hypothesise)

Candidate: I assume so, but it's something that I've never done before. I wouldn't have a clue if it's a lot of money. Here in Beijing it would be considerably more than a rural area, but how it would compare to somewhere like Shanghai, your guess is as good as mine.

Lexical Resource	
Less Common Language	enormous, incredible, assigned, assume
Collocations/Idiomatic Language	by the way, green with envy, for the time being, live in the sticks, your guess is as good as mine
Paraphrasing	countryside→rural areas, outside→outdoors, expensive→a lot of money
Discourse Marker	to me, oh, for me, well, I think, I assume

Well done on getting through all the Part 2s and Part 3s! Hopefully, now you better understand the question styles and the length of the answers.

恭喜学完所有 Part 2 和 Part 3！希望现在你能更好地理解问题的类型和答案的长度。

Some of the Part 2 answers, I have deliberately made a little short, only 60 or 80 seconds, and it might be that the examiner will ask you whether you have any else to say. This is a perfect opportunity to add a little extra vocabulary and grammar range to what you've said already. For example, you could say something along the lines of:

Part 2 的一些答案，我故意写得有点短，只有 60 或 80 秒，可能考官会问你是否还有其他要说的。这是一个补充词汇和语法多样性的好机会。例如，你可以类似这样说：

Well, I know I need to try and talk for two minutes, but there's nothing else I can think of to add to this topic. Is there? No, not really. So, I'm really sorry if the time isn't up yet, but if it's ok with you, I'll stop there.

Or, if you want to try something more idiomatic:

或者，你想说得更地道点：

I'm really sorry, but I'm suffering from a complete brain freeze. There are a few things that are on the tip of my tongue, but I just can't think of them now. If it's ok with you, I'll stop there. I know there's still more time to go, but the words just aren't coming out.

Comparable to Part 1, similar questions often arise in Part 2 (and also Part 3). Examples of this would be:

• Describe a famous athlete you know.
• Describe a foreign celebrity.
• Describe someone on social media.

类似于 Part 1，相似的问题也经常出现在 Part 2（以及 Part 3）中。例如：

• 描述一位你知道的著名运动员。
• 描述一位外国名人。
• 描述社交媒体上的某人。

When preparing for the IELTS exam, many students want to memorise one answer that can be used for all three of these subjects, and, in some cases, that's possible. It's possible that a famous athlete you know is a foreigner who uses social media like Weibo or Facebook to communicate with their fans. In cases like this, yes, it is possible to use one answer for all three topics.

准备雅思考试时，许多学生希望记住一个能适用于所有这三个话题的答案，在某些情况下，这是可行的。你认识的一位著名运动员可能是一个外国人，他或她用微博或脸书等社交媒体与粉丝互动。在这种情况下，三个话题使用一个答案是可以的。

The issue can arise in Part 3 when there are very different questions for each of these topics. If your fluency, for example, suddenly has a multitude of prolonged pausing, it may significantly reduce your score for that element. It may also signal to the examiner that you have memorised this entire answer, which wouldn't be a good thing.

问题可能会出现在 Part 3，因为每个话题下的问题会迥然不同。如果你突然出现大量长时间的停顿，这不仅会非常影响流利性的得分，还可能会让考官觉得你把答案都记住了，这不是一件好事。

An example of this would be:

• What are the advantages and disadvantages of becoming a celebrity? (taken from a Foreign Celebrity)
• What kinds of exercises do Chinese people like? (taken from a Famous Athlete)

例如：

• 成为名人有什么好处和坏处？（选自描述一位外国名人话题下的问题）
• 中国人喜欢什么样的运动？（选自描述一位著名运动员话题下的问题）

The above questions cannot easily be interchanged. 'What are the advantages and disadvantages of becoming an athlete?' is a potentially valid question, but, although 'What kinds of exercises do Celebrities like?' is grammatically correct, it doesn't really make sense as a question. (Why would celebrities like different exercises than anyone else?) However, athletes may well do different exercises than ordinary people depending on what they're an athlete of. This means that you need to be able to answer each question on its own merit, which means that having a 'one answer fits all' strategy is flawed, to say the least.

上述两个问题不能轻易更换。"成为运动员有什么好处和坏处？"是一个可能存在的问题，但是，"名人喜欢什么样的锻炼方式？"虽然语法是对的，但是这么问其实没什么意义（为什么名人和其他人喜欢的锻炼方式会不同？）。然而，运动员喜欢的锻炼方式却可能会因为他们的职业而与大众有所不同。这意味着你需要就问题本身给出针对性的回答，至少可以说"一刀切"的策略是有缺陷的。

My advice here is to be aware that yes, in some limited cases where the topics are very similar in nature, it is possible to use similar phrases in both topics, but just remember that you still need to be able to think in-depth about and around the topic given, so that you can give sensible, extended answers for the questions related to that specific topic. Use the phrases and suggestions that I've given in the beginning of this section, and remember the styles of question given to you in Part 3.

我的建议是，在某些情况下，话题本质非常相似，使用相似的短语是可以的，但请记住，你仍然需要围绕特定的话题深入思考，这样你才能针对特定话题的问题给出合理的、详尽的答案。请使用我在本部分开头给出的短语和建议，记住 Part 3 的问题类型。

Module Tests and Sample Answers

真题模拟及参考答案

Test 1 试题 1

The examiner asks about yourself, your home, work or studies and other familiar topics.

Art

• Do you like art?

• What can you learn from paintings?

• What benefits does painting as a hobby give you?

• What kinds of paintings do people in your country like?

Chocolate

• How often do you eat chocolate?

• What's your favourite type of chocolate?

• Is chocolate expensive in your country?

• When was the first time you ate chocolate?

Part 2

Describe an interesting old person you would like to meet. **You should say:** **Who this person is** **What this person does** **Why you think this person is interesting** **and explain what you want to do with this person.**

You will have to talk about the topic for one to two minutes. You have one minute to think about what you are going to say. You can make some notes to help you if you wish.

Part 3

• Do old people share the same interests as younger people?

• What can old people teach young people?

• Is it easy for young people and old people to make friends with each other?

• Do you think old people should live with their family?

■ Test 1 Sample Answers 试题 1 参考答案

6∂ 286

✎ Art

Examiner: Do you like art?

Candidate: Yes, very much. I have studied art since my childhood. I often paint during my free time now, and I hope I can get an opportunity to study it further, but I'm not sure I'll be able to if I go to the UK to study.

Examiner: What can you learn from paintings?

Candidate: Paintings give me an idea of structure, both in art and real life. I can find a lot of beautiful things in my daily life and have learnt that life is colourful. When we put our creativity and enthusiasm into something, it often turns out to be wonderful.

Examiner: What benefits does painting as a hobby give you?

Candidate: As a hobby, it can enrich my free time so that every day I feel that it has meaning. It also gives me a skill that I can totally use when I need to and helps me feel relaxed. I can also use it as an excellent excuse to get out of the house and spend some time alone.

Examiner: What kinds of paintings do people in your country like?

Candidate: I believe that different people like different kinds of paintings. Old people prefer artwork that shows history and traditions, whereas most young people like me prefer original or new paintings that show interesting things.

✎ Chocolate

Examiner: How often do you eat chocolate?

Candidate: Not very often because I don't have much of a sweet tooth. I suppose, if I had to put a figure on it, maybe once a month, or even once every two months. I try and limit it because I don't want to get fat, and, if I'm honest, I don't actually enjoy it all that much.

Examiner: What's your favourite type of chocolate?

Candidate: My favourite chocolates are those which add milk or nuts because these kinds of chocolate can provide more nutrition, and I also think milk and nuts can make chocolate more delicious.

Examiner: Is chocolate expensive in your country?

Candidate: Chocolates which are indigenous aren't very expensive. However, those which are imported are. I think though, people are more likely to choose the imported ones because they generally taste better.

Examiner: When was the first time you ate chocolate?

Candidate: I had my first chocolate when I was in kindergarten, about six years old. I felt it was very sweet, and I really liked it. But now I care about my health more, not to mention my teeth, and I lost my desire for them, so, like I said earlier, these days, once a month.

> **Describe an interesting old person you would like to meet.**
>
> **You should say:**
>
> **Who this person is**
>
> **What this person does**
>
> **Why you think this person is interesting**
>
> **and explain what you want to do with this person.**

Well, there are actually a number of interesting people I would like to meet, but if I was to have to choose one, it would have to be the founder of a famous company in China. I'm not sure if you know his story, but basically, in high school, he failed the college entrance exam three or four times before finally making it to university and actually worked as teacher for a number of years. It was during this time that he began to develop his company. It may have taken him 20 or 30 years to get where he is today, but it's an incredible achievement considering he is, I believe, one of the richest men in China.

I think he's interesting mainly because he comes from such an unassuming background and wasn't the top of his class, stunningly handsome or from a wealthy family. He simply had an idea, worked very hard and had a little luck. I find it fascinating, recently, that he has stepped down from his role as chairman and, apparently, going back into teaching, or at least education. This shows me where his true love lies. He's made his money and can do anything, anywhere in the world, and yet he chooses to impart his knowledge to the next generation. I think that kind of sums him up nicely, kind, giving, and unselfish.

As for what I want to do with him, to be honest, simply sit down and have a chat with him and pick his brains to see if I can be further inspired and come up with some ideas myself.

Examiner: Do old people share the same interests as younger people?

Candidate: I suppose it depends on what you mean by old. To me at 18, other than my friends, nearly everybody I know is old. Sometimes our interests overlap (重叠) with sports like basketball or football, but generally, gaming interests on the Xbox or PS4 is a younger generation thing (年轻一代喜欢的东西).

Examiner: What can old people teach young people?

Candidate: I think they can teach us a lot if we are prepared to listen. They have a lot of experience in dealing with different problems, whether this be in everyday life or at work or university. The expression 'been there, done that' (过来人), I think, applies here.

Examiner: Is it easy for young people and old people to make friends with each other?

Candidate: Without a doubt (毫无疑问). I wouldn't say that I have loads of older friends, as in, a generation up (上一代人), but I do have a few. Quite often, we meet for dinner, or a drink and catch up with (与某人叙旧) each other. It quite often takes a while because I don't see them that often, and now that I'm in Beijing, it's probably going to be even less. But I thoroughly enjoy the time and usually learn something.

Examiner: Do you think old people should live with their family?

Candidate: Yes, definitely. In my country, we are mostly raised by our grandparents, and I couldn't imagine them not being around and living with my parents and me. I think it's only fair that after they have looked after us for our formative years (形成性格时期), we do the same in their twilight ones (暮年).

Lexical Resource	
Less Common Language	structure, enthusiasm, enrich, unassuming, inspired, overlap, formative, twilight
Collocations/Idiomatic Language	free time, sweet tooth, sums him up, 'been there, done that'
Paraphrasing	paintings→artwork, often→usually, teaching→education, older→a generation up
Discourse Marker	like I said earlier, well, without a doubt, definitely

---

The examiner asks about yourself, your home, work or studies and other familiar topics.

Weekends

• Is the weekend your favourite part of the week?

• What do you normally do on weekends?

• What did you do last weekend?

• Do you prefer to plan how you spend your weekends?

Music

• Do you often listen to music?

• What's your favourite kind of music?

• How do you feel when you listen to music?

• What types of music are popular in your country?

Describe a time when you missed an important appointment. **You should say:** **When it happened** **What was the appointment for** **What happened when you missed the appointment** **and explain how you felt about missing the appointment.**

You will have to talk about the topic for one to two minutes. You have one minute to think about what you are going to say. You can make some notes to help you if you wish.

• Are appointments easy to make in your country?

• How often do you make appointments?

• How important is punctuality in your country?

• Do you think people are born with time management skills, or can they develop them?

Weekends

Examiner: Is the weekend your favourite part of the week?

Candidate: I suppose so, because it gives me more time to do relaxing things. I enjoy what I do, and my study is not particularly tiring. I get to see a lot of my friends during the week, so that's good too. It is sometimes challenging, though, having to get up so early in the morning.

Examiner: What do you normally do on weekends?

Candidate: Sleep. As I said earlier, I have to get up very early in the mornings, so I often have a lie-in on Saturday and Sunday. During the evenings and afternoons, though, I will get together with my friends or family and go out to the cinema or maybe a restaurant.

Examiner: What did you do last weekend?

Candidate: Last weekend, it was actually my friend's birthday, so a group of us got together and had a party. We got home quite late after singing at the KTV on Saturday night, so I think on Sunday I didn't get out of bed at all. I just watched TV in my room.

Examiner: Do you prefer to plan how you spend your weekends?

Candidate: Not really, no. I'm an easy-going kind of person, very happy-go-lucky. If there is a special event, like my friend's birthday, I might plan for it, but otherwise, I just see what happens at the time.

Music

Examiner: Do you often listen to music?

Candidate: Definitely, yes. I love music, and I can't live without it. I listen to it every day, mostly in the morning, but sometimes in the afternoon too.

Examiner: What's your favourite kind of music?

Candidate: Classical music and country music are the ones I enjoy the most. I find that the instruments are soothing and help me calm down if I've had a bad day.

Examiner: How do you feel when you listen to music?

Candidate: Like I just said, when I'm trying to sleep, soothing music can help me relax, whereas if I'm doing sports, music which has a fast beat can get me excited, and I can exercise to the rhythm.

Examiner: What types of music are popular in your country?

Candidate: Well, I suppose Pop music is the most popular one, probably due to its name, Popular. These days western music is well-known here, as well as local Chinese tunes.

> **Describe a time when you missed an important appointment.**
>
> **You should say:**
>
>   **When it happened**
>
>   **What was the appointment for**
>
>   **What happened when you missed the appointment**
>
> **and explain how you felt about missing the appointment.**

A recent situation where I missed a significant appointment was when I was going to my IELTS Speaking test last month here in Beijing. Needless to say, I got stuck in traffic on the 4th Ring Road. I'm not sure if it was just heavy traffic or whether there had been an accident in front of us, but I had rarely seen it this bad on a Saturday lunchtime.

After about an hour, we had only moved about 2 km, and I was beginning to get twitchy and stressed because we only had another half an hour to get to the test centre and my speaking test. About 15 or 20 minutes later, I realised that I had missed the test. I spoke to my mother in tears.

To be honest, I was crying my heart out. Once I had calmed down a little bit, I rang the test centre to say I was not going to be able to make the appointment and that I was very sorry. There was nothing much I could do to change the time at that stage, so I told my mum to turn the car around and go home.

I felt both distraught and furious at the same time because I thought that this time was going to be the last time that I needed to take the IELTS exam, but no such luck. I got home and cried a bit more, but then pulled myself together and booked another test for the following month, and here I am!

Examiner: Are appointments easy to make in your country?

Candidate: Yes, I would say so. The appointment I made for this test was very easy. I simply went online and booked it. Other appointments I would normally make by phone, for example, if I want to book a massage or something like that.

 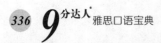

Examiner: How often do you make appointments?

Candidate: Personally speaking [就自己而言], not all that often. Being a student, I don't actually need to make external appointments with that many people. This test would be one of the few exceptions [例外] to that. It might change in the future when I start working, but that's not for another few years.

Examiner: How important is punctuality in your country?

Candidate: Oh, it's crucial to be on time! In my country, it is considered the epitome [典型] of rudeness to be late, especially if you are meeting someone older than you or maybe your boss. I always try to be 10 or 15 minutes early, at least, when I do make an appointment.

Examiner: Do you think people are born with time management skills, or can they develop them?

Candidate: Oh, I think it's very much about nurture rather than nature [后天而非先天]. I think if your parents get you into the habit of being early for things from a young age, it will follow you into adulthood. I think schools can help with this too. They can do classes on things like Time Management, Scheduling [调度], etc. Actually, that is just a good idea for all students anyway.

Lexical Resource	
Less Common Language	soothing, distraught, exceptions, epitome, nurture, Scheduling
Collocations/Idiomatic Language	have a lie-in, happy-go-lucky, crying my heart out, pulled myself together
Paraphrasing	on weekends→on Saturday and Sunday, favourite→enjoy the most, important→significant, punctuality→on time
Discourse Marker	as I said earlier, to be honest, personally speaking, oh

■ Test 3 试题 3

The examiner asks about yourself, your home, work or studies and other familiar topics.

Jewellery

• Do you like wearing jewellery?

• What kind of jewellery do you like to buy?

• Why do so many people choose to buy expensive jewellery to maintain value?

• How often do you wear jewellery?

Schools

• How old were you when you started school?

• What were some of the most popular activities at primary school?

• Have you ever returned to see your old school again?

• How did you get to school each day?

Part 2

Describe an event in history in your country.
You should say:
Where it happened
When it happened
What happened
and explain how you feel about this event.

You will have to talk about the topic for one to two minutes. You have one minute to think about what you are going to say. You can make some notes to help you if you wish.

• How do people in your country learn about historical events?

• What kind of people can appear in history?

• Do people like to learn history?

• What are the differences between learning history from books and videos?

Jewellery

Examiner: Do you like wearing jewellery?

Candidate: I haven't really thought about it before. I suppose, for me it's not all that important, so I wouldn't say I enjoy it. I do wear some, like this ring and my watch, but that's about it. I'm not one of these people that needs to put on different things each day.

Examiner: What kind of jewellery do you like to buy?

Candidate: To be honest, I don't. Not for myself anyway. I occasionally buy something for my girlfriend, like a nice ring or necklace, but not that often. The ring I'm wearing today, my father gave me, and the watch attaches to my phone, so it's more practical than decorative.

Examiner: Why do so many people choose to buy expensive jewellery to maintain value?

Candidate: I'm not sure. I suppose it could be used as an investment. Gold and diamonds, usually at least, hold their value, if not increase, so people could sell them if they fall on hard times. I think others simply like to show off.

Examiner: How often do you wear jewellery?

Candidate: As I said earlier, I have this ring and watch, and I wear them every day. I just don't wear too much jewellery. I think that it looks a bit tacky.

Schools

Examiner: How old were you when you started school?

Candidate: I must've been about 6 when I started primary school. I remember that I was really looking forward to it and meeting new people.

Examiner: What were some of the most popular activities at primary school?

Candidate: Well, I remember that we played in the playground a lot and we always did sports too. The boys normally played football or tag, whereas the girls played hopscotch. I remember that we had some classes too, but not the details.

Examiner: Have you ever returned to see your old school again?

Candidate: I've only gone back once. It was about five years after I'd left. I was in the area and felt like popping in to see some of my old teachers. Wow, the desks were small. I didn't really think I could ever fit behind them. They just seemed really tiny.

Examiner: How did you get to school each day?

Candidate: When I was really small, my mum took me, but when I was about 11 or 12, I cycled to school on my own, or maybe hooked up with (与某人结伴) some friends and went in together. It was only if it rained that my mum would drive me.

Part 2 293

Describe an event in history in your country.

You should say:

Where it happened

When it happened

What happened

and explain how you feel about this event.

Well, there are many important events in history, and I would like to talk about a famous inventor, James Watt, who invented the modern steam engine. When the Industrial Revolution began in Britain, the development of factories was limited because of lack of a stable power source. People still used traditional power sources like animals, wind, and rivers to drive machines. So, there was an urgent need to solve this problem.

He was born into a humble family (贫苦家庭), and when he was young, he couldn't get to school because of poor health. However, Watt was very intelligent, he liked to play with tools from his father's carpenter warehouse, which gave him a good engineering basis. In 1769 he began to try to invent a steam engine, and after 20 years of effort, he successfully invented a kind of steam engine that can be used as the power of the factory. Since then, people began to use steam engines to drive trains, ships and all sorts of other machines; the appearance of society (社会面貌) had been greatly changed. Humans entered the steam age, and soon after that came the Industrial Revolution, which interestingly also started in Britain.

For me, learning this in my history class just showed me that with some will, intelligence, a little luck and a lot of determination, anyone can do anything and change the world. It's not necessarily that I want to go down in the history books (载入史册), but I am coming around (转而接受) to the idea now that I speak more about it.

Examiner: How do people in your country learn about historical events?

Candidate: People in China learn about historical events in different ways. I suppose the most common is for students to learn history from textbooks and teachers. Other ways, I guess, would be from TV and maybe surfing around on the Internet.

Examiner: What kind of people can appear in history?

Candidate: Well, I think mostly heroes and villains appear in history. For heroes, they may have sacrificed their lives to rescue the country or have made a great contribution to the country and improved people's lives, you know, played the role of the good guy. On the other hand, for villains, maybe they be trayed a country for their personal interests or simply were just really evil people. But then, history is normally written by the victors, so you'll always get a one-sided view.

Examiner: Do people like to learn history?

Candidate: It depends. There are those who are really interested in the past and where we came from. There are also those who look back and hope we don't make the same mistakes as in the past, but I'm not sure that works. Everyone learns a little bit of history as it's part of the College Entrance Exam, but I'm fairly sure not everybody actually enjoys it.

Examiner: What are the differences between learning history from books and videos?

Candidate: Well, the obvious difference is speed. It's much faster to watch a video than read a book. I think that if you want to find information though, like a date or a person's name, it would probably be easier in a book. So, there are pros and cons for each I suppose. Some people would prefer the former, and some the latter.

Lexical Resource	
Less Common Language	tacky, investment, humble, villains, victors
Collocations/Idiomatic Language	show off, popping in, coming around, pros and cons
Paraphrasing	like→enjoy, wear→put on, maintain value→hold their value, returned→gone back, heroes→good guy
Discourse Marker	to be honest, well, for me, on the other hand, it depends

---

The examiner asks about yourself, your home, work or studies and other familiar topics.

Outer space and stars

• Have you ever learnt about outer space and stars?

• Do you like science fiction movies?

• Do you want to know more about outer space?

• Do you want to go into outer space in the future?

Small business

• Do you know many small businesses where you live?

• Do you prefer buying things from big companies or small businesses?

• Have you ever worked in a small business?

• Have you ever thought about starting your own business?

Describe a piece of good news that you heard about from someone you know well. **You should say:** 　　**what it was** 　　**when you heard it** 　　**how you knew it** **and explain how you felt about it.**

You will have to talk about the topic for one to two minutes. You have one minute to think about what you are going to say. You can make some notes to help you if you wish.

• How do people share good news?

• How does modern technology affect the delivery of information?

• When do people share good news?

• Should the media only publish good news?

Outer space and stars

Examiner: Have you ever learnt about outer space and stars?

Candidate: Bits and bobs. We learnt about the solar system at school, and I'm a fan of Sci-Fi novels, but I'm no astrophysicist. I know the basics of fusion and fission and that we're trying to harness the power of the sun on earth, but the details and the maths are beyond me.

Examiner: Do you like science fiction movies?

Candidate: Absolutely. As I said, I'm a big fan of the novels, and I do also enjoy the movies. One of my favourite movies recently is called *The Wandering Earth* in English, and I think they're making the sequel at the moment. The *Three Body Problem* has just been turned into a TV series. I haven't seen it yet, but I did enjoy the books.

Examiner: Do you want to know more about outer space?

Candidate: Actually, yes, I do want to understand more. I try and follow the reports about the new telescopes that are going up and what they're finding. I can't wait for the results of the Mars probe and whether they can prove that there was once water, and even life, there.

Examiner: Do you want to go into outer space in the future?

Candidate: Fast answer, yes. Even if it was just low orbit like the Virgin or Amazon guys are doing. There are a number of problems to overcome yet. We're not really adapted to working in zero gravity for extended periods of time.

Small business

Examiner: Do you know many small businesses where you live?

Candidate: Well, I wouldn't say 'know', because I don't visit them very often, but I know OF them. Many of the shops, little supermarkets and restaurants are what would be classified as a small business. They're dotted about all around the campus where I live.

Examiner: Do you prefer buying things from big companies or small businesses?

Candidate: I always try and support the small business around me. Many of them, I believe, are family-run and need the support of the locals. That being said, they don't always have what I need, and I need to go to the larger chain supermarkets for certain items. Decent meat, for one. I haven't managed to find a local butcher yet.

Examiner: Have you ever worked in a small business?

Candidate: Yes, I have. My first internship was with a small company. Actually, it was a company run by one of my foreign teachers. He needed some help with some translation work and setting up [创建] some social media accounts. It was quite an interesting work, and related to my major, not to mention [更不必说] well paid. So, everyone won.

Examiner: Have you ever thought about starting your own business?

Candidate: Yes, it's one of the things I want to look at more properly once I've graduated. I've already got a few ideas that I'm mulling over [仔细考虑]. I just need to take things step by step.

> **Describe a piece of good news that you heard about from someone you know well.**
> **You should say:**
> > **what it was**
> > **when you heard it**
> > **how you knew it**
> **and explain how you felt about it.**

The news that Chinese citizens can go to more than 20 countries without a tourist visa is definitely great news. It means that our passport is again getting more powerful and going up the list. It seems that it's improving year on year. We're still a fair way away from the top of the list, which is Italy from memory, but we're getting there.

I learned the news from my friend's blog on Weibo. It's like China's Twitter. Later, it was reported in the newspaper and put on the big screen, and the Internet. Actually, at that time, you could read it anywhere in the country. For me at least [至少对我来说], it was a big deal [非常重要的事] as it was for a number of my friends too, as they will also be doing some travelling in the near future.

It's great news for those who want to go abroad to travel and further their education. It just became much easier for them. Today, Chinese people can go to more than 20 countries without needing a visa, which means that we can carry our passports and go to those countries any time when we want. It's something that we couldn't imagine a few decades ago when it was impossible for Chinese to go to the other side of the earth.

It goes to show that times are changing, and the whole world is becoming a closer and more open place to live. I hope that one day we will all be able to visit or study anywhere in the world without the barriers that we currently have. It would be lovely to have a truly free movement among the human race.

Examiner: How do people share good news?

Candidate: Generally, I think we share things when we see each other. If it can't wait, you know, if it's really important, we can call someone, or more likely, WeChat them and tell them that way. It would depend if it's one of my dorm mates or not. With them, I can just talk to them face to face.

Examiner: How does modern technology affect the delivery of information?

Candidate: Oh, hugely. The way and the speed with which we can send people information are very different from the past. The Internet has brought a lot of people closer together with faster and more reliable delivery of what we send. We know that it's going to get there and not get lost.

Examiner: When do people share good news?

Candidate: All the time. Or, more specifically, whenever they have positive news to share. If people don't have any, it'd be a little silly. But seriously, we are social creatures who enjoy communicating with each other, so any kind of news will always travel fast.

Examiner: Should the media only publish good news?

Candidate: No, I don't think TV and radio should only broadcast good news. I think it's important to know about what's going on in the world, and whether it's good or bad. However, I would like to see some more good news as it always seems to be one disaster after another, especially because of the recent health scares and changing climate.

Lexical Resource	
Less Common Language	solar, astrophysicist, fusion and fission, sequel, classified
Collocations/Idiomatic Language	bits and bobs, dotted about all around, family-run, mulling over, year on year
Paraphrasing	know→understand, good→positive, media→TV/radio, publish→broadcast
Discourse Marker	actually, that being said, not to mention, generally, you know, but seriously

■ Notes and Final Advice from the Author 作者最后的注释和建议

On this last page of the main book, I just want to wish everyone who reads it – Good Luck! Any exam can be scary, and certainly when it can potentially have such a profound effect on your future. So, show confidence, even if you don't feel like it.

在本书的最后一页，我想祝每一位读者——好运！任何考试都可能令人害怕，尤其是可能对你的未来产生深远影响的考试。所以，即使你不自信，也要尽力表现得自信点。

Also, remember that the examiners aren't monsters. They're NOT there to try and destroy your life; they're there to do a job, and they will do that to the best of their ability. Most examiners I know and have met, above all else, believe in fairness. They truly understand the stakes of the exam and are adverse to the idea of cheating because it's just not fair.

另外，记住考官不是怪物。他们不是来摧毁你的生活的，他们只是在恪尽职守，发挥专长。最重要的是，我认识和见过的大多数考官相信公平。他们完全理解考试的利害关系，反对作弊，因为这不公平。

With this in mind, remember that there's no shortcut to learning any language. It takes hard work, lots of effort and time. My mother always said, 'You get out what you put in'. It means that if you put effort into the learning, you'll be rewarded in kind.

记住这一点，学习任何语言都没有捷径，需要艰苦的工作，付出大量的精力和时间。正如我母亲常说的，"你投入什么就会得到什么"。也就是说，只要你努力，你就会得到同等的回报。

As a learner of language myself, Chinese in my case, I understand how difficult and frustrating it can be, but I also know how satisfying it can be to learn a new phrase or word you can use in conversation.

作为一名中文学习者，我知道学习一门语言有多么困难和令人沮丧，但我也知道学到一个可以在对话中使用的新词或短语有多么满足。

Try not to be too shy, use your English whenever and wherever you can, and try to build your confidence.

不要太害羞，无论何时何地都可以练英语，要自信。

Lastly, when you're outside the exam room, as *The Hitchhiker's Guide to the Galaxy* said, DON'T PANIC!

最后，站在考场外时，正如《银河系漫游指南》中所说，不要惊慌！

So, my final piece of advice is BREATHE!

所以，我最后的建议是深呼吸！